A JOURNEY THROUGH THE WEST

A Journey through the West

Thomas Rodney's
*1803 Journal
from Delaware
to the Mississippi Territory*

EDITED BY

Dwight L. Smith and Ray Swick

OHIO UNIVERSITY PRESS
ATHENS

Ohio University Press, Athens, Ohio 45701
© 1997 by Dwight L. Smith and Ray Swick
Printed in the United States of America

Ohio University Press books are printed on acid-free paper ™

01 00 99 98 97 5 4 3 2 1

Library of Congress Cataloging-in-Publication Data

Rodney, Thomas, 1744-1811
    A journey through the West : Thomas Rodney's 1803
journal from Delaware to the Mississippi Territory / edited
by Dwight L. Smith and Ray Swick.
      p.   cm.
    Includes bibliographical references (p.   ) and index.
    ISBN 0-8214-1179-9 (alk.paper)
    1. Ohio River Valley—Description and travel. 2. Ohio
River—Description and travel. 3. Mississippi River Valley—
Description and travel. 4. Mississippi River—Description
and travel. 5. Frontier and pioneer life—Ohio River Valley.
6. Frontier and pioneer life—Mississippi River Valley.
7. Rodney, Thomas, 1744-1811—Diaries. I. Smith, Dwight
La Vern, 1918-   . II. Swick, Ray. III. Title.
F518.R64   1997
917.704'2—dc21   97-8182
                                          CIP

To Jane, Greg, and Becki Smith

To the memory of Josephine E. Phillips

CONTENTS

Contents

ILLUSTRATIONS

MAPS

ACKNOWLEDGMENTS

Thomas Rodney was a Delaware patriot, politician, and public servant, as well as a brother and father of like-minded Rodneys. He was an inveterate and compulsive commentator and chronicler of all he witnessed, participated in, dreamed of, mused, or imagined. His letters, diaries, and judicial decisions are considerable. He even tried his hand at poetry, ranging from the casual to the epic. Well read, his writings are sprinkled with allusions to classical literature and history.

Having received a presidential appointment posting him to the Mississippi Territory, he had to travel across hundreds of miles of wilderness to reach his destination, half a continent away. Given his penchant for writing, it is not surprising, while on his journey, that Thomas Rodney wrote several letters to his son, which have been published, and kept a journal recounting this travel experience. Fortunately, the journal, heretofore unpublished, was preserved in two parts, the first in the Library of Congress and the second in the Historical Society of Delaware.

David Wigdor, Library of Congress, has implemented our access and use of the first part of Rodney's holograph manuscript journal. The Historical Society of Delaware is the owner of the second part of the Rodney journal. Barbara E. Benson and Constance J. Cooper in particular have been instrumental in granting us permission to publish it. We are most grateful to these persons and institutions for supporting our efforts to bring Rodney's journal to a wider audience.

In preparing Rodney's account for publication, we gratefully acknowledge the assistance of many persons and institutions without which we could not have succeeded. Numerous individuals have provided pertinent information that might otherwise be elusive to archival scrutiny. In West Virginia: Walter S. Carpenter, St. Marys; Robert D. Crooks, Parkersburg; Nina K. Hammett, Vienna; Pamela Salisbury and Rose Stewart, Parkersburg. In Michigan: Susan L. Mitchell, Westland. In Florida: Daniel B. Fowler, Sr. In Tennessee: Lolita H. Bissell. In Ohio: Ruth Lawton (Mrs. Robert E.) Lee, Belpre; Robert E. Putnam, Marietta.

Staff members of libraries and other institutions have eased our research in ways too numerous to list in particularity. In West Virginia, they include: Holly McCluskey, Oglebay Institute Mansion Museum, Wheeling; Nalini Mehta and Lindsay Roseberry, Wood County Public Library, Parkersburg; Robert F. Maslowski, United States Army Corps of Engineers, Huntington. In Ohio: Sandra B. Neyman, Marietta College Library, Marietta; the reference staff, Ohio University Library, Athens; Kim McGrew, Campus Martius Museum, Marietta. Others include: Rob Cox and Susan M. Swasta, Clements Library, Ann Arbor, Michigan; Katharine A. Bratcher, Filson Club, Louisville, Kentucky; Sandee Read, Cincinnati Zoo and Botanical Garden, Cincinnati, Ohio; Longwood Library, Bennett Square, Pennsylvania; Historical Society of Delaware, Wilmington, Delaware.

Staff members of the Miami University Libraries handled a steady barrage of queries and requests in our search for fugitive and elusive sources. They include Elizabeth Brice, Suzanne Haag, Frances McClure, Martin Miller, and Barbara Schutte in Special Collections; the late Inka Blazek and Jerome Conley in the Map Library; Ruth Miller, Scott Parkinson, and Elizabeth Ping in the Instructional Materials Center; and Sarah Barr, James Bricker, Scott Van Dam, and Ed Via in Interlibrary Loan.

John Diller and Mary Hubbard of Access Services steadily facilitated access to the holdings of institutional libraries of members of the Ohio

Library and Information Network (Ohio Link): Bowling Green State University, Case Western Reserve University, Central State University, University of Cincinnati, Columbus State Community College, University of Dayton, Kent State University, State Library of Ohio, University of Toledo, Ohio State University, Wright State University, and Youngstown State University.

Charlotte Newman Goldy, Jeri Schaner, and Allan Winkler of the Department of History, Miami University, extended courtesies that have eased our research and preparation through the several stages of the project. Elizabeth Smith transformed our complicated and difficult manuscript into presentable form for submission to the publisher.

Jane D. Smith, as is her wont, labored long and diligently proofreading a succession of drafts, the final master copy, and then, triumphantly, the page proofs for the volume itself.

Finally, and significantly, we are indebted to the anonymous reader whose suggestions have improved our efforts, and to the staff of the Ohio University Press who have honed and crafted our manuscript into an attractive volume of which Thomas Rodney himself would be proud.

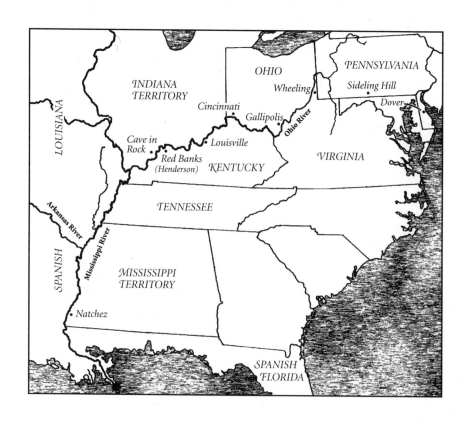

INTRODUCTION

Thomas Rodney, a future pioneer of the West, was born on the shore of Delaware Bay near Dover, Delaware, on June 4, 1744,[1] the youngest of the eight children of Caesar and Elizabeth Crawford Rodney. The Rodneys were of English descent, having emigrated to America in the 1680s.

Only a month short of his first birthday Thomas Rodney lost his father, a tragedy that was to have far-reaching consequences: his mother, following the custom of the time, was not long in remarrying (to one Thomas Wilson), but neither she nor her husband found it necessary to send young Thomas to school—this despite the fact that she herself came from an educated background, for her father had been a minister of the gospel.

Deprived of a father's care, fortunately Thomas was guided by his much older sibling, Caesar, with whom he had a close relationship that in the future would shape and define both his public and private lives. Following his eighteenth birthday, Thomas left his mother's home to live with brother Caesar to help him manage his farm and later to assist him in his public duties. Caesar Rodney held a variety of offices that were the stepping stones to what would become a brilliant political career. He served variously as a county sheriff, register of wills, recorder of deeds, clerk of an orphans' court, and trustee of the county loan office.

He was elected to several terms in the colonial legislature, serving four times as speaker, and was chosen as president of the state.[2] As the Revolution appeared more and more a reality, the pace of Caesar's professional career quickened. He became active in protest against British colonial policy, was several times elected a member of the Continental Congress, signed the Declaration of Independence, and was appointed as a military general. All of this, moreover, was accomplished in the face of severe health problems; the Delaware patriot suffered from asthmatic attacks and eye cancer, painful handicaps which the primitive medical knowledge of the day could do little to relieve.

Caesar's wide scope of activities and powerful political connections served at once as both example and opportunity for Thomas Rodney, who set the stage for his future career by moving with his brother to Dover in 1764. In addition to the employment provided by Caesar, Thomas may have worked occasionally as a surveyor and as a "viewer" in land litigation. But gradually he came more and more into the public eye, as demonstrated by the offices he was chosen to fill. He won election as a sheriff but chivalrously declined to serve in deference to a friend who had also run. Although he may have been appointed earlier, by 1770 Thomas was installed not only as a justice of the peace but also as a member of the county common pleas and orphans' courts.

The following year a great change took place in Rodney's domestic life: he married Elizabeth Fisher and embarked upon the task of starting a family. His first son, Caesar Augustus, named for his grandfather and beloved uncle, was destined to grow up to cut his own wide swath in the political world. The Rodneys subsequently became the parents of a second boy (who survived only eight days) and finally of a daughter, Lavinia.

In 1771, perhaps due to his newfound responsibilities as a husband and father, Thomas attempted to augment his income by opening a store in Philadelphia. This mercantile venture proved not overly successful, lasting less than two years, and so the resilient Rodney returned to Dover to start another store. This second experiment in trade, however, soon gave way before the much more exciting experience of tasting "the bread of office and the wine of politics,"[3] for the awful specter of the Revolution was looming upon the horizon. He soon was again tending to Caesar's affairs and finding himself involved in county politics. Once more he became a justice of the peace, appearing, as part of his duties, before the levy court, the county's tax-fixing and governing board.

Following his brother's lead, Thomas Rodney identified himself with colonial protests against Great Britain, the warming tinder which soon would ignite into war and revolution. He was elected to serve on the county Committee of Correspondence, in effect a chapter of an inter-colonial network responding to Britain's 1774 closing of the port of Boston. What evidence that exists suggests he acted as the committee's secretary.

Following the news of the skirmishes at Lexington and Concord, Delaware organized into local militia companies which in turn were formed into an association. The Rodney brothers were not long in assuming roles in this defensive array, Thomas being appointed captain of the Dover company with Caesar attaining the rank of colonel of the association. The Dover company reportedly gave more time to troublemaking and politics than it did to "martial rigors." In addition, the two would become involved in successive committees and councils at county and colony levels, overseeing militia and protest activities. And while the Rodneys diverged occasionally in their political outlook, both remained firmly committed to the patriot goals of protest, colonial action, and independence. Although the precise details and significance of their roles in Delaware's fight for independence are a bit confused, the Rodney brothers nevertheless could always be found in the midst of the resistance movement.

One of the most intriguing aspects of Thomas Rodney's life history is his entrenched belief that divine inspiration thrust him frequently into the Revolution's most crucial roles. Assuredly, both creative exaggeration and rich embellishment had their share in coloring his memory. Unfortunately, with a paucity of documentary or any other evidence it is virtually impossible to sift fact from fancy in some of his descriptions of his participation in some of history's turning points. At any rate, by his own account he loomed large as a catalyst in Delaware's move to sever its ties with the mother country.

The most famous of Thomas's fanciful accounts of his influence on the course of events revolves around the motion before the Continental Congress, sitting in Philadelphia early in July 1776, to declare the colonies' independence from England. Delaware's vote was the all-important one, being necessary to make the decision for independence unanimous. Two of the colony's three congressional delegates took opposite stands on the matter. The third delegate, Caesar Rodney, whose vote was thus the pivotal one, was unfortunately absent, being in Delaware tending to urgent matters in his capacity as speaker of the assembly and acting governor as well as general of the militia. And to compound matters, he was undecided in the matter. Possessing great respect for Thomas's opinion and knowing that divine inspiration formed the basis of his advice, Caesar consulted with his brother, who convinced him of the rightness of independence. Caesar thereupon galloped furiously to Philadelphia—the famous ride which traditionally has formed such a dramatic part of Delaware's early history—and cast his vote, thus winning the day for independence in the Continental Congress.

After failing to be selected as delegates for the state constitutional convention, the Rodneys turned their attention to the urgent matter of the war. Things were not going well for the American cause in the first year of independence. Defeated in New York, General George Washington retreated southward and early in December crossed the Delaware River to safety in Pennsylvania. The future looked bleak indeed for Washington and the American cause.

It was at this crucial juncture, by his own account, that Thomas Rodney once more became the deciding factor. It is in Rodney's epic, *The Caesariad,* for he was also a poet, that he most fully described his role: his prayers to God brought visions involving an archangel with assurances that independence was not a lost cause and that the right man could save his country. That man, Thomas was convinced, was none other than himself. Then the enemies of independence took him to a mountaintop and offered riches and power if he would not interfere with Washington's acceptance of proffered peace terms; but he resisted the temptation. His advice to persevere was sent to Washington who as a result recrossed the Delaware on the offensive on Christmas night, 1776, thus saving the American cause. Rodney was to recall his key role in these events a number of times during the rest of his life, including once during his 1803 journey through the West.

Even though the truth in Rodney's account is infinitesimal—his biographer calls it a "fairy tale"—his contingent of militia was serving with Pennsylvania militia and did cross the Delaware River on Christmas night to spend the next few days alternately capturing supplies and engaging in some protective measures for Washington's army. Thomas saw action in the Battle of Princeton, and as ranking officer in his regiment, achieved the distinction of guarding Washington himself as he moved to winter quarters at Morristown. Then, his extended enlistment completed, he returned home in January 1777 to open his store, buy some land, and resume his duties in the orphans' and common pleas courts.

With Caesar's election as president of the state in March 1778, Thomas Rodney's star began to rise. Honors and appointments now rained upon this heretofore not-too-successful younger brother: he succeeded Caesar as admiralty court judge, was appointed clothier to the state regiment, declined to accept election as chief justice of the county common pleas and orphans' court, was appointed county probate wills registrar, and was elevated to the rank of colonel of a state militia regiment, a title he proudly used whenever possible for the remainder of his days.

Unfortunately, Thomas's bumpy career was troubled by an episode that does him little credit. In response to a congressional request, Delaware placed an embargo on all shipments of wheat and flour. As the state's president, Caesar Rodney was empowered to appoint a superintendent to oversee such potentially highly profitable transactions as the purchase of wheat and flour for Congress and the French and Spanish fleets. While the records are too incomplete to reveal whether or not Thomas was chosen to serve as superintendent or only functioned as an assistant, he was, nevertheless, deeply involved in the business and in the summer of

1780 moved to Wilmington to be closer to the action. By 1782, having failed to profit in the enterprise, he retreated to Dover, narrowly escaping the tarring brush of scandal, specifically accusations of bribery.

Rodney was chosen to represent Delaware in the Confederation Congress in 1781, a position to which he was reelected four more times during the decade, though he only attended in 1781-1782 and 1786. The most solid fact of his congressional career was his appointment to the Ways and Means Committee. Far shakier are his claims, substantiated by no other source than his own recollections, that it was he who proposed the creation of Congress's administrative departments; outlined a form which the federal government might assume after 1788; was responsible for Washington's having a free hand against General Cornwallis in Virginia during the last year of the Revolutionary War; was to be credited for Robert Morris attaining the office of superintendent of finance; and caused Thomas McKean to be chosen president of the Continental Congress. Rodney's tales multiplied imaginatively, with only one of them, that he was instrumental in getting Benjamin Franklin appointed to the commission which negotiated the peace treaty of 1783 with Great Britain, bearing any verisimilitude.

By this time Thomas Rodney was entering a period which would be the nadir of both his personal and professional lives. He was elected to the lower house of the state legislature in 1786 and 1787 and served briefly as its speaker. Because of a temporary illness he resigned this office. The death of his wife in 1783 was followed the next year by an even greater calamity—the death of Caesar. His beloved brother, the font of opportunities upon which Rodney built his career, had served, too, as Thomas's anchor and mainstay in the rough-and-tumble world of Delaware business and politics. And now he was gone. It was a void which ill prepared Thomas for the difficult days that lay ahead. His lucrative state clerical appointments were not renewed. Then Caesar's large estate, willed to Thomas's son, was sold to satisfy the demands of creditors. Rodney's good name suffered in the confusion when he was accused of having stolen money from the Kent County Loan Office for which Caesar once had served as trustee. Thomas's troubles finally came to a head in 1791 when he was arrested and thrown into debtor's prison in Dover, an incarceration which lasted fourteen months.

After regaining his freedom in August 1792, Rodney adopted a semi-nomadic existence. He lived two years at "Ionia Farm," a property his son had inherited from Caesar, then moved in with Caesar Augustus for a while, and finally was given a room in the Dover household of his half sister Sally. With little else to occupy him, Thomas Rodney devoted more and more time to his books, to his pen, and to the pleasurable diversion of recalling his past.

More specifically, he pursued his lifelong study of history and epic poetry and continued to read intensively in the standard and classical treatises of the law. Thomas Rodney never lost his love for writing, which he now renewed daily through penning letters, keeping a variety of records, and producing lengthy accounts of his thoughts and reasoning on all sorts of public and private matters. He even ventured into the heady realm of poetry, producing his epic, *The Caesariad*. It is not surprising, therefore, that his papers are voluminous or that a perusal of them reveals a paradoxical mentality. Capable of presenting an argument grounded in logic and positioned in authority (he even wrote, but never published, a book about common law and estate inheritance), Thomas could just as easily veer off into mysticism. It was such fertile periods of creativity that gave birth to the visions of divine inspiration which placed him at some of the critical crossroads of American history.

Gradually the worst of Thomas Rodney's difficulties ebbed away and he regained some measure of influence in his community. He was elected a vestryman in his church and president of a new agriculture society and was made trustee of a school. Then, following the Federalists' defeat in the 1801 state elections, the Rodney name once more began to rise, and with it Thomas's expectations of again holding public office. These increased somewhat when his son-in-law became the secretary of Delaware and even moreso in 1802, when Caesar Augustus was elected to the United States House of Representatives. Soon suggestions of possible political positions for Thomas were being bandied about, including his candidacy for the governorship itself in the next election. Nothing came of this, but in December 1802 the governor of Delaware commissioned Rodney as a state supreme court justice, an office which carried with it a judgeship on the appeals court. While the income from these high occupations was not equal to their prestige, they did serve to mark the end of his long exile from political office-holding.

Rodney's friends continued working behind the scenes, even soliciting on his behalf in Washington. Thomas McKean, an old political friend who was serving as governor of Pennsylvania, recommended to President Thomas Jefferson that Rodney should be given serious consideration for patronage. The suggestion bore fruit: in July 1803 Jefferson tendered Rodney an appointment as a Mississippi territorial judge and as a land commissioner for the district of the territory west of the Pearl River. One month later Thomas Rodney set out from Dover for his new assignments. Despite his age, he stood the long and difficult journey to the Mississippi Territory well, making his way overland to Wheeling, (West) Virginia, and then by boat down the Ohio and Mississippi rivers to Natchez. He traveled the last six miles by horseback to Washington, the territorial capital. His August 14-December 1, 1803 travel journal, the text of the present volume, narrates this experience.

In his new career, Thomas Rodney served as an instrument in providing what one historian has called "the transit of law to the frontier."[4] Rodney and his fellow land commissioners were concerned with the Natchez District, where the sovereignties of England, Spain, and Georgia had prevailed previously and where it was now necessary to sort out carefully and somehow reconcile within the framework of American territorial land laws claims established under these jurisdictions. The commissioners did not conclude their work until mid-June 1807.

Rodney's office was no sinecure, for as both commissioner and judge, his bench and circuit duties kept him exceedingly busy. It was a demanding schedule which finally saw the man measure up to the job. There were no more sudden resignations or neurotic retreats into the shelter of his family, for Thomas conscientiously attended to his new responsibilities with unaccustomed deliberation and decisiveness. In the Mississippi Territory, Thomas Rodney finally escaped from his brother's shadow.

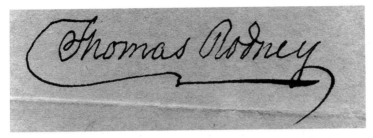

Thomas Rodney's signature to his July 7, 1805, letter to Robert Williams, governor, Mississippi Territory. No portrait or silhouette of Rodney has been found. Courtesy Blennerhassett Island Historical State Park, Parkersburg, West Virginia.

Whether territorial courts such as Rodney's were a part of the federal court system and whether appeals could be made from them to the federal supreme court had never been defined by law or precedent. In such cases and in other gray zones, especially where modification of common law would suit the purposes of territorial justice, Rodney did not hesitate to introduce his own distinct innovations. Rodney's notes and comments, the only such source for the territory, constitute, therefore, a significant record of the establishment of law on the American frontier.

As in his Delaware years, the usual bureaucratic routine and humdrum of Thomas's Mississippi period was occasionally enlivened by controversy. The most famous instance of this occurred with the appearance before Rodney's court of Aaron Burr, whose "conspiracy" came to a boil as he made his way down the Mississippi early in 1807. The judge also became more than a casual bystander in the factional conflicts that raged in the territory, disturbing the tranquility of its citizens and casting Rodney in the role of adversary. One such example was the storm of contention that surrounded the territorial governor, Robert Williams. The governor and Rodney were at odds in 1805 over where the court should be housed, and that the governor should quarrel with Rodney's interpretation of territorial law served to fuel his descending opinion of Williams.

When the unpopular Williams finally resigned his office in March 1809, the citizenry broke out into celebration, making part of their jubilation a nighttime visit to Rodney's home. By torchlight, they cheered and serenaded the old gentleman with fife and drum. This incident was but one example of the acceptance and respect which the judge had attained in his adopted homeland.

Rodney had hoped some day to return to Delaware; but he had sunk deep roots in his frontier post, and this wish was never fulfilled. Thomas Rodney's career in the South was destined to be a short one, for, beginning in 1810, his health began to fail. His vigor steadily declined, and on January 21, 1811, four months and a few days short of his sixty-seventh birthday, he died.[5] His Mississippi years constituted Rodney's triumph, seeing him at last standing alone, building a credible career through his own ability and initiative, independent of family influence.[6]

Thomas Rodney's August 14-December 1, 1803 journey from Delaware to the Mississippi Territory is the physical link between his Delaware years and his Mississippi period. Brief summaries of his travel are recounted by his biographer, William Baskerville Hamilton, and in a few published biographical sketches. A fuller account is rendered in the series of letters Thomas wrote to his son Caesar Augustus during the long journey. These have been published in *Pennsylvania Magazine of Biography and History*.[7] But Rodney's detailed day-by-day narration of experiences, observations, and thoughts are recorded solely in his journal and this has never before been published.

Rodney's manuscript is contained in two separate notebooks, the first delineating his journey from Dover, Delaware, to a point on the Ohio River at present-day Rockport, Indiana. The second notebook takes up the narrative there and concludes it at Washington, Mississippi Territory. The first part of the journal is in the Library of Congress. The second is owned by the Historical Society of Delaware. Rodney's journal is among the most detailed of early nineteenth-century travel accounts by Americans, equaled perhaps only by that of Christian Schultz, Jr., who traveled through the western country a few years later.[8]

As a traveler, Rodney is closely observant and unquenchably curious. These fortuitously combined traits carry him beyond the habit of many frontier travelers of merely recording the monotony of bad roads, land prices, kinds of timber and soil, and the number of islands passed in a day's voyage. He is interested in geological formations, archaeological remains, local history, agriculture potential, battle sites, wildlife, the state of western culture, salt licks, and the personal foibles and behavior of the many people whom he met on his odyssey. And it was a motley assortment of humanity that populated the American frontier: Rodney socialized with war veterans, lawyers, craftsmen, Indians, local social and government leaders, soldiers, and settlers in isolated farms and fledgling towns.

He also met certain individuals who in themselves were important milestones of history-in-the-making. During his lengthy stay in Wheeling, Virginia, the old traveler enjoyed the company of Meriwether Lewis, whose epic exploration with William Clark was in its early stages. Below Marietta, Thomas visited the magnificent island home of Harman and Margaret Blennerhassett, which shortly was to receive national notoriety as the base of operations for Aaron Burr's famous 1806-1807 "conspiracy." Rodney's journal entry stands as the most detailed contemporary account known to exist of the Blennerhassett estate and its proprietor. Above all, the detail with which Rodney records his observations brings them to life for us today, whether it is a "Dutch" (that is, German) graveyard in Pennsylvania, the Ohio River "fogg," "Illuminated with the appearance of Innumerable small sparks of fire which we Took To be the gloworm," or the sinking of his boat.

Rodney exchanged information with other river travelers; traded trinkets and trivia with an occasional band of Indians; added his initials to graffiti-ridden trees, cliffs, and cave walls; and willingly imparted medical advice and nostrums to the sick. With candor and verve he confided to paper his thoughts, spanning the astonishingly wide spectrum of such topics as his traveling companions, the place of classics in his life, his mystical reflections, and his explanations of fossil formation and prehistoric peoples. Through it all Rodney not only kept his sense of humor but also maintained a sense of serenity, even in the face of disasters such as the near loss of his river craft just days before his journey's end. Rodney's account thus gives us a vicarious sense of what it was like to travel in 1803 from a long-settled eastern seaboard state into the wilderness heart of the continent.

Editing an early nineteenth-century journal for late twentieth-century readers is at once a challenge and a dilemma. On the one hand, to tamper with the entries in any way violates the integrity of the journal. It is, nevertheless, sometimes impossible to render a literal transcription from indecipherable penmanship or to transfer the precise flourishes on the manuscript page to the printed page. At best, an element of inference and guesswork is involved in the transcription. Even a photo-facsimile may fail to reproduce all the nuances of the weathered or worn manuscript page.

On the other hand (and at the other extreme), to modernize the transcription of such a journal would erase much of its charm and context. This would inevitably invite comparison with a present-day production, undoubtedly resulting in its rejection by readers.

Our position as editors of Thomas Rodney's journal falls somewhere between these two extremes. We have endeavored to render the transcription as literally as possible without making it so tedious and unattractive as to discourage readers. At the same time we have resisted the inclination to make it so readable as to lose the immediacy of Rodney's account of his travels. We recognize that this constitutes a compromise and that at times we may have erred in either direction from that position.

We have silently employed a few conventional editorial devices to maximize the readability without sacrificing the flavor of Rodney's prose or the integrity of his entries. These concern such things as spelling, contractions, abbreviations, punctuation, capitalization, indecipherable words, and other matters that can benefit from editorial help. An outline of our editorial stance on these matters follows.

Rodney's prose is plagued with misspelling which is, moreover, inconsistent; it is not unusual, in his journal, to find divergent spellings of the same word in close proximity to each other. These idiosyncracies apply to personal names and place names alike. Difficulties with transcription of his handwriting only compound the confusion. With respect to spelling, every effort has been made to render a faithful transcription. To designate each such occurrence would hopelessly clutter the journal.

Accordingly, *sic* is used sparingly. Unless it is reasonably evident which word he is using, bracketed letters are inserted to correct misspellings.

By the same token, Rodney's penchant for contracted words is retained unless his meaning is unclear. In such cases, corrections or additions of letters are made in brackets. Confusion sometimes results when it is not possible to discern whether he is abbreviating or contracting. Abbreviations still in common use are retained and supplied with periods; otherwise they are spelled out silently.

Rodney frequently and inconsistently split many compound words into component parts. These are retained except for some that obviously necessitate connection, such as "a cross" and "to day." "A head," which he uses frequently, poses a particular problem, for it is not always possible to determine whether he means "ahead" or a "head" as in the case of a head wind. In some instances it has been necessary to break up words he runs together.

Transcription was at times difficult not only because of misspellings, abbreviations, and contractions, but because of general undecipherability. Editorial insertions in brackets serve to illuminate such situations. If context and conjecture yield a plausible rendering, this is indicated in brackets with a question mark, such as [boat?]. If not, such is indicated as *[illegible]*. In instances where Rodney left a blank space, as in the case of a person's name, this is shown as *[blank]* in the transcription. A physical condition of the manuscript that presents a difficulty is explained by an editorial insertion, such as *[blotted]*. In general, awkward phrasing will stand, but if an editorial insertion will clarify a passage, a word or two [is added] in brackets.

Superior letters, that is to say those written above the rest of the line, are brought down to the line of the text. The so-called tailed p is rendered as per. The ampersand (&) is written as "and"; "&c." becomes "etc." Inadvertent or unnecessarily repeated words are deleted silently.

Rodney's capitalization of words is at once erratic, inconsistent, and frequent to the point that it is often impossible to distinguish whether he is using lower case or capital letters. As a faithful transcription in this matter is virtually impossible throughout the journal, the editors have chosen to delete or introduce whatever capitalization is appropriate to the needs of each situation.

In another matter of textual transcription, it must be noted that Rodney uses virtually no punctuation beyond flourishes and dashes, a common practice in the eighteenth century. These are sometimes superfluous and sometimes lacking, so they cannot be used as satisfactory alternatives for anything resembling conventional punctuation. What may be regarded as sentences, if he had punctuated them, are sometimes long, tortuous, and convoluted. Editorial punctuation, therefore, is supplied to make the text more readable. In instances where there is superfluous punctuation, it is deleted. Incomplete sentences are retained as such unless they can be corrected with editorially bracketed additions.

Except for the separation of a new day's entry from that of the previous day, Rodney seldom uses paragraphing in the journal. Even though frequently several sentences do not fit together in a paragraph in the usual sense of the word, editorial paragraphing has been introduced throughout the journal to enhance readability.

Following somewhat the same rationale, the editors have arbitrarily divided the entire journal into eleven chapters of approximately the same length. As befits a travel journal, each chapter covers a distinct segment of the journey. This sometimes results in an anomalous situation as a journal entry might overlap the arrival and the departure from one of the locations indicated in the chapter subtitle. As Rodney's daily entries are not always sequential in their accounts of a day's activities, it is impossible to divide them internally to allow for chapter divisions. The integrity of the entries has in all cases been maintained.

The editing of such a journal entails more than transcription of the original manuscript. Editors are obligated to add whatever explanation and orientation are desirable to make the content of the transcription meaningful to the readers. Further, readers who wish to pursue the subject in broader or deeper research may do so with the aid of the documentation.

The paragraphs in italics at the beginning of each chapter introduce the reader to some of the interesting persons, places, and experiences Rodney records for that leg of the journey. Documentation notes identify, explain, locate, add to, or comment upon such things that are essential to the reader's understanding of Rodney and his entries and the progress of his journey.

Keeping this in mind, it has not seemed necessary or desirable to attempt to identify every person Rodney mentioned or encountered. Apart from his traveling companions and a few notable figures, in general only persons having more than a casual relevance to his journey are identified. Beyond that, whatever identification Rodney may give, if any, such as innkeeper, lawyer, settler, or storekeeper, the editors have deemed sufficient.

On the other hand, as this is essentially a travel account every effort has been made to identify all locations he mentions so that readers can follow his progress from Delaware across Pennsylvania and down the Ohio and Mississippi rivers to Natchez. While sometimes Rodney's remarks are sufficient, generally they are not. Many sites inadequately described by name or location simply cannot be identified on modern maps.

For the Ohio and Mississippi portion of his trip, at least, Thomas relied on printed travel aids. Of these, only one can be identified beyond reasonable doubt. What he refers to as the "Ohio Pilot" is Zadok Cramer's *Ohio and Mississippi Navigator,* which ran through twelve editions from 1801 to 1824 and was widely recognized as the standard guidebook for western travelers during this period. Internal evidence shows that Rodney was using the third edition, a forty-page pamphlet published in 1802. Despite its title, Cramer's *Navigator* contained no navigational details beyond the mouth of the Ohio River, giving only general remarks about the Mississippi. Beginning with the fourth edition (1804), however, the book's navigational advice was extended to include "the Father of Waters."[9]

For guidance on the Mississippi River, Rodney relied on Mathew Carey. His few references to "Carey" and "Misisipi Pilot" make it impossible to identify what map, atlas, or "Pilot" source he was using.[10] Given the insufficiency of sources from which Rodney could garner navigational information and gain geographic orientation, as well as the decreasing reliability of such data as one moved further into the Ohio River and Mississippi Valley wilderness, it is not surprising that he was at times uncertain or confused as to his precise location.

Additional factors make it difficult and even improbable sometimes to follow Rodney on modern maps. Nearly two centuries of changes wrought by humans and nature alike have so altered the landscape that an 1803 map or navigational guide would be considerably out of date. Yesteryear's roads, if they still exist, may have to some extent been rerouted. Some thriving settlements have become ghost towns or even vanished from memory or record, such as Alexandria, which once stood at the mouth of the Scioto River. Still others have merged with others or now have different names. New ones have been added to gazetteers. The courses of Rodney's rivers have changed much due to such caprices of nature as earthquakes and floods and other vagaries of time, to say nothing of dams, locks, and deliberate rechanneling.

For the most part, it is possible to identify Rodney's progress on present-day maps. The editors have chosen to do this on maps issued by the United States Geological Survey, a source sometimes supplemented with other documentation.

In summary, the goal of the editorial process has been to enhance Rodney's travel journal to the point of making it understandable for the modern reader; and to enable the reader, by Rodney's able pen, to envision the long-vanished world through which he and his companions journeyed so many years ago. If that goal has been attained, then we have succeeded in our task.

"All my friends lamented"

Setting Out for "Misisipi"

Dover, Delaware, to Sideling Hill, Pennsylvania,
August 14–28, 1803

On Sunday, August 14, 1803, four weeks after he had been commissioned as
a judge and land commissioner of the "Misisipi Terratory," fifty-nine-year-old
Thomas Rodney set out from Dover, Delaware, in a horse-drawn chaise bound
for his son Caesar's home in Wilmington. A week later, having tended to some
personal matters and last minute details for his impending journey, Rodney's
western adventure began.

He was accompanied by his son, daughter-in-law, a friend, and William
Shields. This last-named gentleman, soon to loom large in Rodney's journal,
was a relative, an ambitious young lawyer who was bound for Mississippi in
search of career opportunities. The little party traveled north into Pennsylvania
and then headed west on the turnpike through Lancaster to York. Here all
but Shields said good-by to Rodney and turned homeward.

As the two men continued on their way, they gradually settled into a
routine. In 1803, travel through the settled portions of the United States and
into the frontier beyond was an experience neither easy nor always pleasant.

Rodney, however, seasoned by past troubles and mellowed by maturity, readily accepted whatever circumstance befell him. It is a philosophy that not only allowed him to endure the conditions of his trip, but to actually enjoy them as well. This enjoyment stemmed, considerably, from his continued love affair with the pen. Seemingly missing nothing, he soon proved to be an astute recorder of all that he saw, occasionally leaving his carriage for walks near the road to better note the increasingly interesting features of nature. While Lancaster, York, Chambersburg, and whatever lesser settlements there were in between came in for close scrutiny, Rodney does not neglect to describe people whom he encountered, in all their varying ranks and appearances. These literary practices continued unabated as he penetrated more deeply into the West, adding depth and detail to a journal which was destined to become a unique record of its time.

Book of Accounts of Thomas Rodney Commencing at Dover in the State of Dalaware—August—1803.

On the 17th of July 1803, Thomas Rodney, one of the judges of the Supreme Court and of the High Court of Errors and Appeals for the State of Dalaware, was commissioned one of the judges of the U.S. for the Misisipi Terratory and one of the commisioners of the U.S. for determining the claims of land west of Pearl River, etc., in the said Terratory. . . .[1]

Sunday, August the 14th 1803.[2] Took my leave of Dover to go to the Misisipi Terratory. Set out in my son's chaise and his horse. Called at Charles Hams and took his sister Ann Ham[3] to her cousin Phillip Lewes at Newark.

We called to see Fenwick Fisher at or near D.C. Cross Roads[4] and dined there then went on to the Brick Tavern[5] where we tarried all night. Miss Ham was unwell and was sick all night, but better in the morning. We breakfasted and then set off again.

❁

August 15. Tavern bill paid—17/6. Went over Iron Hill and Gray Hill[6] and thence to Newark where we arrived just before dinner. By this time Miss Ham had got almost well. Stayed at Lewes's all night and breakfasted there next morning.

❁

August 16th 1803. Left Mr. Lewes's and left Miss Ham there and arrived at my sons in Wilmington to diner.

Paid servants gratis, etc.—3/9.

❁

Wilmington, August 17th 1803. Received a letter from Mr. A. Gallatin, Secretary of the Treasury of U.S., respecting my salary and the payment of my commission money: salary to be paid quarterly, etc., and 500 dollars of comm[issioner's] money now, 500 more on the first day of January next, 500 more on the first day of April next, and the last 500 dollars after we report, etc. Received at same time a letter from Th[omas] T. Tucker, Treasurer of the U.S., inclosing an order on A. McLane, Collector of the Port of Wilmington, for 500 dollars, of which gave said collector notice.

Received several letters of information from Major Claybourn who is to go out with us to Misisipi but now is at the Federal City.[7] Mr. Wm. Shields[8] of this place also goes with us.

❁

Wilmington, August [18,] 1803. Allen McLane called on me and gave me a check on the bank of Dalaware for five hundred dollars and took up the treasury order, but [I] shall not call on the bank till Saturday. . . .[9]

In my journey from Dover to New Ark both days, Sunday and Munday were very pleasant. They were broken clouds with a fine western breeze, and a little before we arrived at D.C. there was a very light misty shower and no further rain either day. We assended the Iron Hill from Coudhes Mill and viewed all the best prospects from different parts of the top of the hill. Then crossed the valley by a middle road on south between Elk[ton] and Christian roads throug[h] the Rocky Groves of wood to Chesnut Hill,[10] and assending into the old field on the top. Rested under a large poplar shade [tree] an hour or two to enjoy the prospects round and the pleasant breeze and entwining air.

Miss Ham viewed the grand and beautiful prospects on both hills with great delight and admiration never having been there before. While we rested in our chaise under the shade of the poplar she said that all my friends lamented that I was about to leave them and all these beautiful hills to which I was so much attached to go into so distant a part of our country as the Misisipi Terratory. That she in particular lamented parting with one who had so long been a friend of their family. That her brother, the Doctor, and Mr. Bishop were extremely distressed at my going and indeed all my friends; and begged that I would leave her some token of remembrance which she would always set great store by. I replyed that I would do this with pleasure if I met with any article that I thought would be aggreeable and was sutable as a memorial. And today I bought a small gold ring for that purpose thinking it might perhaps be more agreable to the taste of a lady than any other trifle. It is set with a small ruby collored stone or paste.

NB. This ring I afterwards sent to her by P. L.[11] sealed up in white paper from York Town when he parted with us.[12]

I afterwards wrote to Miss Ham from Wheeling inclosed in a letter to P.L. Have only heard from her since through the Doctor. . . .[13]

Wilmington, State of Dalaware, Sunday, August 21st 1803, 28 year of independance. At nine o'clock this morning I set off from my sons in Wilmington with Mr. Wm. Shields in the carriage with me for the Misisipi Terratory. A great number of friends attended to see us depart and take leave of us. And my son and his wife, Captain Hunn and his youngest daughter Maria, Secretary John Fisher, Mr. Phillip Lewes, Mr. James Wilson, Printer of the Mirror, and his wife, and Messrs. John and William Warner[14] accompanied us eight miles on our way to a tavern where we enjoyed a little refreshment together; and then all of them but my son and his wife and Mr. P. Lewes, and Mr. Shields, a young gentleman of the law who goes all the way with me, turned back. The rest of us went on to Webbs Tavern on the Lancaster road[15] where we dined. After diner we proceeded by Doe Run to W. Lilleys Tavern, where the road to the Gap and that which goes directly to the Philadelphia Turn Pike to Lancaster.[16]

All the country through which we passed today may be said to be verry hilly and some of the hills very high. No country can well exhibit a greater variety of landscape than was afforded us in passing this road. It was continually changing as we assended and decended the hills, like a cloud changing its form with every puff of wind. The country is mostly fertile and the landscape mostly very beautiful and animating.

Munday, August 22d 1803. We lodged and breakfasted at Lillys Tavern, a pretty large stone house, and tolarable accomadations, and then set off and took the Old Gap road which we found very hilly and badly cut with the late rains as well as stony; but this was compensated by the grand and delightful prospects the hills affoarded. Our first stage was 8 miles to the Rising Sun Tavern on this turnpike road, a large stone new house where we had our horses fed, 14 miles from Lancaster.

From the Rising Sun we persued our route on the turnpike to Lancaster. It is a straight and beautiful road. It is formed of the common stones of the country it passes through, broken into small pieces by a hammer or pick ax, and then laid thick on the road, and covered with sand so as to make it level. Yet it is a little ruff for want of plenty of sand on it, which indeed is difficult to keep on as the rains wash it off. On either side of the gravel road is what are called the summer roads that run on the earth only, which are at present very good and pleasanter to ride than the turnpike or gravel road. We arrived at Eioltchs Tavern in King Street in Lancaster about 2 o'clock and dined there.[17]

This town is said to contain about a thousand houses. The streets cross at right angles and are about 30 ft. wide. And in the center of the

THE OLD COURT HOUSE AT LANCASTER.
[Torn down in 1853.—From an Old Print.]

Courthouse, Lancaster County, Pennsylvania. Erected in 1787, this was the county's second courthouse. William H. Egle, *History of the Commonwealth of Pennsylvania* (Philadelphia: E. M. Gardner, 1883), 814.

town where King Street and Queen Street cross there is a small square in the middle of which the Court House stands which is a spacious and very elegant brick building for a country town. The buildings are either brick or stone, generally brick; and most of those built since the Revolution are good buildings. Many of them very good but all in a plain stile. There is a large Dutch Church in this town with a steeple 190 ft. high. Lancaster stands in Lancaster County and in the midst of a fertile country ten or twelve miles from the Susquehanah River and about a mile from Conastoga Creek in what may be called a plain, tho some parts of this town is on rising ground and much higher than other parts. I visited this town in 1778 when it was not more than a 4th part as large as it is now. It is at present the seat of the legislature of Pensylvania and is considered a healthy situation. The inhabitants are chiefly Dutch or the decendants of Dutch.[18] Here we taried all night.

◢◣

Tuesday, August 23d 1803. After taking breakfast we went on to the Susquehana River at Columbia Ferry, 12 miles. The road is a turnpike all the way and passes through a fine country of hills and dales. About 3 miles from Lancaster we passed the Little Conastoga[19] over a bridge. We stopped at the ferry house on the bank of the river and taried till after diner.

In the meantime I took a walk along the river up to the point where it comes through the first mountain. The prospect there was grand and stupendious, the points of the mountain being very steep and composed of granite rocks from the waters edge to the summit. Yet it was so cragy that I assended it some distance with ease step by step to take a more extensive view of the river which at the ferry is about a mile wide but much less where it passes through the mountain. The bottom is covered with rocks which rise all over it almost at this time above the water, so that a little below the gap of the mountain it appeared as if I could have passed across the river in my half boots without getting wet the water being very low at this time. I washed my hands and bathed my feet and legs in the river and then returned.

Columbia at present is nothing more than a villiage but is increasing very fast, there being a great many new buildings going on and lately built chiefly of brick and mostly commodious. The ferry house is a large comodious brick building and we got a very excellent diner there. But there was a very noisy set there, a number of Kaintucky men and horses who had been to Lancaster loaded with money for the merchants of Philadelphia who deal in the back country. They told us they brought down several hundred thousand dollars on 21 horses.

After diner we set out again at 2 clock P.M. for York Town. Two boats went over at the same time. One took us and our carriages, the other the Kaintucky men and their horses and 2 of our horses. The ferry men were all drunk, and those in the different boats ambitious to beat each other and made great exertions and run each other aground on the rocks, and run foul several times and made such work that at length we were obliged to interfere and silence them. We were about 3/4 of an hour passing the ferry and then got safe over and went on to this place, Little York.[20]

It is a very good road from the ferry to, all the way to York Town over hills and dales. Sometimes the hills, one in particular, seemed pretty high yet where we looked on either hand the mountains at about five or 6 miles distant were so high that we appeared to be in a vally between them. We seemed indeed to be in the center of a vast amphitheater formed by nature. The view was very grand and delighting. The soil on this side the river seems even better than in Lancaster County and produces nearly the same kind of wood, walnut, oak, and hickory chiefly. On either hand as we passed the farms appeared very fertile and mostly covered with clover, or Indian corn or fallow. But few buildings on them and those chiefly mean. We saw but two or three good buildings all the way. Yet we are told the land sells in this country for from 40 to 100 dollars per acre. Indeed it is a very fertile country and is chiefly inhabited by Germans or their decendants. We arrived at Little York about 6 o'clock P.M. and put up at the Black Horse Inn, the stage house of this place, for the night.

Wednesday, August 24th 1803. This morning we took a view of Little York. It is a hansome town containing about six hundred houses. Its streets are spacious and cross at right angles. At the crossing of the two principal streets [are] the Court House and publick offices. The former is an old plain brick building but the latter is a new elegant building. On the south side of the main street through which the road passes stands an elegant large new church and steeple about 150 ft. high in appearance, but I did not measure it. But this building is squeezed between the dwelling houses so that you cannot git into the church yard without going through a gate on the back street. This church belongs to Dutch Calvanists. On the main cross street about the same distance from the Court House stands an old stone church of plain structure belonging to the Dutch Lutherans, for the people here are all Dutch except a very few. Both these churches are large and capacious.[21] I went through the yard of the Lutherans to view the tombstones. The writing on all I examined is Dutch. And it appears that most of the persons there died young. I noticed but 2 that reached 70 years and most of them were children and young people which shews that it is not a healthy place. The Cadorus runs through the town and binds around it so that the two main streets cross it at right angles with each other; and there is of course two bridges over it, both wooden except the abutments.[22]

At eleven o'clock our friends parted with us here and returned: my son and his wife and Mr. Phillip Lewes who had accompanied us thus far, so that Mr. Shields and myself hence forward have to pursue our route alone.[23] We all set of[f] at the same time. We persued our route toward Chambersbourgh and dined at the Sign of the Unicorn, a logged house eleven miles from Little York. Then we went on and passed through Abots Town at 4 miles further and stoped and fed our horse at Hartford, 8 miles from the Unicorn. This and Abots Town are but small villages. This however is the largest but both are composed chiefly of logged buildings.[24]

We went on again and passed a very well built stone bridge about half a mile from Hartford over the Canaway Creek[25] where there is also a very large mill house on the east side the creek about a mile from Hartford or perhaps some more. The road to Hunters Town where we intended to tarry all night turns off to the right; but we took the left hand road and went on it four miles to cross road that also lead to Hunters Town before we got set right being then about two miles off.

We arrived at Hunters Town before sun down.[26] This hardly deserves the name of a town there being only three or four houses in it. The tavern is a brick house with 4 small rooms on a floor and would be a pretty good house if repaired but is very much wrecked at present. It is rented too by very poor people who have but a bed or two and 2 or 3 chairs. Yet we got a very good supper here. The poor people did the best they could but our bed was very ordinary. But the situation is very fine and pleasant and deserves a better inn but Dixon the tavern keeper says it belongs to a poor judge who cannot repair it.

Our rout today was through a fine country as to landscape and also pretty fertile. It abounds in clover and buckwheat. The road all the way was hill and dale and very good only stoney in some places. After passing the Unicorn we began as we passed over the hills to have a distant view of the South Mountain or Blue Ridge rising as it were to the sky while on our left appeared the lofty hills which run from the Susquehana westward. The prospect of course was very grand and dignified, and kept our minds cheerful; but the sun shone so warm in our faces all the afternoon together with jostling over many places of [the] small stoney road that this evening for the first time I felt a good deal weary.

Thursday, August 25th 1803, Horns Tavern on the top of the South Mountain at the part of it called Black Gap.[27] We left Hunters Town after taking breakfast at 1/4 after 7 o'clock A.M. and reached this place about 1/2 after 12 o'clock.

Here I will take a little retrospect of the road[s] from Collumbia Ferry on Susquehana. From the ferry to Hunters Town and for 7 miles on this side they continued much the same as to goodness, and generally at this time are pretty good carriage road[s] being only now and then a little stoney for a small distance; but from 7 miles back they kept growing more and more stoney for about 4 miles, and then we had nothing but stones to roll over to this place and esspecially when we drew near the mountain; but we assended the mountain without any other difficulty. The road runs round the end or break in the mountain called the Gap which is made by a valley or ravine that penetrates the mountain.

The timber and soil in the country appeared to decline as we approached the mountain, but we were compensated for this by the grand prospect the mountains afforded as we passed over the lesser hills. The woods on the first mountain was chiefly chestnut and oak with hickory and several other kinds of wood and pretty good, but the more northern and eastern part of the mountain beyond the ravine appears to be covered on the summit by pine and ceader.

We have been well entertained here with good meat, veal, and bacon, etc., and good butter, etc., etc., and Horn says they frequently have vinson.[28] He also says he has sometimes bought fine oysters here, of the wagons that go to Baltimore with flour, on their return home, and he also has good spirits, Lisbon and Madeira wine. These things were beyond my expectation on the mountain, and being pritty w[e]ary by rolling over the stones so far we determined to rest and go no further today. This country abounds in fruit trees quite to the mountain but very little fruit on them.

Since passing the Susquehana in all our rout including all the towns, we have not seen half a dozen women or ladys genteely dressed, and two of them was in passing a logged house about 2 miles before we arrived. In our travel we meet with more or less people every day from the Ohio or near it and some who have been down to the Natchis.[29] One of them gave us a bad account of the women there. He says indeed they are very hansome but all of them whether married or single are of leud conduct and ready to imbrace any body, that Natchez is worse than Philadelphia for strumpits.[30]

Our host Mr. Horn proposed sending his son with us in the morning to Chambersbourg, that his son may ride in the carriage and I have his horse to ride over the stoney parts of the road which I accepted of. 5 wagons came by here today from Baltimore where they had been with flour.

Distances on the road we have travelled

From Wilmington to Webbs Tavern	12 miles
Thence to Doe Run	9 miles
Thence to Lilleys Tavern	5 miles
Thence to the turnpike road near Old Gap	8 miles
Thence to Lancaster	14 miles
Thence to Susquehana at Columbia	12 miles
Thence across the river at ferry	1 mile
Thence to Little York	12 miles
Thence to the Unicorn	11 miles
Thence to Hartfoard near Canaway Bridge	8 miles
Thence to Hunters Town	6 miles
Thence to Horns Tavern on the South Mountain	14 miles
Thence to Chambersbourg	12 miles
in all	124 miles

The b[e]aring of the road from L. York to Canowaga Bridge is nearly west by south, thence to Hunters Town nearly west, thence to the mountain nearly west by north, circular over the mountain, then west and west by north to Chambersbourgh.

Through all the country since we entered Pensylvania or rather Lancaster County, the people are mostly, as I observed before, Germans and much uncultivated as to dress and manners. Even in this town which is composed of so many neat and I may say elegant houses, we have hardly seen even a woman genteely dressed.

Chambersbourg, Fryday, August 26th 1803. We left Horns Tave[r]n this morning after breakfast at 8 o'clock A.M. and arrived here at 12 o'clock. We decended along the side of the South Mountain about a mile and then crossed a little stream in the bottom of the vally between two projecting tonngs [tongues] of the mountain while the sumits on each hand were at least half a mile perpendicular hights above the stream. About 2 miles further on we passed a small bridge over a branch of the Conococheage Creek where the side of the South Mountain terminates on the border of the vally.[31]

Here I assend the end of one point of the mountain on our right on horseback to near it[s] sommit, and thence had an extensive view of the N side of the S. Mountain and of the plain or valley lying between it and the North Mountain and a distant view of the N. Mountain itself, which appeared a little obscured in smoke and its head or ridge rising to the clouds while a more distant and darker shade of the Alegany seemed rising above it. At the distance of 5 miles we met with the first solatory landscape.

All the way till we decended into the valley the tall timber on the mountain was pine, not very large, and on the decline with age. The undergrowth was small oak bushes from 2 to 4 feet high and loaded with acorns, a fine pork country tho fit for little else. It was 6 miles before we reached the open cultivated country in the valley, but thence the country is pretty well cultivated to this place but far from fertile. The whole valley seems to be a bed of rock mined with clay, and the surface generally very stoney. Yet it produces in the bottoms very good grass but Indian corn appeared very feble everywhere.

Chambersbourg is situated in respect to the Conococheage just as Little York is in respect to the Codorus and is laid out in the same manner, but the streets are wider and the houses in general hansomer.[32] Yet we have hardly seen a person of genteel dress or manners in the town. They appear like honest industrous people but very rustic in their dress and manners.

The Court House may be said to be a plain brick building and except that it has a cupelea or bellfery looks more like a prive than a public building. Their gaol [jail] is a large strong look[ing] stone building.[33] Just to the NW[34] of the town the Conococheage divides into several branches. The forks exhibit fine ceadar groves and romantic scenes of rock and stream and evergreen shades. A large new church stands by the side of one of these groves, and the burying ground is chiefly in the grove.

Saturday, August 27th 1803, Chambersbourg. Wrote to my son C.A.R. and J. Fisher yesterday and to P. Lewes this morning. Very warm yesterday and so it is today. We gave out [our] cloaks to wash yesterday and only wait for them today till 12 o'clock. Goods are as cheap here as in Wilmington. Butter very plenty in their market, everything else scarce. The wagons returning from Baltimore in the winter when they have no other loading bring back oysters to this town so that the street about this tavern is covered with shells, and what is remarkable they are sold here as cheap as in Dover in Dalaware. We stayed here till after diner, received our cloaths from washer woman, and proceeded on our journey.

The road for 8 miles was equally good with any in New Castle County, and continued pretty good to Camels Tavern, 10 miles from Chambersbourg, where we rested awhile and then went on 4 miles further to Stingers near to Ridles Nob of the N. Mountain.

Here we had a night view of that nob and two others not much inferior to it, all very lofty;[35] but we had horreble lodging. The house was a large loged house with two rooms below but the loft all in one where the family slept in 5 or 6 dirty beds. I retired from this scene and had a bed laid in one of the rooms below. The bed and bedding [were] very durty as was everything else about the house, yet they gave us a pretty good supper. The old lady was drunk but all of them seemed inclined to entertain us as well as they could. They spread a clean cover over all the durty bed and on this I laid in my cloaths and slept very well.[36] The night was bright and beautiful.

MConnels Town, August 28th 1803. We rose early in the morning and were on the road by sun up. We found the road pretty stoney to the N. Mountain and up the mountain which has a horrible rockey and stoney appearance; but we found the road not more so than the S. Mountain, indeed hardly so bad.[37] The assent to the summit was gentle but the decent very steep. We were 3 hours in passing it and 4 1/2 in all from Sting[ers] to this place, which is 8 miles.

This N.M. is very lofty from the summit. We saw over all the valley and inferior mountains we had passed and northward over the inferior mountains and valleys to Allegany. Thus we had as grand a prospect as perhaps the world exhibits anywhere. Nor has the road been so bad. Yet as I expected and yet all agree that we have passed the worst road there is between Philadelphia and Pittsbourg; but the mountains before us tho not so high, except the Alegany, look horrible presenting an aspect of rocks and stones and starveling trees squeezing up among the rocks; but none of them can be worse in that respect than the N. Mountain. The timber growing on all these mountains is pretty much alike.

Here, at MConnels Town which is put at the N foot of the N. Mountain in the valley, we halted to breakfast at Daviss Tavern, Sign of the Black Horse. It is quite an elegant stone house commodious and everything about it new, neat, and clean; and we got an excelunt break-fast and were attended by Miss Davis, the tavern keeper['s] daugh[t]er, a young hansome girl and genteely educated, an honor we have not experienced before. Indeed our entertainment here made ample com-

pensation for our lodging last night and I confes I feel here a high degree
of pleasure in having rolled this North Mountain under our feet this
morning and now being so happily situated.

Impromtu, I began the following verses of prais yesterday and continued them with vast pleasure today

> Glory to Him in the highest
> Who formed the mountains!
> Glory to Him in the highest
> Who formed the fountains!
> Great are his works from Pole to Pole
> Glory to Him in the highest who formed the whole.

This little town or village is composed of about 30 houses, all of them
but 3 or 4 of logs, one of brick and 2 or 3 of stone, which are neat
buildings. It is situated in a narrow cove or valley among the mountains.[38] Here Mr. Clark and Mr. Brown, two gentlemen of the barr on
their way to the court at Bedford, came up with us. We rested a few
hours and then proceeded to Beckwiths Tavern at the south foot of
Sideling Hill.[39] In our progress there we passed a very ruff and hilley
road. Have rolled over no less than five mountains on our way. Some
of them very high so that the road at different places exhibited a great
variety of grand and extensive landscape.

At Beckwiths we met with an old soldier of Carlile who knew me
as he thought and called me General Rodney; but it was my brother
Caesar who he remembered when he commanded at Trenton in January 1777, and repeated several incidents that happend there. Also a Mr.
Jordan was there who had been a seaman and remembered my brother
when he was Governor of Dalaware and said he was universally hon-
ored and beloved.[40] And the old soldier said that he was beloved and
highly respected by all the army at Trenton, etc., and he heard me with
great pleasure repeat some of the incidents of that period, etc., etc.
The old soldier and part of his family were on their way to the Ohio
state where some of his children are settled. We had very good entertainment at this place.

CHAPTER TWO

"Grand and beautiful scenes"

Into the Western Wilderness

Sideling Hill to Wheeling, (West) Virginia,
August 29–September 5, 1803

As Thomas Rodney slowly made his way through western Pennsylvania, he was repeatedly impressed by the timber and beautiful mountains, a virtual "region of the clouds"—scenery which he variously characterized as majestic, magnificent, "stupendious," and romantic. The scientist in him speculated on how such natural features came to be formed. While the "feasants," "patriges," and "dear" did not escape his attention, he never tired of chronicling the condition of the roads, just as soon he would describe every stretch of the rivers which were to carry him toward the Mississippi Territory. The all too often deplorable condition of the taverns somewhat lessened the degree of comfort which Rodney enjoyed on this, the land-bound portion of his journey.

For pleasure and to mitigate the effect of the trip's exertions, Rodney wrote letters back home, and hunted whenever the chance presented itself. He first turned Nimrod while descending Laurel Hill Mountain, where he killed a pigeon. "I never saw a fatter bird." With great gusto he mingled with local inhabitants, for example, as at the Sign of the Eagle in Bedford, where he fraternized with the "gentlemen of the barr."

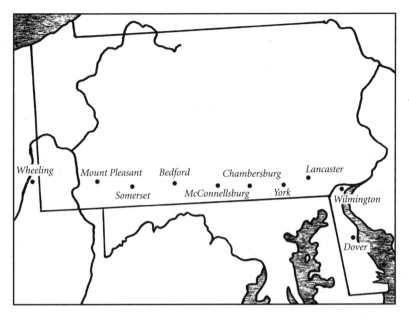

Thomas Rodney's Overland Journey
Dover, Delaware, to Wheeling, [West] Virginia. August 14-September 5, 1803

His journal, however, remained his delight and favorite pastime throughout this phase of his westward trek. It became a literary refuge in which he nightly committed to paper all he saw during the day that had struck his fancy and intrigued him. Rodney indeed proved himself a master of the pungent obser-vation, whether describing a religious service of the "Presbyterians that may have got in the same frenzy of shouting and falling down that the Methodists have long been at," the use of coal in a region, the taverns, "durty and swarming with bed bugs and fleas," a pretty serving girl, or a horse-operated grist mill.

Finally, with mountain travel almost behind them, Rodney and Shields neared the Ohio River. They then entered western Virginia and approached the river port of Wheeling, which would be their longest stop and an important milestone on their journey. After crossing Wheeling Creek no less than sixteen times, the two finally reached Wheeling, but not until Rodney climbed a high hill to get a bird's-eye view of both the town and the Ohio, the great highway flowing west and south toward his destination.

33

Munday, August 29th 1803. We set out this morning at sunrise and continued our rout over Sidling Hill, which is a very high mountain, and several other hills and mountains to old Col. Martins Tavern at Juniata where we breakfasted; and here we found the most ordinary entertainment we have met with. The road to this place was some of the very worst we have passed, yet the assent of Sidling Hill which we had been so much alarmed about was some of the best part of the road. We were however amply compensated for the badness of the road by the variety of grand and dignified prospects it afforded us. The very worst part of all the road we passed this morning to Juniata was the steep decent tho short down to that stream at the foord.[1]

From Col. Martins the road runs generally on very high ground along and near the Juniata to Wainsbourg or Ville.[2] 4 miles, and all the way is very hilly up and down continually, yet it was better than any of the road we had passed before not being much stoney. We stoped at Stantons Tavern in Wayn Ville and rested our horses and refreshed and fed our horse. Then proceed on a pretty level road some times along the bank of Juniata, mostly on level ground to Bedford formerly called Fort Bedford.[3]

In this short rout we passed two grand and beautiful scenes which I enjoyed with great felicity. These were where the Juniata passes through the Warrior Mountain about a mile above Wayns Ville, and through Bedford Mountain about a mile below the town of Bedford.[4] These scenes are grand and magnificent. The mountains are at least 500 feet high above the stream and are cut down by the stream just in the manner we may suppose it was naturally done when the land and water of the world were first seperating from each other, when the valley being full of water began to break over the ridge of mountain at that spot being accidently a little lower than the rest; and as the torrent increased it cut down the ridge more rapidly, so that the passage kept narrowing till it got to the bottom of the mountain, and such is its present appearance; but the stream by time has narrowed so as to occupy now only about a third part of the bottom space or gap between the point of the mountain. Yet in great freshe[t]s in the spring it evidently sometimes overflows the whole.

The ends of the mountains present huge piles of rock upon rock from their base to their summits, yet they are mostly covered with wood growing up among the rocks. There are some spots however where the rocks will not admit any kind of growth and rise in great upright crags perhaps 20 or 30 feet perpendicular, and so rock above rock to the summit of the mountain, with jagged tops of points very stupendious and romantic in appearance. I walked along the bank of the stream through each gap and viewed the wonders of nature at my lezure while my companion Mr. Shields road on in the carriage and waited for me at the end of each gap.

After enjoying the cast of these scenes we went on and arrived at Bedford about sundown having passed two branches of the Juniata within a mile of the town over wooden bridges that deserve no particular notice. The stream is very low at this time and may be forded anywhere. It is only in the spring that it admits of boat navigation when the waters are swelled by the melting of the winter snows, etc.

The town of Bedford, Tuesday, August 30th 1803. We put up here yesterday evening at Smiths Tavern at the Sign of the Eagle where Judge Ridle and Mr. Clark, Mr. Dunlap, Mr. Brown, and Mr. Ridle, all gentlemen of the barr lodge. We saw none of them in the evening but spent our time alone investigating our maps and assertaining the roads we have to perrsue.

The first thing I did this morning was to git stuff for a new riding coat and git the taylor at work, my old one being torn too bad to ware any further. Soon afterwards Mr. Clark came into the parlour to see me and invited me upstairs into the dining room where he introduced me to Judge Ridle and other gentlemen of the barr and we all breakfasted together. Judge Ridle is a lusty well looking man of dark complexion, is very conversable and intelligent. Says he came from Ireland to this country in 1785, and has lived at or near Carlile ever since. He is now President of this Circuit.[5]

After breakfast Mr. Clark who is a genteman[l]y affable man walked with Mr. Shields and myself to take a view of the town, but there is nothing very remarkable about it only that it has a very hansome situation and is very healthy. There is a variety of landscapes round of mountain, hill, and dale. The town too is supplied with water from a fountain or spring that issues from the foot of a mountain SW of the town, and is so high that all the families who will be at the expence of conveying it from the public conduit may have the water drawn from casks in their own houses; and several of them enjoy this benefit. The best buildings in town are brick or stone but there is not one to be called elegant. Their Court House and prison are both under one ruff and have no pretensions to elegance. The town is but small and does not exhibit any prospect of increase tho in time perhaps it may be the seat of many manufactories.[6]

We determined yesterday to rest our horse here today and make use of the opertunity to write to our friends, etc. I wrote to Caesar[7] and Bishop and when I went to the Post Office enquired for Major Claybourn. The postmaster said that he knew him but that he had not been here.

In the evening I took a rural walk along the Juniata till it entered the wood above the town and washed my feet in the stream. All over the bottom land along the stream there is cuts and breaks made by the current of the overflowing water where the mountain torrents come rushing down. The bottom land is rich and mellow. There are some lots near the town upon it and the growth luxuriant.

The top of Alegany Mountain, August, Wednesday the 31st 1803.[8] We left Bedford this morning at sunrise and breakfasted at a tavern 5 miles from there. The road hilly and stony but not to say bad. From this tavern to within two or three miles of Aleganey the road was hilly but not much stoney and great part of the road very good. We were all the way for twelve or fifteen miles on what is called the Dry Ridge and were mostly in the region of the clouds except when crossing several steep valleys, but even in the bottom of them we were as high as the tops of the small mountains. The higher parts of the ridge seemed to lift us to a level with the tops of the highest mountains, except Alegany; and the ridge is in some parts not more than a hundred feet wide and is but narrow all the way, a deep valley being on each side.

We decended from this ridge into a steep valley at the foot of the Alegany and crossed a small stream in the valley where Boones Tavern stands; but we did not halt there but proceeded immediately up the mountain about one mile and a quarter to the top of the south spur or nob to a tavern where we stoped and dined. We had been told that the assent was so gentle that we should not know when we were assending it but found this information erronious, for the assent is as steep as that of the Sideling Hill and very much like it as to road.

Long before we reached the top we found we were raised far above the tops of all the other mountains; and when we reached the top we found our view extended to the eastward and southward as far as the eye could see; and all the mountains in that vast space which had before appeared to us so elevated were now sunk down apparently into little hills dispersed over a vast plain. So much superior grand and dignified is this majestic mountain above all the rest, and yet we were not on the highest part of it.

Near the tavern on the top are several fine springs whence the tavern is supplied with water. We for the first time dined on venison at this place. The timber chiefly chestnut and oak is the largest and loftiest on this mountain of any we have seen in the mountain country and the soil also appears of the best kind we have seen among the mountains. We frequently saw wild pigeons, and several flocks of feasants crossed the road before we reached the mountain; and on it we saw two flocks of potriges, and the dear is very plenty in all this country.

After diner we proceeded on our journey and immediately decended into a small valley on the mountain bound by the stream of a spring, and assended the north spur or nob of the mountain, which is considerably higher than the south side where the tavern stands; and in assending it being pretty steep and stoney the tonge of the lower buckle of our collar strap broke out, being the first accident that in any way impeded us on our rout, but was soon remedied by extending the buckle to another hole in the same 4 strap. And then we proceeded.

The road is stoney till we got quite clear of the mountain, but the decent is hardly so steep on the N as on the S side. Afterwards we entered into a plain called the Glades[9] where we beheld beautiful meadows on either hand as we passed, the road being some times good some times very stoney, and so it continued to the tavern aforesaid where we suped and lodged all night, and the people gave us a very good supper and good beds but full of bugs and the house durty and disagreable being a waggon stage. Mr. Shields killed two young wild pigeons as we went along which we had for supper. Mr. Shields played his flute in the evening and there was a soft and sweet ecco from a wood N of the house.

Summersett, the County Town of Summerset in Pensylvania, Thursday, September the 1st 1803. We came on 8 miles to this place to breakfast this morning and put up at Websters Tavern. This town is quite new and mostly logged buildings except the Court House offices and prison which make a neat and decent appearance. In coming to it we passed over a wooden bridge across a small stream of the York or Youhagana Creek.[10] It is situated in a plain between Alegany and the Lorrel Hill. The stream abovementioned is the first water of the Ohio that we have met with. We saw a tract of woodland on the road about 5 miles before we got to this town of the finest and largest chestnut timber I ever saw and there was little other growth among it; but the wood or old timber generally in this country has got its growth and is on the decline; but the young growth is rising to supply its place and so thick that it can hardly be passed through on foot.

After breakfast we proceeded onward 12 miles to the top of Lorrel Hill and beyond its sumit, and stoped at Bremers Tavern at 4 o'clock P.M., and determined as the road had been bad all the way to go no further today;[11] but we did not find the hill worse than other mountains we had passed but much like. It is near as high as most of them except Alegany. In passing up the hill we saw the remains of a large rattle snake which had been killed in the road.[12] The chestnut timber is also large and lofty on this hill and we saw some evidence of a coal mine; but we saw nothing to entitle it to the name of Laurrel. It is 2 or three miles from the foot of the hill where we passed a branch of the Youhagana called Laurel Hill Creek over a wooden bridge.[13]

◍

Top of Laurel Hill, Fryday, September 2d 1803. We put up here at a Mr. Bremins. He married a daughter of Webster in Summerset. They are young people and both modest and obliging. They live in a logged house covered with puncheons and floors little better than the covering, yet we were well entertained and got good lodging and had silver handled knives and forks to eat with; and a very hansome modest girl of the name of Betsey Lockwood lived with them, a relation of the Lockwood family in Kent. She had a very fine person and features and would have made a figure if dressed. Her modesty had a softness and sweetness in it seldom met with among hiring girls. Her mother lived in a house next door and her fathers heirs owned the tavern and land around it.

We stayed to breakfast there, and then proceeded on our journey down the Laurel Hill and found it a bad road indeed, but not so bad as reported. We passed over it six miles and stoped at Joness Tavern to feed.[14] The land the whole way was good and covered with very heavy timber chiefly chestnut. We then proceed up Chestnut Ridge after passing a bridge over a branch of the Youhagana.[15]

We found the road in part very stoney for near a mile, the rest pretty good to the fork of the road at Hartmans Tavern; and about midway we passed over a small hill of remarkable fine land, it being equal to the best in Little Creek or Jones's Neck in Dalaware. It was chiefly covered with black walnut timber and very large, some trees being 3 and 4 feet diameter. I should not have forgot to mention that on coming down the Laurel Hill, I being on foot took the gun out and shot a wild pigeon. This was the first time I had fired the gun, and I never saw a fatter bird. They were flying about in flocks today, but I had only a single one to shoot at. The flocks were distant and we had not time to go to them.

It is to be noted that there is both a tavern and smiths shop where the road forks to Pittsbourg and Washington, but a durtier looking tavern I never met with. Tho they are mostly so on this road, we have seldom met with a decent one. We fed at said tavern and proceeded for Mount Pleasant, 8 miles. We went on a road mostly very bad till crossed Jacobs Creek, a branch of the Youhagana, and indeed till we got to within 2 miles of Mount Pleasant.[16]

The road till then was very rocky and stoney and passed one place at 5 miles that presented a vast bed and pillars on blocks of rock thrown as it were in great confusion and piled one upon another and yet quite seperat in a most wonderfull and romantic manner. We stopped and went up on them to view them. In one place an oblong block 15 feet long, 5 ft. thick, and 8 ft. wide lay with one corner upward on the top of 6 or 7 others which lay below, as if all of them had been thrown by hand on[e] upon another promiscusly. Yet it is evident that they must all have grown as they were as there was no mountain near them from which they could have fell or any land higher than where they lay. We also shot several pigeons as we went along.

When we got within 2 miles of Mount Pleasant we crossed a little branch and bottom where there was a fine meadow; and thence to M.P. was white oak land and clear of stones and good road. We soon got to town and put up at the Sign of the Ship about 5 o'clock P.M.

Mount Pleasant. This little town is on perhaps the highest hill between the mountains and Youhagana; and from the highest part of the hill where 2 new houses are building there is a very fine view of the mountains eastward and southward and of the valley or lower country between this and the mountains. There is not more than 10 or 12 families in this town and all the building[s] are of logs, most of [them] 2 stories high and pretty neat. We are informed that we are over all the stoney road on our way which affoards us great pleasure. The soil and timber round this town are different from all we have seen since we reached the mountains. The timber is almost all white oak.

Saturday, September 3d 1803. We left Mount Pleasant after breakfast and went on our journey. We found the road very hilly and the up and down steeps and hights as bad or worse than the mountains till we reached the Yohagana. This is a branch of the Monongahala and about fifty yards wide. We foarded over it, the water being very low, and dined at a very ordinary tavern on the other or west side, and then proceeded on and found the road much better across the fork to the Monongahala.

About 3 miles before we reached the latter we decended a very high hill into a steep valley; and after crossing it we road [sic] along the side of the western hills, considerably elevated above the bottom of the narrow gully for a quarter of a mile, on a causway of logs or rails till the gully opened, and then decended into the bottom land and persued it on a level road, to the river about a mile; and then road along the bank of the river on a beautiful level road near 2 miles to the ferry, where the river is about one hundred yards wide but the water very low so that we foarded over. No part of it took the horse higher than his knee with a stoney or rocky bottom as all the streams of this country are. We crossed at Parkinsons Ferry as it is called and put up at Parkinsons Tavern on the west side the river.[17] The course of the river where the road runs along it is near W by N.[18]

After passing the Youhagana the soil and wood changed in some degree. We saw some small pieces of walnut land but mostly white oak and black or red oak indeed very much like the land in New Castle County [Delaware] between New Castle and Red Lyon. The Monongahala is a beautiful river, is a beautiful stream as far as we had a view of it, the bottom [h]as livel land along side of it about 50 to 100 yards wide and the land or hills on each side very high hills.

There is a small town at the ferry of about 20 small houses mostly logged. The tavern house however is pretty large. They tell us here that there is a wonderful spunk[19] at this time in the religious way among the Presbeterians that they have got in the same frenzy of shouting and falling down that the Methodists have long been at and that the people assemble together from 20 or thirty miles round, etc. Meeting is today about 4 miles from the ferry on the west side the river.

In all our travel today the squirrels and pigeons were plenty in view but we wou'd not stop to shoot any. The squirrels are mostly black but there are some grey and some fox squirrels. Near to this place is several fine coal mines. The tavern keeper has opened one of them and uses the coal and made us a fire of it. It is in appearance equal to any English stone coal and burns as well. He says it is very plenty all over this part of this county but has not been found further west than Licking River in Kaintuky. He says it answers better than charcoal for smiths work. The vien *[sic]* is about 30 rod wide and 5 feet thick and covered by slate rock.

Parki[n]sons Ferry on the Monongahala, Sunday, September the 4th 1803. The weather still continues fine and we have had moonlight nights ever since we set out. We lodged here all night and was to breakfast this morning. All the river and valley between the hills this morning was covered with thick fog while the hill tops ran above it. Old Mr. McGreggery and his wagon with his daughter and son in law who are going to settle in the Ohio state came up with us again here and tarried all night. We overtook them first at the foot of Sidling Hill and have fallen in with them several times since. We set off again after breakfast and stoped only once to feed our horse at the halfway house and then rode on to Washington to diner.

Put up at Morris's, said to be the best tavern in town but the family were all at meeting and we could hardly git our diners. The Court House and offices are plain brick buildings and the prison stone, and there is a bell and bellfry on the Court House. The town is in a hilly valley and makes but a mean appearance. Most the houses are wooden, logged, or framed. There is however a few of brick or stone but none that display any taste or elegance. We sent for Captain McCannon who is Prothonatary[20] of the county and was an officer in the Dalaware Regiment but he was at meeting and we did not see him.

After diner we proceeded 5 miles and put up at the Sign of General Wolf where we got poor accomodations; however this is what we have got used to for we have not yet met with but one decent tavern, to wit Davis's at McConnel Town. All the rest have been more or less durty and swarming with bed bugs and fleas, etc. Be it so, our object in this rout is to see the country and the people as they are.

Munday, September 5th 1803. We set out from the General Woolf early in the morning and proceeded 5 miles to breakfast. Then proceeded on to a little town called Alexander, ten miles from Wheeling and one half a mile from Virginia and Pensylvania line. Stoped there to feed our horse. The house[s] are a logged in this little town and about ten or 12 in number and even the Presbeterian Meeting is a logged building.[21] I went to view it, and the graveyard indicated its being not a very healthy situation tho situated on a high hill. The graves were numerous for such a new settlement. Yet in all this country on this side the mountains we have remarked seeing the children very numerous; and I have often expressed my pleasure at this as promising the improvement of this new country.[22]

In proceeding one mile further we decended into the Valley of Wheeling Creek along which the road runs near nine miles, so that in going two miles we crossed the creek, which runs a serpentine course through the valley, 8 times; and then stoped at a tavern to see a new horse grist mill which we saw working with two horses. It was on the usual construction of such mills but her works rather heavy so that she grinds only 41 bushels a day with two good horses; but this is very benificial to the country. Now all the mill streams of water are dry and great complaint in the country for want of bread.

We proceeded on along the valley and crossed the creek 8 times more before we got to Wheeling. We stoped on our way to view a large coal mine on the N. side this creek which the town gits coal from. Indeed the banks of this creek on both sides appear to have a stratum of coal 5 or 6 feet thick, and indeed the high hills, or I may call them mountains, on both appear to be in great part coal, and so we were informed they are by the inhabitants.

For several miles and particularly one mile before we got to Wheeling the valley creek and mountains on each side presented the most romantic scenes we have met; the sides of the mountains being very steep and covered with wood and stupendious rocks. We g[r]aduly assended the mountain along the north side of the valley till we reached the summit on the brink almost of the Ohio where the river and town at once presented themselves to our view, the town being on a narrow strip of land at the foot of the mountain and between it and the river; yet this strip is 50 or 60 ft. above the river.

When we got to the summit we halted to view the town and river. Here I observed that a strip or spur of the mountain run off to the south parrallel with the river and back of the town with the valley of the creek behind it, and saw that it ran into a nob behind the town much higher than where we were. I therefore left Mr. Shields to proceed to town in the carriage and I walked up this strip or spur of the mountain to the summit to take a more ample view of the river and country round. I found it in some parts not two [sic] wide for a single carriage and very steep, almost perpendicular towards the valley, but not so steep towards the town, tho too steep [to] decend but where the road passes over it.

After indulging my mind with [the] view and paying my tribute of thanks, adoration, and praise to the Most High God, I decended to the road again and so to the town and found Mr. Shields put up at Geo. Knoxes at the Sign of the Black Horse, etc. Here we took up our abode.

CHAPTER THREE

A Sojourn on the Ohio

Wheeling, September 6–19, 1803

Wheeling was founded, traditionally in 1769, more likely in 1774, by three brothers: Ebenezer, Silas, and Jonathan Zane. During the American Revolution, its Fort Henry was besieged by the British and Indians, served on one occasion as the backdrop for Betty Zane's famous powder-carrying episode, and was a base for raids into Indian country. In the 1790s, the town, flourishing as a shipping point for the area's export of grain and flour, was designated by the federal government as an official port of entry. Many travelers and emigrants came to favor it over Pittsburgh as their westward point of embarkation either down the Ohio River or by land over Zane's Trace.[1]

A traveler passing through Wheeling a year before Rodney described its new courthouse as "A Stone house Unfinished without a door or window a part of the roof uncove[r]ed & Not a Florr in the building except some loose boards over apart. . . . [It] appears to have Stood in this Situation for a Number of years—but the Carpenters had that day commen[ce]d work in the upper part of it. . . . I was present at one [of] their Courts[.] The Judges, Sherif & Attorney were Seated around a Small Table & Serounded by a Croud of uncouth Men every one Speaking that pleased—I must Say I was much at a Looss which wer Judges or peasants—"[2]

45

Ebenezer Zane home, Wheeling, West Virginia. Zane was a founder of the settlement in 1769. He built this house about 1800. This photograph was made in 1868, shortly before the building was razed. Courtesy Oglebay Institute, Wheeling, West Virginia.

At Wheeling, faced with the prospect of becoming a sailor for the remainder of his journey, Rodney tackled the all-important task of providing himself and his party with a suitable boat. He lost no time in hiring two young men to construct a "batteau" thirty feet long and eight feet wide, to be equipped with four oars, a square sail, and four berths covered by a painted canvas. He next set about obtaining supplies for the long voyage ahead: food, bedding, and other necessities unobtainable or hard to find in the wilderness through which he soon would pass.

For a while, Rodney was in a quandary about what to do with his horse and carriage. Not receiving any offers he judged commensurate with their worth, he determined to take them with him to Mississippi, but finally sold them to a local merchant in exchange for goods from the man's store.

Here, Rodney was joined by some more traveling companions: Major

Richard Claiborne, a Virginian on his way to assume the post of clerk to the Mississippi land commissioners; a Mr. Buchanan (Rodney never reveals his first name) who signed on the boat crew in exchange for passage to Natchez; and finally, two carpenters who joined as hands.

The wait in Wheeling proved to be a protracted one for the travelers, who were increasingly eager to be away. Rodney filled the long days and early evenings pleasantly enough by poring over his books and papers, writing letters, stalking the post office in the hope of hearing from his family and friends, talking to frontiersmen about the land along the Ohio and its tributaries, and forming part of the audience for several musical performances by Claiborne (who always appears as "the Major" in Rodney's journal) and Shields when they enlivened their roughhewn surroundings by playing "fiddle and flute."

Rodney's pastime which proved most valuable to posterity, however, was his tours of the town and nearby countryside. He depicted these excursions in such a vivid manner and with such detail that they constitute one of the finest firsthand descriptions ever penned of this section of Virginia in frontier times. Among the most exciting and valuable passages are his accounts of visiting Meriwether Lewis, then just embarking upon his historic exploration of the Trans-Mississippi West. Intrigued by Captain Lewis's barge and his rapid-fire "air gun," the judge listened intently to Lewis's account of his expedition's goals. When the time came for Lewis to cast off, Rodney was on hand to bid him farewell, but not before sharing with him "a parting drink and part of a water mellon."

Rodney's own leave-taking was soon at hand. On September 17 his boat, christened Iris, was launched into the Ohio, upon whose clear waters "she sat like a sea gull." "She will certainly carry us quick down the river," Rodney wrote hopefully. Within a few days, he and his party would be on their way toward new adventures.

Wheeling on the bank of the Ohio, Tuesday, September the 6th 1803. The landlady being in the straw³ it was late last evening before we got supper, but it was very good when it came. It being monthly court the sheriff and one or two of the justices supped with us; and a Doctor Spencer, a Yankee who lives 8 miles below Muskingum, lodged in the same room and was very inquisitive about our journey and business.

This little town is the Court of Ohio County in Virginia. The Court House stands [on] the east side [of] the Main Street and is but an ordinary stone building. The town appears to contain about a hundred houses, some pretty good framed houses, and a few of brick chiefly in one street and about half a mile long. It stands on the bank of the Ohio above Wheeling Creek and under a lofty hill or mountain. There is two or three boat yards here for building river boats and a number of taverns and merchantile shops and a variety of mechanics.

We agreed today with two young men to build us a batteau 30 feet long and 8 feet wide, to have 2 births on each side towards the stern of the boat which is at that end to be 6 1/2 wide at least. The births will take up 12 feet on each side from the stern forward, and are to be covered with painted canvas, and the top with half inch board in the manner of a stage waggon or coach; and so far as the births extend, the sides of the boat are to be raised 20 inches above what they otherwise would be. She is to be finished complet and neat, with 4 oars, a mast, and two spars for a square sail. The boat at 1 1/4 dollars a foot in length including the oars, mast, and spar and frame for covering stern as prices fixed in agreement. We to buy sail cloth, roaps, etc., and pay them for making sail; also to pay for painting and for canvas and painting for covering stern and for under irons, etc., and for any thing else we may propose not mentioned in agreement.[4]

After we had agreed as aforesaid and just before diner, Major Claybourn arrived, which gave us great pleasure as he is one of our company to Natches;[5] and he tells us that he was told on his way that Mr. Lewes, Private Secretary to the President, is at Pittsbourg and that his baggage is in this town; but we had heard nothing of this before. Indeed I expected he was at the head of the Misourri before this. Lewes, it is said, is aground up the river in his barge, and that was the reason of his sending his bagage down here by land.[6]

Wheeling

Wheeling, Wednesday, September 7th 1803. The weather fine and cooler than it has been since we set out before. The post arrived at 8 o'clock A.M. and immediately after breakfast, Major Claybourn, Mr. Shields, and myself went to the Post Office to look for letters but none came. We stayed awhile to read the [news]papers and then returned. Major Claybourn and Mr. Shields took boarding at a Mr. Zanes.

Afterwards Mr. Shields and myself took a ride in the carriage three miles up the river. The road runs along the bank of the river on the bottom land between the river and mountain. The road having the river on one hand and the mountain on the other presents a rout not to be exceeded anywhere for beauty and grandure.

The river (above the island which lays opposite Wheeling and divides it into two streams) asumes its own majestic and noble form in one intire stream. We road along it two miles above the island. Its shores are a gravely grey yellowish sand, and several barrs of the same appeared bare in places; but generally the water flowed from shore to shore above the sandy shore. The bank is a gravelly clay very rich. The river, where not broken by islands, appears to be about 2 or 3 hundred yards wide above Wheeling.

We passed several little farm[s] on the bottom land and stoped at a new field on it where the trees had been lately deaded and the field planted in corn, which was very stout and strong indeed; but what most drew my attention at this spot was the monstrous vines that run on almost every tree in the corn field and still hung on the trees tho cut off and the trees dead. Many of the vine stocks were thicker than my thigh and run to the tops of the largest trees. Many of them hung like ropes to a ships mast single and perpindicular for 70 feet without a branch and then spread out over the trees. In all my life I never saw so grand a native vineyard and they seem to have spread in this manner over ten acres of land from the brink of the river to the mountain.[7] Never was there a finer place to plant a vineyard; but the native grapes are small and sour and not yet quite ripe. They are however a spici [species] of our September grape.

On this rout along the river we saw the bottom land, where not cleared, abound in luxuriant woods: buttonwood, black and white walnut and hickory, and the buckeye nut, which tree looks like hickory and the outside hull something like a hickory nut, but the nut has a soft hull like a chestnut and of the same color, and the meat or cernal is also like that of a chestnut, but the nut is larger than horse chestnuts, yet it is said not to be good. We cut several and tasted them. Their flavor is most like that of a hickory nut. The trees of this kind were loaded with nuts not quite ripe tho near it.

The hickories are also loaded with nuts and also with squirrels but we did not take our gun. The Major and Shields have a pike of 15 lb. for diner today and came over for me to dine with them at Zanes; but I am too busy to go. Wrote a letter to my son[8] and another to P. Lewes. Then took a walk and returned to coffe, after which retired to my books and maps in my chambers.

Bought a pound of powder and 2 lb. of pigeon shot today, 15/-.

Thursday, Wheeling September 8th 1803. The weather clear and pleasant. Wrote another letter to my son.[9]

Visited Captain Lewess barge. He shewed us his air gun which fired 22 times at one charge. He shewed us the mode of charging her and then loaded with 12 balls which he intended to fire one at a time; but she by some means lost the whole charge of air at the first fire. He charged her again and then she fired twice. He then found the cause and in some measure prevented the airs escaping, and then she fired seven times; but when in perfect order she fires 22 times in a minute. All the balls are put at once into a short side barrel and are then droped into the chamber of the gun one at a time by moving a spring; and when the triger is pulled just so much air escapes out of the air bag which forms the britch [breech] of the gun as serves for one ball. It is a curious peice of workmanship not easily discribed and therefore I omit attempting it.[10]

Major Claybourn, Mr. Shields, and myself then all went to Caldwels store and bot stuff for mattrasses and beding. I got 5 yds. of fine ticking at 7/6 for mine and 6 yds. of linnen @ 3/6 for sheets and pillows and 2 1/2 yds. of chintz for a coverlid. The mattrass and pillow to be stuffed with wheat straw, and delivered them to a Mrs. Laurence to make for me.

Then I dined at Mr. Zanes with the Major and Shields and Captain Lewes on the great Ohio pike which was not dressed yesterday, and I found it to be a very good kind of fish; and we had a cleaver diner. Mr. Linsey, a lawyer, and Doctor *[blank]* were both introduced to us there. Zane is a son of old Jonathan Zane of Philadelphia[11] who I was formerly acquainted with and brother to Joel Zane of Wilmington who I am acquainted with.

After diner the Major, Shields, and myself went over to the island and the Major shot twice at a squirrel but did not git it. This island is all of it river or what is called bottom land tho pretty high ground and very rich. The part not cleared is covered with wood mostly black or white walnut, hickory, elm, etc., etc., and elder and rich weads very luxiurient. After viewing this we returned and went on board Captain Lewes's barge to eat watter millons and then returned to coffee.

Wheeling, Fryday, September 9th 1803. Tuesday and Wednesday morning were foggy, yesterday morning and this morning cloudy, yet all the days have yet been clear and pleasant afterwards. This morning, however, looks very much like rain yet.

Captain Lewes's object is to assend the Misisipi and to visit the Lake of the Woods, to assertain accurately its lattitude and longitude and as well as the head of the Misisipi, and then to return to or cross over to the Misouri and explore those parts and branches of it that are yet unknown and the country of Louisana west of the Misisipi. He says that the Brittish or the Canadians under the Brittish, by means of what is called the Company of the West trading under the direction of Sir Alexander McKenzie, the northern and western traveler in America,[12] now trade from Canada through the lakes and up the Fox River from the Green Bay on Lake Michigan and down the Consin to the Misisipi, and up the River St. Pear or St. Peter,[13] and so across the country to the north bend of the Misouri, which course of trade comes considerably within the terratory of the United States east of the Misisipi and will be more so on the west side when the cession of Louisana is ratafied. This may in future be the cause of dispute and trouble between the United States and G. Brittain unless early prohibited.[14]

Captain Lewes is a stout young man but not so robust as to look able to fully accomplish the object of his mission, nor does he seem to set out in the manner that promises a fulfilment of it. He sits out in a vessel 56 feet long and completely equiped with sails and 18 oars, with as many soldiers and rivermen as are necessary to man her, and a Mr. Clark, son of Genl. Clark as his companion;[15] and his vessel fitted with very nice and comfortable accommodations with great stores of baggage and cargo so that she draws 2 1/2 feet water and will be very heavy to go up against the stream of the Misisipi and other rivers.[16]

This will be the cause of great delay in assending the rivers so far as this vessel may carry him; but he has what he calls a portable boat, the frame of which is made of iron, to proceed in; yet it seems to me that he had better have adopted the long experience of the Canadians and used the bark canoes that are used by them in their northern trade. He has already been delayed a long time in the Ohio waiting for his boat, which cost 400 dollars, and in gitting this far, and now is obliged to use three or four Ohio canoes to light him over the riffs or ripples below this [place], so that it is likely we may yet overtake him before he gits down tho he goes off today and we cannot git away till Tuesday or Wednesday next.

Mr. McCannon, a stout young man who has been several times down the river to Natches and has business there, offers to go down with us as a hand on the most cheap and reasonable terms we can git a hand and cheaper than any other. He appears a decent young man and I ventured to engage him and requested him to git us another good hand.

After breakfast, the Major and Shields being busy writing, I took Mr.

Rolo, a young merchantal gentleman who is about to settle at Wheeling, with me in the carriage, and crossing over Wheeling Creek road about three miles down the river on the river road which runs close along the bank of the river and is level and beautiful as a road can well be, and the river itself is very hansome and delighting; and on our left as we went the bottom land from the river to the foot of the mountain is covered with fertile farms but not yet in a high state of improvement. We saw only one good stone house and none of brick on this road. The rest are ordinary wooden houses; but in time the road along the river, which seems extending every year, and the farms on the bottom land between the mountain and river, combined with the river and mountain, must exhibit very enchanting landscap's. Indeed as far as the road and farms extend it is now a beautiful scene.

Just after diner Captain Lewis called on me to bid me farewell. The Major, Shields, and I went down and took a parting drink and part of a water mellon on board his boat and then bid him adieu and stayed on shore to see him depart, and I waited till I saw him over the first ripple.

I have met with several Dalaware families in this town: first a Mr. Coulter, scoolmaster who formerly lived at Lewes Town. His son is one of the young men that is building our boat. Secondly a Mr. Stuart who married a sister of Steph. Alston. She has 4 daughters by Danl. Cole, her first husband, grown up but not married and 4 children by Stuart. He came from Frederica. Also a Mr. Moffit, one of the Moffit family in the forrest of Janess hundred; and a Mr. Grave who has 11 children all married but one. He is only a labourer.

Wheeling, Saturday, September 10th 1803. There fell a good deal of rain last night and it is still cloudy, but have not been out yet to view the river. The young men had our bark on the stocks yesterday evening but we only saw her from the top of the hill. Went into Carters store and bought letter paper. Received a letter from my son by the mail. All well.

He hints his coming here. Fisher was to have been at Wilmington last Saturday. Wrote a letter to Fisher, one to Doctor Ham, and one to Mrs. Miller, Dover.

Sunday, Wheeling, September 11th 1803. Broken cloudy. I thought [of] hearing a Babtist preacher in the Court House but the water of this place gave me a little lax[17] and I stayed in. [This] afternoon ten persons, Babtists, were to be babtised in the river. They all left the Court House in a body and sung hims down to the brink of the river. I went out to see the ceremony but the preacher spoke so long and the sun braking out very warm I could not stay. Came home and wrote to my son.[18]

In the evening Major Claybourn came and told me Peter Stout and N. Drew were come and put up at Bells Tavern and wou'd see us in the morning. Shield this morning took the horse and carriage and Mrs. Richardson, Mr. Zanes daughter, rode out with him to Major Sheperds, 6 miles out of town, where they were well entertained and got fine millons, etc.[19]

Wheeling, Munday, September 12th 1803. Morning rainy and it rained last night. I wrote another letter to Fisher and one to the President of U.S. and one to Mr. Gallatin, and put all my letters in the Post Office.[20] Went to see the boat boys at work. Went to Caldwell about my horse. He tried him and refused buying. I of course stoped gitting goods of him. Carty came over to buy horse and carriage in the evening. Tried his own horse in the carriage. Drew rode with him. He asked till the morning to consider.

I was not quite well of my lax today and amused myself with Denons Travels in Egypt and the Odyssee, etc.[21] P. Stout came in the evening and sat with me and we agreed we would all dine together tomorrow at Bells Tavern as Mrs. Knox is in the straw. The Major was about his rowing machine but gave it up for the present. Many came in at different times to see his poling machine and all agreed that it was very ingenius but would not do for want of a regular bottom to work on, etc. It rained a good deal today.

Wheeling, Tuesday, September 13th 1803. Cloudy but clearing up. I have used at times a little gin and wine and my lax has ceased today. After breakfast Peter Stout and I rode up the river and returned. We measured a cycamore tree on the road that was 36 feet round 2 feet from the ground and was solid.[22] Carty came and tried my horse and carriage. Offered 150 dollars for them. Told him I would not take it. P. Stout agreed to take my horse back and I determined to take my carriage to Natchez.

The Major, Stout, Shields, Drew, and myself dined at Bells. Had a good diner and Madiera, Lisbon, and peach brandy. Were all very chearful and happy. The Major and myself told some good anectdotes with which the young men were highly pleased. Our club was only 5 dollars. I paid 3 dollars, the club of the Major, Shields, and myself. The Major agried if I did not sell my horse that he would ride him with P. Stout through Kaintuky to Bairds Town, near which he also had land, and thence through Tenessee to Natchez while we go down the river, etc.

Then I ritired to my books. Stout and Drew came and spent the evening with [me] and agreed not to set off till the ten [o'clock] mail arrives in the morning but that Major declined going with them.

Wheeling, September 14th 1803, Wednesday. Have neither sold horse or chaise yet and today I must be fast gitting ready. Morning verry foggy tho the evening was very clear. An old backwoods man of the name of Johnson lo[d]ged in my room last night. He has travalled over most part of the New Country, has sold his land between this and Washington, and is on his way to buy on Mad River in the Ohio state.[23] He says the finest land he has ever seen is at Illinois and from that towards the Wabash and would cho[o]se to purchase there but cannot persuade his family to go so far. He has been up the Misisipi to Illinois, has seen the

Great Rock which stands in the middle of the river and is a hundred feet high, called the Great Tower.[24] There is a Great Whirl Pool near it which on the top of the rock you may see down into a great way. He has seen it suck in trees 40 feet long. They woud decend perpendicular down and appear no more. How is this whirlpool made? The river is deep there and very swift. The rock stops the water most towards the bottom where it is no doubt the widest. The water, therefore, that passes by the sides of it nearer the top runs round and decends suddenly to fill the casam at bottom.

This effect is perpetually continued by the waters swiftly running away from the bottom; and of course the whirlpool seems as if the water decended into some subteraneous river; but the old man had no idea of this and thought it inextricable phenomana which no one could decend to examine. Yet this would be easily proved by droping in it noted peices of wood that would float and such if attended to would be seen to rise to the surface of the water again some considerable distance down the river; for as they wou'd be sucked down to the bottom and the current from there being very swift, they may be carried some miles down the river before they would rise to the surface of the water again.

Today we shall hurry our selves to gitting off as soon as possible as our boat will be nearly done. Went out this morning and sold my horse and carriage to [blank] Carter, merchant, for 160 dollars, to take the price in goods out of his store in such articles as we want, and such as he has not got he will procure for us, reserving the use of the horse and carriage till I go away from here. Then I went to see the boat. She is to be launched tomorrow. Called on the Major and Shield. Informed them of my bargain, and directed them to git our covering made and painted as soon as possible, and hurry every thing. All this before breakfast.

Went several times to see the boat and back and forward to Carters to whom we now apply for everything he can furnish us with. Got 30 yds. of linnen for covering boat of him and Shields set the [sadler?] at work to making. The Major was busy about his propelling machine. I wrote several letters, etc.

Wheeling, Thursday, September 15th 1803. Broken clouds and a rain bow appeared this morning and soon after the cloud thickened; and we had rain all the fore part of the day, and cleared up in the evening. Got cloth and trimings for a short coat of Carter @ 45/- per yd. and set taylor to work. Also got 2 books @ 15/- and an umberello 37/6 of Carter, etc. When the rain held up visited boat several times and hurried workmen.

We all dined, including Peter Stout, at Zanes today on a fine buffillo fish which is not quite so good as black drum tho exactly like it otherwise. After diner Shields and Stout went agunning and killed ten pigeons and sent me two. I attended to the boat and spoke to tinnman [to] make us a cook stove which is to be done Saturday afternoon.

In the evening I went to Zanes, and the Major and Shields played fiddle and flute till nine o'clock when I returned home. Put five letters in the mail today: 1 to my son, 1 to Fisher, one to Bishop, one to P. Lewes, inclosing one to A.H., and 1 to J. Dickenson.[25]

Fryday, Wheeling, September 16th 1803. Foggy morning. Changed to broken cloudy. Carpenters got our boat turn'd up for corking this morning. Two young ship carpenters who want to go to Lime Stone applied to work their way down. Engaged to take them and set them to work at the boat to help finish her so as to git of[f] tomorrow. Bought a bottle sweet oil, a 1 lb. of tamarinds, and a loaf of sugar of pothercary and sent them to Carters. The young carpenters I mentioned are going to build a ship at Limestone for Gallahar. Carpenters got the boat corked and payed with pich and rudder hung. Stout and I rode out in my carriage along the river road where Stout got pasture for his horse at one Denny's. Stout lent me 5 dollars to pay in part to Coulter, one of our carpenters, when we were in the carriage as I had no change in my pocket and could not turn back.

One of our new carpenters says that one shilling a yard is enough for painting vessels, whereas Mr. Shields agreed to give 2/- per yd. and the other painter asked 3/4 per yd.; but the people in this place are all sharpers as to strangers and little is to be got of them without paying dear, esspecially their workmen, which in the end will be a great disadvantage to their town. Otherwise it would become an important place for hundreds come and go every day.

❧

Saturday, Wheeling, September 17th 1803. The morning foggy and thick; but the fogs here are not so damp and unpleasant as in the low country owing probably to their being chiefly exhaled from the pure and pelucid water of the river. The fogs here are soon dispersed by the rising sun and the day was fine.

All hands were busy in expediting our bark and gitting ready. We got her on the water and she sat like a sea gull on it. Got her painted and oars, mast, spars, and sail made; but towards evening I saw that we could not git our berths and cover completed and therefore gave up gitting away till Munday, and return'd home to rest for I had exercised much in running about to prepair every thing. Stout determined to go off tomorrow morning but have not seen him since tea.

After resting went to Zanes to see the Major and Shields but they were abed. I returned and went to bed, too, earlier than usual. It rained in the night but the showers were light, however they changed the air more cool so that I had to git up and put an aditional coverlid on my bed.

❧

Wheeling, Sunday, September 18th 1803. Morning cloudy and cool, wind NW. When [I] went down, found a fire in our breakfast room. The day continued broken cloudy and sunshine. If we had been ready to go this morning we might have been near Miskingum tonight. Our boat looks beautiful on the water. She looks like a sea nimph, but we coll [her] however the *Iris*.[26] She will certainly carry us quick down the river.

I dressed and went to the Court House to hear a Babtist minister before diner; and after diner took a walk along the river and on the mountain alone; then came to my chamber, and finished a letter to my son[27] and one to Fisher, the last I shall send them from here, with one to Doctor Ham, to go by the mail tomorrow.

I cannot leave this little town without some observations on it. We were directed on the road to a tavern kept by a Mr. Knox, who is a captain of militia and a justice of the peace, and is a pretty likely man in the prime of life but rather indolent in his turn of mind tho not wanting pretty good sence. Yet his tavern is a durty hovel and his beds swarming with bugs; yet I had a very good bed perhaps the best in the house and elegant chintz furniture and being newly painted green the bugs did not much disturb me;[28] but there were three other beds in the room very ordinary and all swarming with bugs so that no decent person could rest in them till Mr. Shields made a rout and made them wash two of them. All the rest of his beds and room I believe were worse, for mine was the best room and the most decent company put there; nor was there any regularity in the management of the house.

The servants all appeared idle and worthless, and sildom was the chambers in any decent order, and their table was still worse regulated and in general ordinary, tho some times we got things pretty good, but it was rare; and there was nobody seemed to care whether it was well, or ill done. The only excuse for this was the confinement of the landlady in the straw. Her eldest daughter, a very pretty girl of 15, was up tho not much minded by the servants nor was it much better after the landlady turned out; and there were two other taverns in town worse than this, but the 4th kept by a Mr. Gooding below the hill and near the river is said to be a much more decent tavern than either. There is no distinction in this or the two others or very little between wagoners, labourers, and gentlemen as in equality.

There [are] eleven stores in town and most of them well stoc[k]ed with goods; yet they appear to be [poorly] constructed and narrow in their mode of dealing without generous spirit and assiduity which would make this a place of great importance. They deal indeed more like sharpers with strangers and ready to take advantage of them rather than to oblige and accomodate them; and thus strangers are discouraged from taking this otherwise most convenient way down the Ohio, which in time may turn them some other way, to the great injury of this place.

Indeed this part of our country wants much very much light and knowledge deciminated through it and the polish of dress and man-ners.[29] I therefore incurraged them in all their little towns to employ singing and dancing masters, and I consent even to the young peoples reading novels where it tends to improve their dress and manners and to rub off that rusticity which is the parent of so much filth and want of neatness and decency. The poor as well as the rich may keep them-selves as well as their houses clean and neat; and surely it is more pleasant to live in a clean cabbin than a durty pallace [where] one must wade thrugh dust or mud to be devoured by vermin.

While I was writing the foregoing observations the Major and Cap-tain Shields with Doctor Patterson and Doctor Forsyth[30] waited on me in my chamber and chatted an hour or two. This is the first time any of the gentlemen of the town have directly waited on me tho we have frequently been together below and at other places accidently.

Wheeling, Munday, September 19th 1803. The morning thick foggy but cleared up pretty soon. Last evening a boat came down from Pittsbourg in five day[s] with a Mr. Andrews and his wife on their way to Natchez, and the[y] left this [place] early in the afternoon; but with all the exertions of all our workmen they could not git our boat quite finished. Part of our berths still are unfinished so that we are obliged to stay till tomorrow; but we got most of our accounts paid and may be ready by ten o'clock in the morning to sail; and as this is the third time, trust we shall not be delayed longer.

Finding we could not git away we met at Mr. Zanes in the evening to have a little music by way of relaxation; and several gentlemen of the town joined us to spend the evening, to wit Mr. Parsons, Doctor Patter-son, Doctor Forsyth, and Doctor *[blank]*, and another gentleman. The Major and Mr. Parsons played on their violins while Doctor *[blank]* and Mr. Shields alternately played on the flute and one of the gentlemen sung so that we had a chaste clever little concert. At nine o'clock I came home to my books and papers.

CHAPTER FOUR

The Launching of the *Iris*

The River Journey Begins

*Ohio River: Wheeling to Gallipolis, Ohio,
September 20–28, 1803*

As Iris *began making her way downstream on a rainy Tuesday afternoon in
late September, 1803, a new world unfolded before Thomas Rodney and his
little band — the world of the river. As they soon learned, the Ohio made
definite demands on those who chose it as a route for their travel. The necessity
of learning and practicing navigational skills softened and blurred the distinction between the passengers and their crew. Not only did Rodney, Shields,
and Claiborne acquire the practical knowledge of how to operate a boat, they
also came to respect the nature of the river: its vagaries involving currents,
depth of water, sand bars, riffles, and floating obstructions, the "fogg" which
often enveloped their boat by night and early day, and the many islands which
studded the stream. They had to discern when fickle nature would cooperate
with them and when it would go its own way.*

*The autumn landscape passed very slowly before the travelers' curious gaze.
Without oar power, a flatboat moved at an average rate of only two to three
miles per hour — four to five miles if the water were up and moving more swiftly.*

Barring obstructions ashore, an able-bodied man or woman could outwalk these sluggish water craft. Such a pace, of course, was favorable to Rodney's journal-keeping as it allowed him more than ample time to observe and record what he saw.

On the upper reaches of the Ohio, where settlements were more common than they were lower down, sights were exciting enough to interest even the most jaded traveler: Marietta with its neat houses and shipyard which "appeard like a phenomany so far in our interior country;" the elaborate, European-style estate of Harman and Margaret Blennerhassett (soon to become nationally notorious as the scene of Aaron Burr's "conspiracy"); the French-settled Gallipolis; and lesser curiosities such as a tree etched with Indian carvings.

To add variety to the voyage, Rodney and his companions took lengthy walks through the forest, collected fossils, and initialed rocks and trees. When Iris nearly sank at Amberson's Island, Shields was so unnerved that he started home on horseback. It would not be the last such danger the argonauts had to overcome.

◆

Wheeling, Tuesday, September 20th 1803. The morning foggy but soon cleared away before the rising sun. It was near or quite 2 o'clock before we got all on board and ready for setting off and all our accounts settled. Paid 65 dollars for our boat and smith bills. The Major and Shields went up to settle Majors accounts.

I put off in the boat in the midst [of] a heavy rain, and put into the creek to take carpenters baggage on board. Major [and] Shield were not come. Sent Brown ashore in the skiff for to wait for them. Just as we came out of the creek Shields came and we took him on board and went on, leaving Brown to bring the Major.

It continued to rain heavy and we got five miles before the Major and Brown came up with us. By this time we were all as wet as drownded rats for our painted canvas cover leaked like a riddle[1] so that all our beds and baggage got much wet. We sent ashore however and got fire and cooked dinner which we had to eat after night without candles

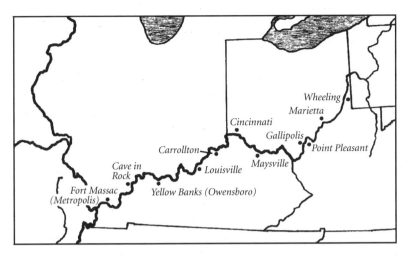

Thomas Rodney's Ohio River Journey. September 20-November 9, 1803

which had been neglected. The rain ceased about 8 o'clock and we continued on till passed the sand shoal just above Grave Creek[2] and got below that creek and ankored in 10 ft. water. I went out in the skiff myself while we were on the barr to find the chanel and directed them off, for there was water enough but Bucanan[3] did not keep the channel which was close under northwest shore.

Here we laid till morning and had an uncomfortable night all of us being wet and all our beds; and in the night the wind blew very cool for an hour or two, yet we all got more or less sleep. All of the crew but myself put on more or less dry cloths. After the rain ceased I laid down in my wet cloths and wet bed but coverd warm and towards day got some sleep so that [the] boys had got several miles before I awoke. Thus we got about 14 miles the first day.

Ohio River, Wednesday, September 21st 1803. The boat was one or two miles on her way before I awoke. There was no difficulty in the river till we arrived at Captinah Island.[4] We took the chanel next the Virginia shore and found a bad riffle at the lower end of the island divided into two riffles. The first had 2 chanels with a barr between them. We took the channel next Virginia shore which was the best, as we found by sending the skiff ahead at the lower riffle which is but a little way below. The first we crossed in a single channel turning short toward the other side the riffle and got safe through both without touching. This island is 20 miles below Wheeling and is about one mile long with a plantation on it.[5]

From this the water good to Statton Island, 26 miles from Wheeling.[6] Here we followed the direction of the Ohio Pilot and took the channel next the Virginia shore, and found it floting [or shifting] from the island as well as from the Virginia shore and full of timber towards the shore; but we went safe to the powder mill by keeping a good look out; yet the water was shoal quite across most of the way till we got to the powder mill at the mouth of Fish Creek opposite the lower end of the island on the Virginia shore.[7] Just below the powder mill the channel contracts and uniting with Fish Creek runs rapid but is not shoal or dangerous and only wants care to keep the boat from being forced by the current on one of the shores. We passed rap[id]ly and safely and found the river good below at its union after passing the island.

Just before we got to this island Brown and the Major went ashore to git chickens for diner; and we passed the island so rapid and having had a fair breaze since. They are not yet returned, tho we left the island at 12 o'clock and it is now one o'clock and we are several miles below the island. This island is a mile and a half or 2 miles long. What the channel is on the other side [I] cannot tell but likely it is better than the one we passed for it looked so. Captinah Creek falls in below 1 1/2 miles below [what is] now the NW shore.[8]

We arrived at long reach in the evening. It soon after became dark and I laid down. Before I got up the boys changed watch. Bucanan said he had passed several island[s] and Brown was directing the boat. After he laid down to rest about eleven he got in a riffle, and I got up; and after gitting throug[h] we came to ankor in 6 ft. water under this Ohio shore, the fog being so thick we could not see the shores, and lay quiet there till day light.

Ohio, Thursday, September 22d 1803. Morning very dark and foggy yet we weighed ankor at day light and proceeded. We passed 4 or five islands with riffles at all of them; but our boat tuched only on two and then we were not in the best water. At the lowest riffle, which was the worst of them all, the man who lived opposite to it told us that Andrews boat passed there at 9 o'clock in the morning. We passed it at about one o'clock P.M. That is about 4 howers after him tho he left Wheeling 30 hours before us.

We run about six or 8 miles and there passed three other islands, one a small one but none aboard knew their names, and the Ohio Pilot and our guide McCannon disagreed about them. We passed the last at 5 o'clock P.M. and saw no other island in view below, the river being open from barrs and islands till sun down.

We observed settlements frequent on both shores and on several of the larger islands but several of the smaller islands were not inhabited. The Major and Shields went on shore after breakfast on the Ohio side and walked 3 or 4 miles. Then Shields came on board; and the Major crossed in the skiff to the Virginia shore and walked 5 or 6 miles further, and came on board at 2 o'clock and brought us 2 lb. of butter.

We proceeded on till dark and after dark passed a boat laying close in with the NW shore which hailed us; but she was so far off [we] could not learn what boat it was, but they said they were from Pittsborgh and hence we conjectured it was Andrews. They asked the channel by the next island. We told them on the NW shore; yet not knowing we were near the island we proceeded till moon down keeping the middle of the river and just as the moon went down run on the barr above the island.

I took Brown with me in the skiff and immediately run across to the northwest shore along the uper side the barr and returned so far above as to keep in water that wou'd float the batteau; and so found that the channel run close under the NW shore, and that by returning back a little way we could take the batteau across to it; and so proceeded and ankored at ten o'clock close to the NW shore in 10 ft. water.

We were so near the shore that the trees hung almost over our boat; and here we saw the shore illuminated with the appearance of innummerable small sparks of fire which we took to be the gloworm. By this time the fogg grew very thick so that if we had wished we could not have proceeded; yet it is a little extraordinary that these foggs which obscure the shores of the river when you are in the middle of it renders things on board the boat and just around us much more conspicuous than they were in the night when there was no fogg, in so much that several times when I awoke in the night things appeared so conspicuous in our cabin that I thought day was dawning.

All the rest of our crew went to sleep while I sat up writing; for this was the first night we had candles since we left Wheeling, Shield having forgot to have them brought on board; and tho we sent on shore every day along the river, never could obtain any till today; nor could we git any eggs or chicken; but having sent Brown ashore in the evening to git milk, he returned with milk, candles, eggs, and boiling corn and cucumburs. Our cabbin has been open at both ends till this evening; but tonight we shut out the fogg by spreading our sail over the front and spreading flannel and my su[r]tout coat across the after part, so that tonight we are more comfortly accomodated than any night since we have been on the Ohio; and it was not till today that all our beding got perfectly dry.

Fryday, September 23d 1803, on the Ohio. The fog was very thick this morning yet we weighed ankor at day light and run down the channel on the NW the island at the lower end of which was a very bad riffle. In passing it we had to run so close under the island shore that our mast carried away a large bow of one of the trees; but we passed safe. We run down the NW shore till passed three island[s] all in a string called The Brothers, but we call them Shadrach, Mesheck, and Abednigo.[9]

After gitting below these islands and a long narrow sand barr below the last, we came into a wide part of the river. Shoal quite across the river and the deepest water lies close along the Ohio state shore; but in going too far out we got aground; but a person on shore told us where the channel was and we passed in to it and got through easily, tho the water was scant even in the channel.

Soon after I went on shore for the first time, and as the boat went but slow I kept up with her. Soon after I got round a point on the Ohio shore, saw 8 or ten squirrels runing down to the river to swim across to the Virginia shore. Others saw me and run back into the wood. Our boat, after the squirels had got half way, put out the skiff and killed them both. While they were at this I saw a third enter the river and was so near him that I threw stones beyond him and frightend him back, and as he came to shore killed him with a stick; thus we got three of them, and Major Claybourn who is very fond of them skined and dressed them, and the boys, after we arrived at Muskingum, cooked them for diner.

Soon after we got these squirrels the boat arrived and a riffle and McCannon missing the best water run on ground. This induced me to turn back but they soon got her off and then sent the skiff for me. We soon after passed the mouth of Little Muskingum 2 miles above Marrietta and were now in sight of Muskingum Island which we soon reached.[10]

Our guide Buchanan said the best channel was next to the Virginia shore; but as it looked much the worst at the entrance he took the NW shore channel; but we found it so shoal all the way that it was with difficulty we got through it. The drift wood also was strewd from side to side in it; but as there was a great deal of river grass in it where the pike conceal themselves and as the boat frightened them, they fled in flocks from it; but we had no harpoon on board or might have got plenty of them.

We arrived at the lower end of the island and ankored abreast of Marrietta[11] at 12 o'clock in 4 feet water a little above the riffle at the lower point of the island barr. [This is called Duvalls Island.][12]

Muskingum River falls to the Ohio just below the town and a little below where we come to.[13] There appears to be several good brick buildings in the town and near it and several very cleaver frame buildings.

The Major and Shields immediately went on shore but I have not been up yet. We only come to here to git bread and try to git our cover tarred.

Muskingum Island is long and narrow being a mile and half long and not over a quarter wide.[14] There is a plantation on it as I suppose as I saw cattle driving from there over to the Marrietta side.

The Major and Shields returned to diner and on consultation we deturmined to have our boat covered with thin planks under our canvas instead of tarring it. Sent Shields to procure the board[s] and nails and Brown agreed to cover it immediately. Then I went on shore; and the Major and I walked up the bank of the Muskingum to the ship yard, and thence to the uper part of Marrietta, and by the Court House and rope walk back to the Golden Ball Tavern on the hill opposite where our boat lay, where I called for a pint of wine.

Shields had in the mean time procured stuff and Brown was at work when Shields came to us and shared part of the wine. Then he and the Major went away; and soon after Judge Green, cousin to Genl. Green,[15] came in to wait on me, and after some little chat he invited me to breakfast with him tomorrow, and desired me to bring the Major and Shields with me, and he wou'd invite Judge Pigot[16] also to breakfast at his house with us.

Then I went to the boat and found Brown almost done and sent Shields to pay for the materials; and soon as Brown was done I ordered the boat to proceed to git across the riffle. By the time they were ready Shields returned and we pushed off tho the Major was still behind. We got over the riffle with some difficulty and ankord of[f] the lower mouth of Muskingum just at night fall to wait for the Major; and the boy went to cooking supper; and after Shields and myself were done and the boys eating, the Major arrived in a canoe. Before supper was over it got too late to proceed, the moon being almost down.

Marrietta is at the confluence of the Muskingum and Ohio and chiefly on the east side of Muskingum, but there [are] two very genteel building[s] on the west side. There are several elegant buildings too on the east side, some of brick and some of wood but scattering; there are 8 to 10 dwelling houses built and building in good taste. The Court

House however has but little elegance about it tho it is a very good frame building and suitable enough for a County Court. It has a bellfry and bell. Near it is the school house of not much note, only it is now conducted by a grandson of old General Putnam.[17] The streets run parrellel one way with the Ohio and the other way with the Muskingum, crossing at right angles.

Up the Muskingum between the northern and southern part of the town are two ship yards, one on each side the river. That on the east side had a ship on the stocks of about 160 tuns burthen more than half done, her timber chiefly black walnut. On the other side were 2 brigs or schooners of about 100 tuns each, both of the same size and apparently of the same form and rather more forward than the ship. These sights appeard like a phenomany [phenomenon] so far in our interior country.[18]

The ground about this town does appear very fertile; and all the ground on which most of the town stands about three years ago was over flowed by the swell of the rivers so that the inhabitants were dreadfully alarmed. This flood lift[ed] the almost intire body of a solid tree 6 ft. diameter on the highest ground in the town, and this tree is still there remaining as a memorial of the flood. This is the hansomest town that we have seen in the new country except Chambersbourg; but there is hardly a hundred houses in it, but most of them are neatly built.

When the Major came on board he said that Col. Sproat an old officer had come down to invite us to sup with him but found the boat gone.[19] After the Major and Shields and all the hands were asleep I concluded here half after eleven o'clock P.M. and then went to bed.

Marrietta, Saturday, September 24th 1803. We weighed ankor at the mouth of Muskingum a little after day light. The fog was rather thiner than usual. At 3 miles down we came to Muskingum Island. [This island 3 miles long.][20] Here the Ohio Pilot says the channel runs close to the island.[21] We followed his direction but from the current which run over the riffle fell to the NW shore, and we soon found we were wrong; and our guide put the boat back and found the best water on the NW shore. I put out in the skiff to examine the island channel but there was not water, even for the skiff. This riffle is opposite the sand barr at the uper end of the island. About a mile below this island commences the 2d [island] below Muskingum.[22] The uper end is a sand barr. The whole island about a mile long, channel on the Virginia shore, the riffle being on NW side. The middle and lower part of this island is cover'd with wood, but not large. One mile below this commences a third island, a very hansome island a mile long and cultivated.[23]

1 1/2 mile below this is the Little Canawa, a very hansome river 150 yds. wide at the mouth, and falls into the Ohio from the east.[24] There is an old block house on the point and a small village round, all wooden buildings, and a few logged buildings on the other side; and opposite to the mouth of the [Little] Canawa on the NW side the Ohio is uper Belleprie.[25] A fine level country round it, but only 3 or 4 wooden building[s] near the river. Indeed the country here appears pleasant on both sides of the Ohio. The Major and Shields went ashore at Belleprie for milk and butter. What little wind has been today was mostly a head so that we have only come 12 miles, the distance from Marrietta to the Little Canawa, by 12 o'clock at noon.

The next island we came to was Blaney Hazzards,[26] 2 miles below the Little Canaway. This island as to buildings is very elegantly improved. The dwelling house struck our view as soon as we turned the point of Belleprie; and when I came opposite the house and waited for the Major and Shields, and as soon as they came the Major and I went on shore to view the island and its improvements. Mr. Hazzard came to us, but I had got in the garden first and he and the Major came to me; and after viewing the garden which was new and but small he excused its condition. There was nothing peculiar in it; however it was a good Kitchen Garden, and the plants in it were luxurient.

He pressed us to stay and dine with him, which as his diner was ready we assented to. We had a small piece of ordinary bacon and two roasted chicken[s] and secondly perserves and cheese and good brandy and wine and musk mellons or cantelopes and Malacatoon [malagatune] peaches,

The reconstructed Blennerhassett Mansion, Blennerhassett Island Historical State Park, Parkersburg, West Virginia. 1992 photograph by Brian B. Schroeder.

which were full ripe and good and the first we had seen on this side the mountains.

He pressed us to stay all night. Our time would not admit of such delay and therefore I begged to be excused. He excused his not being better prepaired, his wife being ill, and mentioned the cause of her illness and unpleasant situation; and the Major mentioned my having some knowledge in medicine tho not a physician; and I recommended a bath warm or cold or alternate and to rub on coming out of the bath with perfumed dissolved oil; and he came on board with us and I supplied him with enough to last six months.

His house tho only framed and covered with boards is built with taste. It is large and has two wings back. The front is towards the south [i.e., west] and both front and back project out about 4 or 6 inches from the middle half way towards each end which had a good effect. There was two windows on each side the door at equal uniform distances one being in the out set and the other in the other part towards the end; and the second story was uniform. On the back of the house were two wings each apparently, for we were not in them, composed of one room below and each like the other in all respects and both very neat and painted white as well as the house.

From the main house there is a simecircular piaza extending from each back corner (including a door) to each of the back wings, which stand about 20 ft. further back than the main house and as much further beyond each end which forms a comodious yard back and has a good effect. The concave side of the piazas are towards the said yard and the convex side outward towards the front yard, which is large and open and contain[s] perhaps half an acre of ground, etc. The whole has a pleasant appearence.

This Island like all the rest in this river is very rich. The grass in particular is fine on it. Hazzard owns 400 acres of it but we had not time to see every thing worth observation on it. Hazzard is a sort of a quack and musician and he and the Major had their chat on music and mechanics, etc.[27]

As soon as we returnd on board and Hazzard left our boat we made sail. Hazzard appears to be a cleaver man and fond of society, and expresses a fondness for music, phiysic, and chimistry, etc., but has some thing wild and excentric in his aspect; he is an Irishman and asked me if I was of the Rodney family in England. I told him yes, but he said nothing further on that subject. If any thing not connected with our public business could have delayed me, I should have spent a night on this island which, considering its situations and improvements at this time in this now wild country, appears like an inchanted island.

There is a small island on the east [i.e., south] side of this which, from the appearance of both at this times, seems to have been part of this and since seperated by some overflow of the river. The large island is called Bacus's Island, p[r]obably from some man of that name who first lived on it, or from some Bacanalian [bacchanalian] frolic on it.[28] Lower Belleprie is opposite the lower end of this island and 2 miles lower we passed the mouth of Little Hockhocking a small creek that falls in on the NW shore.[29]

Here I laid down and fell asleep and lay till the boys waked me up to supper when it was dark and we were in good water near a fine looking improvement on the Ohio shore. As it was cloudy so that the moon gave but little light, I ordered the boys to cast ankor; and after supper they all went to bed, but it being warm and very still could not sleep and got up again. We advanced only 21 miles today.

Ohio River, Sunday, September 25th 1803. Morning cloudy and moderate. Steady rain. We weighed ankor at day light and proceeded. Came to Newberry settlement, sand barr island, half a mile below where we lay all night; and one mile below the barr passed Mustapha Island and barr, channel on the NW shore. [Went] by both and not difficult, tho the river is lower now than ever known before. The shores and river however by both these places are rocky but without any danger with due care.[30]

At half after 8 o'clock A.M. we passed Big Hockhocking. This is a larger stream than the Little but is not more than 50 yds. wide, but is deep; however, [it] has very little water at this time. New Lancaster stands on the head of this Little river in the Ohio State. Three miles below this Lees Creek falls in from the Virginia shore. [This is a small creek now dry but appears to be a deep narrow stream when the water is up.][31]

About a 1/4 of a mile above the creek is a rocky or stoney shoal and riffle. Two channels over it, the largest and best next NW shore. After passing this there is another riffle commencing past below the creek on Virginia side and runing oblikely across the river to the other side opposite Belle Ville. The channel nearly in the middle of the river till you git over the riffle, then it runs near to the Virginia shore along Belle Ville; but we found sufficient water over both the above riffles for our boat which draws about ten inches.

Belle Ville is on the Virginia shore and only contains a few logged houses and one pretty good framed house. The shore and country however looks very cleaver. We passed Belleville Island at 11 o'clock, 2 miles below Belleville.[32] Channel here on NW side. Riffle at the upper end not dangerous at the lower end. Two channels one near the NW shore, but the best turns short round the lower end of the island barr. The channel on Virginia side, the island quite dry. All the islands we have yet passed have two riffles, one at the uper, and one at the lower end. There is no perceptible increase in the breadth [i.e., depth] of the river yet, but the riffles are not so bad below as above Marrieta.

At one o'clock being about 6 or 7 miles below Belleville, the wind being hard ahead, that is at SW, and the river WSW, we cast ankor, for the boys to git their diners; and I went on shore, and walked about a mile through the woods where the river turns to the west and then gradually round to the SW forming a simecircle. The land in this bend is the richest I have seen on the Ohio. The hickories, walnuts, elms, beaches, etc. were commonly 5 to 6 ft. diameter. On many of the beaches were the initials of various names marked and dates from 1776 to 1802. On one tree was an Indian king drawn with his crown, smoking a pipe. On another an Indian queen with her Indian dress but her front was bare and naked an[d] even her privy part was deleniated in a conspicious manner. The king appeard to have been drawn about twenty or thirty years ago, but that of the queen seemed to have been drawn 60 or 70 years ago. I left my own name and the year 1803 on a large beach tree, and returned to the river.[33]

I met the boat at the out bend of the river, and walked out to her on a large stoney sand bar where there was a riffle and rapid. They took me in at the lower point; and half a mile below we came to another large sand barr and rapid, where a small creek falls in from the Virginia shore, which we took to be Devils Hole Creek.[34] The channel by both these barrs is near the NW shore. We struck a rock in passing by the last, but there was plenty of water. We passed the last barr at 5 o'clock.

At 6 o'clock we reached Ambeltons Island where there is a worse riffle than any we had yet passed.[35] We ran too low for the uper channel next the island and ran on shore. We pushed back and got in to 4 ft. water and cast ankor. I then took the skiff and Brown to see if there was better water next the Virginia shore. The water was deeper there, but very rocky, so that we could not pass in the night. We got aground with the skiff among the rocks. It was now dark, but the moon gave light through thin cloud. I got out and after leading the skiff out from among the rocks, I walked the riffle to the uper channel where there was not water to float the batteau; but I thought as the bottom was small stones and loose sand, we could git her over, which indeed we accomplished; but in so doing broke a hole in her bottom, so that we were forced to take her immediately to the island shore, in front of the farm house, where the water ran in her as high as it could do, she being on the bottom.

The water was 6 inches in our cabbin; yet the Major, Shields, and myself lodged on board, our beds being 6 inches above the water. This imbarrasment was viewed by all the crew as a terrible accident, and attributed to my anxiety to cross the barr in the night, instead of waiting till next morning. I only smiled at their lamentation, and made light of it; but Shields terrified with prospect of such a voyage determined to set of[f] on fout [sic] in the morning and thence to return home and go to the Natchis by sea, etc.

Ambersons Island in the Ohio, Munday, September 26th 1803. The boys were all up early this morning and rouzed us for we had all rested very well, and I had got no cold tho I had waded so much last night, nor any of us by sleeping in the wet cabbin. The boys soon got all our goods out tho it was raining, small rain, and with the help of two horses, we got the batteau on shore, and Brow[n] being a ship carpenter mended the hole in about 2 hours.

We launched in the water again, and found her tight, then got our diners and put our baggage on board and were under sail at two o'clock Post M. with fine fairwind; but Maindal and Buchannon having had a quarrel yesterday while I was on shore, Mandal alledging his hands were blistered and swelled so that he could not work, applied to be discharged, which I granted, and he marched off. Indeed he turned out to be a very worthless hand, and did not earn his provisions. All the crew were glad when he left us, tho we stood in the utmost need of help at the time; but poor Shields never mentioned a word today of returning home, etc. The Major at first was much alarmed but after collecting himself resumed his philosophy again.

While on Amersons Island I observed many enormous black walnut trees, and went with him[36] and measured one in the woods that was 22 1/2 feet round; and he said there was a cycamore in his field that was 16 feet diameter or 48 ft. round, but hollow.

We passed Big Sandy Creek at 3 o'clock P.M. said to be 4 miles below the said island.[37] Half a mile below this creek there is a large sand barr in the middle of the river, channel next to the Virginia shore, and pretty near the shore; the channel crosses to a point on the NW shore runing pretty close round the point. (The Ohio Pilot is defective in not noticing said sand barr.) The ledge of rocks he mentions on the Virginia shore opposite the above mentioned point are all dry now and 4 or 5 feet above the water, and the channel lays between them and the point.

About a mile above Rocky Island[38] we passed a floating mill ankored in the river. She was placed on a flat or scow and a canoe [was fastened] without it for the axes of the water wheel to lodge on; and both were connected and held together by a frame of square logs above and below. The water wheel appeared to be about 10 or 12 ft. diameter. On the same axes was their largest cog wheel which turned a trunel on the same axes, with another trunnel that turned the trundle of the stone. All the parts were on board the flat but the water wheel. The stones were boxed up and the hopper over them without any cover. The whole was on a small scale compaired even with a horse mill, yet seemed simple and convenient. She was near the NW shore.

We soon after passed a rocky island which we mistook for Goose Island, keeping on the Virginia shore; then crossed over to a point on NW shore without any difficulty. We found water plenty in the channel and met with no impediments afterwards till 7 o'clock, when we drew near to Goose Island;[39] and not chusing to risk passing the riffle in the night, altho the moon shone very bright, we cast ankor in 4 ft. water in the middle of the river and prepaired for a calm nights rest, our batteau being dryer, since repaired, than at any time since we left Wheeling.

There has been but few settlement[s] on the river from 10 miles above

Ametsons Island to this place tho the bottom land on each side has appeared as rich as any on the river. Large ledges of rocks have appeared from Goose Island to this place, some times on one shore, and some times on the other that are dry now, but covered when the river is ful.

✺

Ohio River, Tuesday, September 27th 1803. We ran at day light but the fog was so thick we could not see our way. Got breakfast immediately. By this time 7 o'clock A.M. the fog cleared up, and we saw we were just above the sand barr at the uper end of Goose Island.

We took the channel on the NW side of the barr; and on our right hand there was a stoney barr spreading from the NW shore forming a narrow channel between it and the sand barr, where the current is very swift and deep, till you come opposite the upper part of the island. Then a riffle extends from the stoney barr on NW shore, which riffle ends in a sand barr at the lower end of the island, and in the middle of the river. We proceeded down the channel next to the island till we got about half way down the island. Then the channel suddenly crosses the riffle just where the stoney part reaches the uper end of the sand barr, over close to the NW shore, over which we found plenty of water for our bark; but the channel across was narrow. The river assumed its usual size and stillness bellow the lower barr; for where there is no islands or barrs the river is still and placid, and the current moves but slowly. The channel in such parts is generally in the middle of the river, and the shores are commonly flattey.

Three miles below Goose Island we came to the two islands above Letarts Falls. Here we kept the middle of the channel next to the NW shore (having a pilot on board to take us over the falls) till we got near the lower end of the first island. Then we drew nearer to the island; and then run near along the spit of sand at the lower end of the island, till the channel suddenly crosses the sand barr, over towards the upper end of the second island. Then we proceeded quietly round the point, the river turning here from W to N by E; and just after turning the point half a mile below the last island, we crossed Letarts Falls, which are very rocky but had planty of water for our boat; nor did I see any difficulty in passing them, tho so much was said of the danger, which had induced me to take a pilot on board.

We could have carried her over as well our selves, for Buckhanan is a better pilot than he was, and the torrent and the white caps over the falls was a sufficient direction. There was no danger but one large rock in the midst of the falls, which was easily seen; and the Ohio Pilot directed us close on the left of it, which road our pilot kept, and we were over them in an instant; and when safe we set the pilot ashore, and gave him 3/9 for his trouble.[40]

About a mile below the falls we passed a sand barr on the NW shore but without any riffle. At two miles below the falls we over took the red French boat; but they put of[f] from shore, and out rowed us. Soon after the river turned to NN west and the wind being hard ahead we came to ankor at one o'clock, and dined partly on an Ohio salmon, which Buckhanan spiked with his setting pole.

Here I went on shore in the skiff and placed my name by ingraving it on a high rock being the highest of a numerous pile put on the margin of the river; I had to go on the hill and clamber up a scrubby willow to git on it. For want of better tools, had to use a mallet and corking maul. The boys hurried me, or I would have put the year on it. It is a white looking rock of sandy stone and not very hard. It stands just below, or in, the convex bend of the river, 3 miles below the falls. There is a large cillender faced single rock a little way below it on the same side of the river. I observed by leaves hung on the bushes near that the Ohio some times swells to the top of this rock, which must be at present 25 or 30 ft. above the water; and as the river is said to be lower now than it ever was before I shall indeaver if I find a convenient place to ingrave this at the surface of the water on some rock along the shore.

4 miles below the falls we passed West Creek and 4 miles lower down a riffle a little below the lower point of a large sand bar on Virginia shore.[41] Channel through the riffle near the middle of the river, very rocky on Ohio shore. A mile lower we came to another riffle, channel near the middle of the river, very rocky bottom, but water enough. This

riffle near half a mile long, but we have not been stoped for want of water. We cleared this last riffle at 5 o'clock P.M. The Ohio shore very ricky below it for some distance, about 5 ft. above water. We passed Sliding Hill a little after sun set, and Sliding Hill Creek[42] just at dusk. The shores were rocky, but plenty of water in the river.

We went on about 2 or three mil[e]s further, and came to ankor in 7 ft. water, having come only about 20 miles today, the wind being ahead all the way. From Goose Island and for 3 or 4 miles below LeTarts Falls there were settlements on both sides of the river, but we have seen but few since, on either side; yet the bottom land and islands are pretty much alike all the way down the river, and sells for only 30/ or 4 dollars an acre. Amberson bought his rich island at that price. Such land would bring one hundred dollars an acre, any where within 50 miles of Philadelphia. Their distance from market makes the difference; yet they sell to us as dear as the same arti[c]les woud bring in Philadelphia to wit—7d. per for bacon, 3d. qt. for milk, etc.

Ohio River, Wednesday, September 28th 1803. The morning foggy as usual but being in a clear part of the river we weighed ankor at day light and proceeded. When we were opposite a Mr. Jones's on the Ohio shore, we observd the face of a rock about 200 yards from the river, on the Ohio State shore rising perpendicular like a castle in the air, which appeard at least 200 ft. above the water in the river. I ordered the boat to come to by Jones's house, and the Major, Shields, and myself proceeded to examine this phinomina.

I, with Shield[s], assended the mountain from the point of it which ended in Jones's field. We got about half way to the top of the rock when the assent become too difficult to proceed any further; and Shields turned back, while I tarried and ingraved T.R., the initials of my name, on the top of the rock I had assend[ed] to, and then deceded to the Major, who had proceed along the foot of the rock, and had in his hand two fosils, one allum, one salt peter. We then returned along the foot of the rock in front, and examind this phenomena.

The salt peter was in a yellowish earth among and under the dissolving rock; and above this was a thin stratum of dark fosil, about 2 inches thick, like coal, which was about 2 ft. above the ground. Pervad[e]s the whole rock, in this part. The bottom or lower part of the whole mass of rock appeared to be a yellow earthy calcarious stone, without sand, which still as it rose higher turned gradually to a whitish grey, and on the top was brownish grey; and by the present appearance of the front of this ridge of rock, only half of it remained, the front half having broken off and rolled down to the foot of the ridge, where many massy [massive] blocks of it still remain, or [seem] to have dissolved away; but both of these effects has evidently been the case.

In proceeding further along the foot of the rock, tho still of the same kind of stone, darkened from bottom to top, as if it had been smoked or colored by coal; and the stratum of coal run along this as well as the other part of the rock; and it was under this dark part of the rock, where it was evidently dessolving or decomposing that we found the allum, mixed with the decomposed earth of the rock in the same manner of the salt peter tho less cristalised, and having a meally appearance. Thus it is evident our country contain evidently plentiful sorces of these valuable articles. We took samples of all these fosils. That which looks like a stratum of coal, may be perhaps some other fosil; and still others perhaps may be found in this rich hill, which lies 14 miles up the Ohio above the Great Kanhawa. Jones owns a hundred acres of land there, which includes the SW point of this valuable hill.

About 4 miles below the salt peter, and allum rock aforementioned we came to what is called 8 Mile Island,[43] that is it is 8 miles above the Great Canhawah. This is a small island surrounded by a fine large sand barr. The island and bar about a mile long. Channel on the NW shore. The channel next to Virginia is small, and now dry. Between the white rock and this island, we passed two small creeks both dry, one a mile below the rock, on the NW shore, the other 3 miles below it on the Virginia shore. We passed this island at 12 o'clock at noon. At half after one we passed 6 Mile Island.[44] This island is 2 miles below the last and six miles above the Great Canhawah River, and is but a small island but rather larger than the former. The channel is on the NW side, that on the Virginia side being small and now quite dry. No habitation on either.

Just below the last, Major Claybourn and Captain Shields went on shore on the Virginia side to walk to Point Pleasant. Shields had run me eleven rifle bullets, and I was hammering them when they went on shore. The wind has still been ahead today so that we could not use our sail and have made but slow progress. Since we passed the white rock which I call the Castle, the shore of the river has been hansom on both sides and frequent settlements along both banks, but all logged buildings except one frame house on the Ohio shore. This was painted, the roof and windows red, for it had glass windows below, but was not finished in the second story.

We passed Tyger Creek half a mile below the last island and Campain Creek two miles below, both on the NW shore.[45] General Lewes after the Battle of Point Pleasant carried the war into the Indian country by way of the last creek, but they are both dry now. The latter is 4 miles above the Great Canhawah. At 4 o'clock we reached the Great Canhawah.[46]

This is a noble river in appearance. We saw the Major and Shields on shore at Point Pleasant and the Major requested me to come on shore; and I ordered Buckhanan to throw out the ankor and I went on shore on the point. The Major had several human bones in his hand. A Mr. Pryor was with him and informed us there was 40 ft. water in the Canhawah and that a 70 gun ship would go 50 miles up and a boat of 5 tuns about a hundred; but beyond that there was so many rocks and falls there was no navigating it.

Point Pleasant is a pleasant place and so is the point and land below the river. Indeed this is by far the most noble and pleasant place we have seen along the river but the country round is all a wilderness. General Washingtons heirs owns a hundred thousand acres of land up the river begining in sights of the town only settled by miserable tenants and 20 thousand acres up the Ohio just above the town of Mount Pleasant in the same situation. This Pryor said prevents this fine situation from being improved. The town of Mount Pleasant contains only 8 or 10 houses logged and framed and look but mean for such a place.[47]

Here Du[n]more was in 1774, and here General Lewes had a battle with the Indians.[48] Many bones still remain but slightly burried and here was once a large town of the Indians extending, Pryor says, 3 miles up the Ohio from the Cawhawah. There is still great evidence of this. We saw one of there great funeral mounds on the highest land near the point. It was raised 8 or 10 ft. high and perhaps about 30 yards diameter. It was circular. Pryor said there was many of these up along the Ohio and so near the bank that the freshes were often washing their bones bare and that their heads were all laying towards the river.

As I went on shore I met Mr. Shields at the waters edge with the servant of Mrs. Bennet, Doctor Bennets wife, who lay ill and had sent me some butter, sweet potatoes, and a loaf of bread and requested a little wine and coffee which I sent her.[49] On my return from viewing the point, the town, and Canhawah, I met Mr. Shields at the shore with his cloths, etc.; and he told me he was determined to return and had got a horse for that purpose, that he never the less was determined to go to Natches by sea, have left his chest, beding, etc. on board. I was in haste to git on board, and after wishing him a safe and pleasant ride bid him adieu; and returned on board and only waited for the Major to return with jug of whisky which here sells at 7/6 a gallon as at Marrieta and cost me a French crown. Then we put of[f] again at 5 o'clock P.M.

At the mouth of the Canhawah in the Ohio are several small sand barrs and one large one extinding oblikely downward so that we were obliged to go almost close to the NW shore. About a mile or more down below Canhawah we reached the uper end of Galliopolis Island a pretty large island a mile and a half or two miles long.[50] There is a riffle at the uper and lower end of this island and a rapid from one to the other. The channel is next to the Virginia shore but was room enough in passing both tho it required care in passing the lower one, it being rocky; but the draft of water shews the way over all the Ohio riffles when a person gits used to them if it be day light.

The town of Galliopolis is on the NW shore a little below the island. It being just at sundown when we got there, we took the bark to the shore, it being bold water and the Major and I walked up to see the town. The hill is high and above all the freshes of the Ohio; but back of the town a little way the country appeared sunken and low and the place is said to be sickly. The main street of the town is parrallel with the river and is half a mile long; but the houses are scattering and all logged houses but the Court House which is an ordinary framed building. There is a hansome square on the main street and the principle cross streets which are at right angles with the main. The houses are but mean and the inhabitants (who are mostly French) very poor.[51]

When we returned the boy[s] were done their supper and it being growing dusk we set of[f] again to go 6 miles further by moon light to the next island. We came to ankor at 9 o'clock close und[er] the Virginia shore about half a mile above the island in 8 feet water.

CHAPTER FIVE

Wood Nymphs and Other Adventures

Ohio River: Gallipolis to Cincinnati, Ohio,
September 29–October 6, 1803

As Rodney continued downriver, a large part of his journey was characterized by the mundane reoccurrence of creeks, sand bars, rapids, rocky bars, and shallows, all of which, however, he dutifully chronicled in his journal. There were diversions, nevertheless, which varied from the small pleasures of taking brief excursions on shore to buy necessities and to seek information; conversing with travelers on passing boats; and engaging in a "sublime chat" with the Major (who must have listened wide-eyed to Rodney's theory of the universe and his account of the divine visions he had had during the Revolution); to more exciting pastimes such as hunting geese and ducks and dining on such of the Ohio's delicacies as a "very tender and lushious" turtle and a "remarkably fat" sucker.

Although settlements were becoming more infrequent amid the seemingly endless panoply of trees, Rodney visited Alexandria at the mouth of the Scioto which already bore the marks of its impending death, and Limestone, Kentucky's thriving major port on the Ohio. Here, while Iris was "overhalled

84

and new corked," he scrutinized the town's physical layout and its inhabitants, whom he concluded were a worthless set of idlers. Here the ship's carpenters debarked, reducing the company to Rodney, Claiborne, Shields, and the pilot, Buchanan.

Personal adventures added spice and color to the judge's daily record: being pursued by a mysterious frantic man in a canoe who turned out to be Shields, who had repented his decision to abandon the voyage and was nearly exhausted trying to catch Iris; *and Rodney's encounter with the Ohio's seductive "wood nimphs." He saw the first of these winsome creatures near Augusta, Kentucky, "a very handsom blackeyed woman" from whom he obtained a drink of water and some information about the local geography. This proved to be a mere dress rehearsal for an even more stirring episode a few miles downstream. While his companions slept, Rodney experienced the pleasure of watching three or four girls bathing and frolicking in the water near where the boat had anchored for the night. Next day the amorous-minded Shields and the Major, much to Rodney's amusement, heaped scorn upon him for failing to waken them. Truly the Ohio possessed enlivening scenes not listed in any guidebook.*

Ohio River, Thursday, September 29th 1803. A very thick fogg this morning. Never the less we weighd ankor and put off. Passed the riffle at the uper end of the island close under the Virginia shore; and then gradually gli[d]ed near to the island barr, and crossed through a small channel over the lower riffle that turn short round the spit of sand bar at the lower point of the river on the left towards the Virginia shore, being flatt and very rocky. Then we run along the lower spit of sand bar below the island veering toward Virginia at the lower point of it. The whole of this riffle and rapid is about a mile and there the river assumes its form again. The cours[e] of the river in the reach above the before mentioned island is SE. The reach by the island is S by E, and in the next reach below the course is S by W.

At 1/4 before eleven we passed Little Quiendot, Virginia shore.[1] A riffle opposite to it. Very narrow channel over it in the middle of the

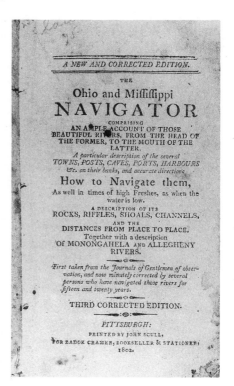

Title page, Zadok Cramer, *The Ohio and Mississippi Navigator*, 3d edition (Pittsburgh: Zadok Cramer, 1802). Thomas Rodney used this edition for Ohio River travel guidance. Despite its title, satisfactory Mississippi River coverage did not appear until later editions of this guide. Courtesy Special Collections, Miami University Libraries.

river and the whole stream of the river here between the bars on both sides only a hundred yards wide. It is the narrowest part we have seen. Another riffle half a mile below this channa[l] over it near the NW shore. At quarter past eleven we passed a creek on the NW shore; and I omitted to mention that we passed a creek at 7 miles below the island and another at *[blank]* miles before we came to Little Quiendot which is 14 miles below the island; and the last creek we passed is about 2 miles or more below Little Quiendot. The river has been rounding for the last 5 or 6 miles from SE to SW by W and then to W by S.

At 10 minutes before 12 at noon we passed a creek on Virginia shore. We have seen settlements on both shore scattering along all this morning. 10 minutes before one we passed a small creek or run on NW shore about 3 miles below the last creek. At two o'clock we passed a riffle, channel on the Virginia shore. Here I lost our spliced pole. At half after two we passed a creek on the NW shore. At 3 o'clock passed another on the same shore. At half past three passed a creek on the Virginia shore. All this time we were sailing at the rate of 6 or 7 miles an hower and awhile after when we got in the reach above Great Guiendot we dined. A high yellow hill appeared at the end of the reach and on the point bellow the mouth of the river. At 5 o'clock we passed a creek on the north west shore in said reach.

At half past 5 o'clock we passed the mouth of Guiendot and the ugly riffle opposite the mouth of it.[2] The channel begins on the Virginia shore and then runs at right angles to the NW shore and there crosses the riffle; but we could cross the river and took channel across the riffle in the middle of the riffle. The rapid below this riffle continues to a creek a mile below the river. This river is 13 miles above Great Sandy.

We got in sight of Woods boat at ten o'clock this morning, and by 12 o'clock she left us; but we came in sight again in passing the last riffle. We were mistaken. We took this to be Woods boat but when came up with her in the evening we found it to be the 2d French boat, which we had passed yesterday. She went by us in the night, while we lay at ankor. We kept on tonight till 9 o'clock and finding we were in a strong current cast ankor near the NW shore. Last night we lay near the Virginia shore. We were opposite a house where Brown went on shore to lodge. We came about 45 miles today.

⚜

Ohio River, Fryday, September 30th 1803. We set off this morning before day, the moon being very bright, and having passed two riffles the last one just above Sandy. At seven this morning we passed the mouth of that river.[3] It is a large fine river but not so fine a river as the Great Canawa. Here we over took Woods boat at the mouth of Sandy and she set of[f] with us. This river is the division between Virginia and Kentucky. 4 miles below we passed a creek on the Kaintuky shore and 7 mile further passed two creeks one on each shore opposite each other. Here we overtook Wood again at half after 10 o'clock.

He had given us a soft shelled turtle in the morning which the Major had prepaired for cooking. These turtles I believe are peculiar to this river and are plenty in it. They are neither like the loggerhead or sea turtle but are of a make between both; but their upper and lower shells are more like the sea turtle. Both shells are thin and no part of them so hard as that of the sea turtle, and the upper shell has a soft border all round it as soft as leather. This soft part flows round juting out beyond the fleshy part of the turtle. The belly both shell and skin is white, a milky white, and the back is the color of the back of a flounder.[4] When we over took Wood again he was endeavouring he said to harpoon me a fish and struck at a good many but did not git one.

We have had a pretty strong current all the way today as far as the two creeks and some distance below them. A mile below this we came to another castle of rocks on the face of a mountain on the Ohio State shore.[5] We came too; and the Major and I went on shore in the skiff. Between the river and foot of the mountain we met with several old woods camps. At the foot of the mountain the people bled all the sugar trees; and others had been making millstones out of the monstrous blocks of rock that had fall[e]n off and rolled d[o]wn from the mountain. I passed them and assended about 200 feet higher to the foot of the castle. The rocks assended perpendicular from this base to apparently about 400 feet, like the wall of a castle; all the rocks on that side facing the river having decayed or falln off and falln down to the foot of the mountain.

The rock was of the same kind of that of the castle we had viewed before, was decomposing in like [manner] so that in various parts great caverns and holes appeared and esspecially toward the base; and I saw many rattle snake dens under them at the base and dens and covers of other beasts; and many parts [of] the face of the rock seemed so broken into caverns and large ovens as it were that it seemed likely that the foundation of some of the very highest part of the face of the castle woud soon give way. Indeed they looked so dangerous that I was afraid to explore the lower caverns least by removing any small matter might bring part of the superstructure down on me in a moment; otherwise I doubt not I should have found the same production of salt peter and allum here as at the other castle. It was evident that vast quantaties of the rock had returned to a black and rich earth which covered the mountain from the base of the rocky castle to the foot of the mountain.

While the Major and I were gone the boys took the batteau to the other side of the river, and we crossed over in the skiff; and I went up to a house that was on the hill and found the family there had come from Sussex in Dalaware about nine years ago of the name of Short; and I sat awhile to answer their questions about Dalaware; and here I got the best water I have tasted since we came to the Ohio, and got some milk of them and returnd.

There being a good breaze we made sail and passed Furgusons Barr a mile below at 2 o'clock P.M. We had a rapid from said bar to Little Sandy which comes in from the Kaintuky shore and the rapid continued a mile below.[6] While we were going over this I shot twice at a flock of 5 wild geese (the first we have seen), but they were too far off and we killed none. In the mean time the Major dressed our soft shell turtle; and it was superior to any thing of the kind except our bay tarripins and perhaps not inferior to them. They are delicate and very tender and lushious.

At half after five we passed a creek on the NW and a rapid opposite and below a riffle channel in the middle of the river, and a little to the left of a large rock now 2 ft. above water. We proceeded after night till we over took Woods boat again one or two miles above Little Sciota and cast ankor near where they lay by the shore. There were settlements on both sides of the river most of the way we came today but some times scattering. We came 37 miles today tho we sailed but little. The current evidently increases as we proceed down the river.

The Major and I had some sublime chat this evening; and as he asked questions, I explained to him my idea of the universe, of the wisdom and goodness of its creator and ruler; whereupon he said he very much approved what I had said that it corresponded very much with his own sense of things. Then, in speaking of the Revolution, I informed him of the special interposition of the Most [propitiating?] God in December 1776 and January 1777, and the manner in which it had been done in some degree thro' me, and that of course I am a strong witness of the truth of His special interposition at that time, and know it to be sacredly true.[7]

After we came to ankor the Major went on shore to see Wood; and I put out my fishing line, and then sat down to bring up my journal. The moon appeared full and bright in the evening. This being the last day of September it makes the 47th day since I left Dover.

Ohio River, October 1st 1803. The morning became after sun up very thick and foggy, yet we put off and so did Wood. 2 miles on we passed Little Sciota and a rocky bar just below it.[8] We passed the bar at the upper end and then run along the side of it across oblikely to the Ohio State shore, this reach of the river runing west SW. We proceed a mile and came to a long sand bar on the Kentucky shore and kept the channel which is close to the Ohio State shore (the Ohio Pilot says it is next to the Kaintuky shore but is mistaken or the bar has altered).

We met with no further impediment to Great Siota which we arrived at about half after eleven; and I went on shore to git some whisky and to see the town of Alexandria, which stands on a hill of high land on the uper side of the Sciota but facing the Ohio.[9] In a street parrallel with the river there is about 20 ordinary logged houses and cabbins in it and one framed and one stone house, but few of the buildings finished and the inhabitants miserably poor. Chillecothe the seat of government of the Ohio State stands on this river 60 miles up it. The Great Sciota is some thing larger than Little Sciota but is but small at the mouth tho it is said to be a hansome river. The reach of the Ohio by Alexandria is SSW. Wood left us while we stopped.

It was just 12 o'clock at noon when we left Alexandria. 5 miles below passed Turkey Creek and a large sand bar on the NW shore.[10] Just after we had left Alexandria some person hailed the boat away behind on the shore near the lower end of the town. We thought it was a man who had disputed a dollar Brown had paid him and we would not stop again. They put off in a canoe and persued us trailing from time to time. At length he got out on the bar and seemed in great distress. The Major went to him in the skiff while the batteau persued her way. It was Shields who had persued us by land and got to Alexandra just time enough to see the boat. The Major brot him on board fatragued [*sic*] half to death for when we saw them coming the boy slacked rowing for them to come up.

At 3 o'clock we passed Canoconneque Creek on the Kentucky shore.[11] This is a fine creek and the only one we have seen that was not dry. There was a flow of water out of this; but there is two ugly bars here, one runing of[f] from the mouth of the creek and one from an island on the NW shore; but we found a good channel between and round them by passing between them and then runing over to and along the Kentucky shore a little way and then gliding off into the middle of the river between the island and Kentucky shore. After passing said island the river assumed its natural form again.

Here I recollect that I omitted to mention the appearance of a cuerious rock on the mountain on the Kentucky shore just before we saw Alexandra round the point. It was an oblong laying like a table on one edge and the upper corners ovalled off a little. It stood on the top of a nob of the mountain and perhaps was 60 ft. long and 15 ft. high. The face was green as if covered with moss and the top edge was crowned with a row of ceadars.

While passing the last island we came in sight of Woods boat again but the wind slacked and he has got out of sight again. At 1/4 before 5 o'clock P.M. passed a creek on the NW shore and a stone bar just below it. Good channel close under the Kentucky shore. We overtook Woods boat at Vance Ville where he had incamped for the night and we come to ankor just above him. There is a very hansom settlement and little town here on the Kentuky shore and a salt works 1/4 mile out of town on Salt Lick Creek.[12] The Major and Brown lodged on shore. This 17 miles below Sciota and 28 miles above Lime Stone. 20 ft. water by the shore.

Sunday, October the 2d 1803. We weighed ankor at day light tho the fog was very thick. In earnest to reach Limestone today to git our boat repaired as she leaks too much, esspecially every night. Wood over took

us about 3 miles on the way again. Just time enough to pass over a
dangerous riffle before us. The best channel was on the Kentucky shore
but we followed Wood and crossed short over the middle of the riffle
in the middle of the river. They rubed hard and we just touched as we
passed over. Just below this riffle we passed Pond Run on the Kentuky
shore and Stouts Run on the NW shore, and 4 miles below there past
Prestonville a little town of ten or twelve poor logged houses on the
Kentucky shore, and passed a riffle just below the village. Channel good
on NW shore.[13]

2 miles below we passed a small island surrounded by a large sand
barr. Channel on NW shore but next to the barr at the uper end and
at the lower end over the riffle at the mouth of a creek on the NW
shore. Keep nearest to that shore and then the middle of the river by
the floating mill, and thence toward the Kentucky shore by the mouth
of a run or small creek on that shore. Thence the channel inclines over
towards the NW shore but is good from the middle of the river to that
shore and no danger any where but by timber near the shore; but low
as the water is both Woods boat and ours passed the island without
touching. This is the uppermost of what is called The Three Islands.[14]

At 2 miles below the island we passed Cycamore Creek on the
Kentucky shore, at 11 o'clock A.M. No riffle here. The Major and Shields
went on shore in the skiff for wood and fire where Woods boat had
landed on Kentucky shore and are now persuing us. At 40 minutes after
11 o'clock A.M. passed Donelsons Creek on the NW shore 2 miles below
the last creek.[15] At 12 o'clock we passed a long sand bar and creek on
the Kentucky shore a mile below the last creek. We go now between 3
and 4 miles an hour there being no wind ahead on stern. (The last
mentioned creek and bar are not mentioned by the Pilot.)

At one o'clock we entered it into the channel on the Kentuck shore
at the upper end of what the Pilot calls the Two Islands. The upper one
we call Tinn Pan Island because the Major here droped one of our tinn
basons overboard and then persued it in the skiff and took it up again.
The lower island we called Manchester Island from the little village of
Manchester on the NW shore opposite the lower end of it. This villiage

has a very hansome situation and contains about 20 wooden houses, some of them pretty decent looking ones.[16]

Wood gave us an Ohio sucker which we had for diner boiled and butter with it and found it a good fish. It was remarkably fat. Before cooking we took near at [a] pint tin cup of leaf fat out of it which lay all along its back interior. It would have weighed as we suppose about six pounds. It was in shape or form like a fatback and in color like a yellow perch. It lives by suction on muscles, etc.

Below the last island the river resumed its natural size again. There is a ridge of mountain on the Caintucky shore opposite these island[s]. Indeed the mountains have appeared on both shores for two days past, and thereby spoiled our wind so that we have had but little sailing.

At 1/4 after 3 o'clock past a small creek or run on the NW shore and a fine extensive settlement along the river below it. At half after 3 o'clock we passed a small creek on the Kentucky shore. A pretty neat logged house and small settlement below. A person passing by told us this is Cabbin Creek 6 miles above Lime Stone. We passed Crooked Creek while I was laying down two miles back or higher up.[17] At half past 5 o'clock we passed another small creek or run, and 10 minutes after passed another just above Brooks's settlement and a sand barr on the NW shore opposite said settlement, which is on the point on the Kentucky shore.[18] As soon as we turn said poi[n]t we saw Lime Stone about 2 miles off and arrived there at 7 o'clock, that is just before dark, and came to ankor.[19]

Limestone on the Ohio, October 3d 1803. This morning after some trouble got the batteau up and got her overhalled and new corked by Brown and another carpenter and got off again at 4 o'clock P.M. Wood waited for us till 2 o'clock and then went off. While there I wrote a letter to Caesar my son[20] and one to J. Fisher and put them in the Post Office; and the Major and I took a walk to see the town and ship yard.

There is about 50 houses in the town and a few large good houses but I observed but one of brick. Mr. Gallahar has a very fine ship of about 240 tuns on the stocks and will be done by the swell of the river. We viewed her and she appears to be well built and of excellent stuff such as mulbery, locust, white oak, etc. Crispin is the master workman and he told me people and mechanecks at that place are the idlest he ever met with. Indeed this appeared to be the case. I saw no body at work and no body about the town took notice of us or offered to afford us the least assistance except one poor man; and we had to pay extravagantly for every thing we bought or had done only [except for] the assistance of Mr. Woods men, our fellow travellers. Indeed, the present disposition of the people on this beautiful river is very unfavorable to its improvement. They mostly seem as if they were only waylayers to take advantage of travellers in[s]tead of aiding and incurraging the navigation of the river. Every thing raised in the country even, is as high here as in the market towns near the Atlantic.

We saw a very few genteel people in Lime Stone. We were introduced by Mr. Wood last evening to a Major Brown tavern keeper and we invited him to drink a glass of wine with us in our cabin and we were back and forward at his house today but he paid very little attention to us. Mr. Gallahar indeed was obliging enough to let us have what we paid for.

We left Limestone at a little before 5 o'clock P.M. and at a 1/4 before six passed a creek on the NW shore. P. Stout had passed Limestone 10 days ago. Here Brown and his companion ship carpenter left us and we had only Buckhanan our pilot beside our selves, 4 in all; but expect to git another hand. Coud not meet with one at Limestone; but our batteau goes better with one hand now she is dry than with two before. We travel about three miles an hour, without wind. The town at Limestone is called Maysville. I know not why. As to the Limestone Creek it is but a small stream and is now quite dry. This place is a great thorofare and more might be expected of it than is seen.[21] The situation is pleasant and gives a good prospect of the river. I here discovered that I had omitted to leave letters brought to J. Rumford at Washington and a Mister Taylor at this place as well as all J. Lees letters to Connels Ville, such has been my haste and attention to my journey.

We dropt ankor at 7 o'clock in the evening near the Kentucky shore opposite a little town called Charles Town the Cou[n]ty Town of Mason County.[22] The Major and Shields went on shore to see the place tho [it was] after dark. It contains only about 20 or 30 houses. The river below Limestone is said to be navigable for loaded boats at all seasons of the year and but little danger any where but at the falls; nevertheless I shall continue my observations on whatever may seem worth notice as we go.

The Major and Shields returned with a nice line [loin] of veal and half a bushel of sweet potatoes as a present from a Mr. Mitchel of Charleston aforesaid whose wife is sister to Mr. Ignatious Smith of Natchez. This is an instance of the greatest hospitality we have met with on the Ohio, not evin excepting Mr. Blany Hazard. He lives in a decent loged house and every thing decent round them, etc. Such men do honor to this wild uncultivated country. It is only to be lamented there is but few of them in it.

Our boat has been quite dry since her dressing at Limestone and floats much lighter by that, and by gitting clear of the young carpenters and their baggage and tools so that she goes faster now with Buckhanan alone than 2 rowers before.

Ohio River opposite Charles Town, October 4th 1803. The morning foggy as usual but we weighed ankor at half after 6 and proceeded. Soon passed a large sand barr on our right, and creek mid way opposite the bar on Kentucky shore; and after passing the bar passed Eagle Creek, a large creek on the NW shore.[23] At 1/4 after 8 A.M. we passed another creek on the NW shore with a high stoney bar at the mouth of it but deep water close along side the bar. Having no wind we have gone this morning about 3 miles an hour, which is generally our progress when there is no wind for or against us. At 20 minutes after 9 we passed a creek on the Kentucky shore and a small sand bar at the mouth of it.

At 1/4 before ten we passed a long stoney sand bar in the middle of the river but rather nearest the Kentucky shore, and a fine settlement on that shore just below the bar, and a ferry over from that settlement to a small settlement opposite on the NW shore; and from the appearance of the road on the Kentucky side it is a highway much used. There was a ferry also near the last creek we passed. At ten o'clock we passed a small creek just below the settlement above mentioned on Kentucky shore. We know not yet wither this settlement is Augusta or not.

At half past ten we passed a large creek on the NW shore and sand bar at the mouth of it, which extend[s] half a mile down the river and at the lower end runs more than half way into the river; and there is a riffle from it quite across to the Kentucky shore and a small creek on the Kentucky shore about midway the aforesaid barr. I landed 2 miles above the barr, on the Kentuck shore, and walked better than 3 miles with my gun on shore, and went on board again near a mile below the barr, and found by my walking that the boat went near on quite 4 miles an hour tho the wind was ahead. At 25 minutes after ten we passed a small creek on the Kentucky shore. Very rocky at the mouth on shore. Two or three houses on the point below at the foot of a mountain.

Half a mile below we came to a large sand barr on the Kentucky shore extending half a mile or more down the river; and half way across it at the lower end there is a short ridge of mountain on the Kentucky side [which] runs one end of it down to the river just at the uper end of this barr; and pretty extensive settlements on both sides the river along the bar; and on the NW shore a hansome creek falls in about half way the barr, and just above the lower settlement on that side. We passed the last creek at noon. A little lower on the Kentucky shore behind the bar falls in a small creek; and there is a 2 story framed house on the point below the creek in a pleasant situation. At a 1/4 before one our course being west and the wind hard at west, we cast ankor near the NW shore and went to cooking diner, and determined on a viel cutlet.

After diner I went on shore with my gun and in wa[l]king a mile on the NW shore crossed two deep creek[s] that had no appearance save at the edge of the river and woud not be noticed by any body on the river unless when the water is high. Many such streams as these we have no doubt passed without notice for all those small creek[s] which we see apparrently now braking into the river when viewed a little way back are deep large streams. At the last of those little deep creeks I saw a fine spring in the bottom; but the bank was so steep I could not git at it, and tho very thirsty was obliged to pass it.

I turned down to the river to see where the boat was which I had directed to meet me there; but she not being up I turned into the woods again some distance below the creek and set down. Heard a dog bark behind me and saw a very hansom blackeyed woman coming from the spring towards me with a pail of water. When she came near I asked her what creek that was on the opposite shore? She said Bracken. I asked her where Augusta was? She said a mile below the creek.[24] Then she gave me a drink of water, and said she lived a little further down, but her house was not in sight.

I then went down to the shore opposite Bracken Creek which appears to be a fine large creek on the Kentucky shore, called the boat and went on board, and ordered them to row down to Augusta. The wind being strong agai[n]st the current there was such a rough swell as we have not found in the Ohio before. I told the Major of my fortunate adventure with the river or wood nimph that I met with on the shore and he lamented his hard fortune at not being in my place.

A little before sundown we cast ankor opposite to a large brick house in the town of Augusta. This little town which contains about 20 houses has one of the most pleasant situations that we have seen on the Ohio. The river is not less than 500 yds. wide here; and there is a straight reach of about 2 or 3 miles about the middle of which the town stands fronting the river, as all the towns on its banks do that we have seen. The reach is WSW and ENE. A large tract of bottom land lays round this town quite level; and there are some settlements opposite on the NW shore at the foot of a high hill or mountains. The Major and Shields went on shore and got soap, candles, and whiskey while I was dressing and returned to tea. At 10 o'clock P.M. I rouzed up Buckhanen and we weighd ankor and proceed till 12 o'clock at midnight, the moon giving sufficient light, and then came too [sic] about 6 miles below Augusta.

[N.B. After the Major and Shield had gone to bed and while I was writing, 3 or 4 girls came down and bathed in the river near our boat and made a great flouncing splashing in the water. The Major and Shields were su[s]picious when they were told of it next morning because I did not wake them while the girls were bathing.][25]

Wednesday, October the 5th, on the Ohio. The morning foggy but not so bad as usual. We weighd ankor at day light and at 6 o'clock passed a large creek on the NW shore; a la[r]ge framed 2 story house just bellow it a little off the river with a large avenue before it to the river; a large sand bar just below this creek on the NW shore extending near a mile below. A little below but almost opposite the above creek is one on the Kentucky shore, and some thing like a villiage, and a ferry over the river. There are good settlements on both shores along here[26] which is about 8 miles below Augusta.

At 1/4 before 9 we passed a sand bar near the middle of the river, but nearest NW shore a narrow strip half a mile long. The fog was so thick at one time this morning that the boat was rowd round which brought the wind aft which was ahead; and now thinking it fair, they hoisted the sale and had returnd half a mile before they calld me. I immediately orderd sail down and ankor out till rowers got breakfast and then set them right by the compass and current.

The fog has now cleared away but a stiff wind at west right ahead so that we make but little way. We are now passing a creek on Kentucky shore. Small settlement just below it but none in view on the NW shore. At ten the wind got heavy and we cast ankor again; and I went on shore and walked into the woods after turkies, having left word for the boat to proceed as soon as the wind slacked.

I met with creek in the woods, and persued it to the river 2 miles above where I landed, and went down to the river at the mouth, and saw a bald eagle pouncing at three ducks in the river on my right. I judged that the ducks were so frightend by the eagle they woud fly, and I walked on towards them. Indeed they on seeing me seemed to proceed towards me to avoid the eagle and he on seeing me flew to the other shore and waited the event.

I fired and crippled one of the ducks and as the others did not fly began to load again. The crippled duck was carried by the current down the river. By the time I was loaded the boat came up and the skiff came for me. By this time the eagle saw the crippld duck and immediately pounced at it, and at the 3d attempt took the duck before the boat could git to it, and flew off with it to the woods on the right. I persued but suppose he went to his nest. I walked on 2 mile further on a very fine pathway on the high bank with my gun but saw nothing more to shoot at; and then having got to the end of a sand bar that run the whole way I had walked and seeing the wind blew too hard to proceed, I called the skiff and ordered the boat to cast ankor.

Went on board and weighed [anchor] and went a little lower down to a spring on the Kentucky shore near a house and came to and got diner. The owner of the house come on board and asked assistance for a sick child which lay ill with worms. I went up and prescribed and furnished mercury pills which I got of Shields, and the woman gave us some eggs; and we returned on board. It is very sickly all along the river on the bottom land and all its inhabitants are very pale colord. In my rout on shore before diner I passed through a fine tract of land. The chief gro[w]th was honey locust and cycamore. The honey locust trees were frequently 5 and 6 feet diameter. This tract is said to be 25 miles above Columbia.

On my return from this rout I discovered that I had lost my gold ring off my finger but could not recollect when. I had obsirved before and supposed I had lost it where I pulled my gloves to load my gun after shooting the duck, or had lost it last evening when I washed and dressed at Augusta; but had to give it up for lost at any rate. But as I conclude that [it] must have come off in the bucket when washing and that it was cast out with the water in the Ohio and I consolate my self for the loss by its being in the Egyptian stile a weding of the Ohio, and surely I could hardly have a more beautiful or prolific mistress unless the incident had happened with Misisipi her parent river.

[I must not omit on this occasion the pleasant banter that passed among the Major and Shields [who] were vexed that I did not wake them when the girls were bathing and swiming near our boat at Augusta; and the instant I enquired if any of them had seen my gold ring or knew where it was the Major replied "O yes, I know where it is." Where? "O by d, that blackeyed girl, that wood nimph you met with yesterday has got it." Shields joined him. I replied that this suggestion was to repay me for not waking them when nai[a]ds or river nimph[s] of Augusta were swiming round our boat; that I expect they had come down agreably to assignation with [us] but they [the Major and Shields] were so fond of sleep they had not pations to wait their arrival, etc. The Major swore he knew the object of my errands on shore, that they would hear of more gold rings lost before we got to Natchez, etc.][27]

While I was on shore the boat past 2 la[r]ge creeks on the Kentucky shore and we have passed two since and one on the NW shore; but these creeks are so numerous that they are hardly worth mentioning unless any peculiar circumstance should require it, for they are all dry at this time; and in future I shall pass them by unless a shoal or riffle, etc. may be distinguished by them. I shall only note rivers. We have seen several flocks of geese today flying up or down the river. Just at dusk we ankored on the NW shore near a settlement, 26 miles above Cincinnatti.

Thu[r]sday, October 6th 1803, on the Ohio. Thick fog. We put off at 6 o'clock A.M. and passed Indian Creek on NW shore and a large creek on Kentucky shore a mile below.[28] Our course from there NNW after turning a point on Kentucky shore at said creek. About mile further we passed a very large creek on the Kentuck shore. It is probable this is what was calld Big Indian Creek by our host last night.[29] The fog cleard early this morning and the weather mild and pleasant. Indeed it has been so ever since we left Wheeling after the first day and night.

A mile below the last creek is a flat bar that spreads quite across the river with a riffle at the lower end. There was only 9 inches water on this bar. We kept the middle of the river. The current fell over the riffle towards the NW shore, and we crossed about half way, being guided by the current. At the lower end of the riffle there is a sand bar on the Kentucky shore and a large creek on NW shore just below where we crossed the riffle. Half a mile below the said riffle and sand bar is a la[r]ge creek on the NW shore after turning a point, and another on the Kentucky shore nearly opposite but rather lower down, we suppose about 10 or 12 miles above the town of Cullumbia or mouth of Little Miama.

There is a large creek on the NW shore about 9 miles above Cullumbia where a rapid begins and about a 1/4 of a mile below a long sand bar in the middle of the river which extends a mile down; but there is a wide channel over the riffle at the uper end of the bar next to the Kentucky shore. The course down by this bar is nearly NW. There the river veers more to the west toward the lower end of the bar. There is a smaller creek on the NW shore.

The next reach below this bar veers to WNW. Indeed the river from where we set out this morning has been constantly veering from N by W to this point; but at the next turn below, it veers to the northward again, that is about 4 miles above Cullumbia, having passed 5 Mile Creek just before we entered this reach, and is 7 miles from the Little Miami to Cincinnatti.[30] About the middle of this reach is another rapid, a stony bar in the middle of the river, and a sand bar on Kentucky shore; but there is a good channel between them. The riffle was over the end of the stoney bar. It is rather nearest to the NW shore between 4 and 5 miles above the Little Miama. Half a mile below this there is a sand bar in the middle of the river or rather on NW shore channel on Kentucky side till you pass the lower end of the bar, then glides over to the NW shore to avoid a bar and riffle on the Kentucky shore.

By keeping too long near the middle of the river, we grounded and all get out but the Major, and easily carried boat back a little way and then passed over to NW shore. The rapid continues 4 or 5 miles in passing all these bars. In the next reach below the river rounded to NW and in the next to N by W.

At half past 3 P.M. we passed the mouth of the Little Miama. This is a handsome river about 70 or 80 yds. wide. There is a large sand bar at the mouth. The last reach that we passed to the mouth of this river is nearly due north. There is not much water comes down it now.

Here we put on shore a Yankee that came on board eleven miles above and helped to row the boat to this place. He is a millright by trade. There is a flat bar and a great deal of it extending along the NW shore down to the uper end of Cullumbia which is a mile below the river.[31] There is a creek on the NW shore at the lower end of the town, and a little below a larger sand bar on the Kentucky shore extending a good way down the river, and a riffle at both ends, but plenty of water near NW shore.

A mile lower ther[e] is another sand bar on the Kentucky shore and riffle midway of it with but a narrow channel over near the NW shore; and afterwards water in the middle of the river till you git near the point at the uper end of Cincinnati; then keep towards the NW shore; then keep near the middle of the river to avoid wood on both sides till come to the middle of the town, opposite the mouth of Licking River.[32] It is 8 miles from Little Miama to Licking, 7 from Cullumbia to Cincinnati. The river winds from the mouth of Miama round to SW in its course to Lycking and is at this time a rapid almost all the way. After passing [Little] Miama we riged all 4 of our oars. Buchanand worked two and the Major and Shields the other two and I steerd, so that we got to Cincinnati and cast ankor a little before dusk.

Some gentleman came to the shore and enquired if Col. Rodney was on board. The Major being out answered he was but woud not be on shore till morning. He said he wantd to see Col. Rodney, but it woud do in the morning. The Major and Shields presently after went on shore; and little below us we saw the fire and heard the horn of Woods boat; but the Major and Shields on going to her contradicted this. Wood had left here 4 hours before we arrived. We then had the fiddle and flute awhile at play to salute Cincinnati and then went to rest.

CHAPTER SIX

Earthworks, Prehistoric Bones, and Two River Towns

Ohio River: Cincinnati to Louisville, Kentucky,
October 7–18, 1803

Rodney's stops at Cincinnati and Louisville provided him and his companions their last experiences of urban life before reaching Natchez, still many miles away. In 1803, Cincinnati, with a population of more than eight hundred, was the third largest town in the Ohio Valley behind Lexington, Kentucky, and Pittsburgh. Here, new sights and cosmopolitan pleasures ranged from the social delights of a tea and card party, where "The ladies were all genteel and agreeable," to conversing with General Arthur St. Clair, recently retired as governor of the Northwest Territory. Here, too, the town's prehistoric Indian earthworks set his mind to turning on how, when, and by whom they had been created. During Iris's day-and-a-half pause at Cincinnati, young Thomas H. Williams joined the party. Natchez-bound, he agreed to work for his passage but not to come aboard until Louisville.

Leaving Cincinnati, the company agreeably passed its time by listening to Shields play his flute or by brief hunting forays in pursuit of turkeys and ducks. They also amused themselves by naming islands, whether or not they

103

already had names. But most interesting of all was a side excursion to visit the intriguing "Big Bone Lick," a Kentucky salt spring some miles inland from the river where the monstrous bones of prehistoric animals once had lain. Few of these fascinating relics remained by the time Rodney arrived, his friend Meriwether Lewis having been there before him and "carried off all the larger bones." But Rodney managed to secure a tooth as a souvenir.

Louisville, much smaller than Cincinnati, held but one cultural attraction for him: more Indian mounds to examine and ponder over. What excited him more was a natural wonder, "the falls of the Ohio," a series of rocky rapids which formed the chief obstacle to navigation on the river. In Rodney's words, it was "a terrable place to pass through." But, guided by a skillful hired pilot, Iris did pass through it and continued on her way deeper into the wilderness.

◁▷

Cincinnati on the N bank of Ohio opposite the mouth of Lycking River, Fryday, October 7th 1803. A very thick fog this morning and cleared up. Summer warm. Early in the morning Mr. Thomas H. Williams came on board the Iris and delivered me a letter of introduction from Captain Lewes, etc.[1] His business was to git a passage with us down to the Natches. He said he had no baggage except what he had brought on horseback and wood take such fare on board as we had to spare and shift as well as he could; whereupon I consented to his going if he would lodge with the Major, as our spare berth was allotted to P. Stout at Louisville if he should meet us there.[2]

After breakfast Shields and I took a walk through the town to view it, and visited the Court House and old Fort Washington etc.; and returned by the tavern where we met with the Major and old General St. Clair, and stoped and sat awhile with the General.[3] He pressed us to take a family diner with him, but I excused myself as I had ordered diner on board, but wou'd wait on him in the afternoon. Shields and I returnd and the Major went with the General.

The Court House is a large stone building with a cupala and belfry on it and will make a neat appearance when finished. For the large room now intended for the Court has an arched raling for the advantage of

Cincinnati in 1802. Henry Howe, *Historical Collections of Ohio*, 3 vols. (Columbus: Henry Howe & Son, 1891), facing 2:44.

sound in speaking, and there is a gallery on one side and the sealing is 18 or 20 ft. high. The whole buildin[g] appears in good proportion and contains room for the publick officers, etc. There are 4 niches in front, of size for a statue to stand in each, but for what purpose intended do not know. As I went to the Court House I passed through the burying ground which exhibited a vast number of graves indeed for so young a place. From the Court House we went to view Fort Washington.[4] This appears to have been origionally nothing more than a kind of block house fort calculated only to frighten or repell Indians. It covers about half an acre but is now partly in ruins and the whole will be so soon as it is of no longer [any] use.

This town, when we consider the recentness of it[s] date, the ground being all in woods only 14 years ago, is astonishingly large.[5] It now contains about 400 houses and a great many new ones building and many of them large good houses. It has nearly a south front on the Ohio. The lower town is evidently built on what was once an island, as the vally between that and the hill back (where the Court House and uper town is) shews evidently that it has been once one bed of the river, but having got choaked up has risen in the course of time and united the island to the main land. Several other islands are now in this progress, the smaller channel round them being dry and no doubt yearly filling up as the larger channel becomes more roomy; and this effect is also apparent at many other places along this river. Indeed, all the bottom land on this river appears to have been united to the highland in this manner.

In the afternoon Mr. Shields and I walked up to Genl. St. Clairs and the Major soon after came to us there w[h]ere we stayed and drank wine while with the Genl. and then returnd. The Genl. came with me and we called again to see the Court House. Then the Genl. came with me to the bank, and we took leave of each other; but as we came along he spoke of the antient fortifications just beyond the town which upon reflection I determined to see in the morning before we go.

Soon after I got on board the Major came down and brought Mrs. Finley['s] complements for us to drink tea there, and the Major and I went. Mr. Williams, Doctor Sulman and his wife, and a Mr. Vaughn and his wife, and a Mr. and Mrs. *[blank]* were there. Mr. Finley introduced us to them all and we drank tea with them.[6] Then whist was proposed and Mrs. Finley and myself played against Mr. Vaughn and Mrs. Sulman, and the Major and Mrs. Vaughn played against Mr. Finley and Mrs. *[blank]*. We ended at 11 o'clock and we returned on board; but while we were playing, the Majors partner sang "Drink to me only with thine eyes and I will pledge with mine." I expected to hear the Major reply in the next verse, "Or leave a kiss within the cup and I'll not look for wine;" but he hung his head and was beat. So he lost a paper of pins. Thus politely treated we spent a pleasant evening at Cincinnati. Mr. Finley is receiver for this district. At our table we left off even games. The ladies were all genteel and agreeable.

Cincinnati on the Ohio, Saturday, October 8th 1803. Foggy morning as usual. As soon as I got up I went alone to examine the old supposed fortifications a little to the westward of the Court House. They are in the form of a regular uniform circle with an opening of about a hundred yards on the eas[t]. The surrounding wall is about 6 feet high and uniform in hight and size all round. The area within contains about ten acres. The trees that grew on it are cut down. The larges[t] stump remaining counted 150 years groth. This grew on the highest part of the ridge. There is no appearance of mote or ditch round it, nor could there be after such a length of time; and therefore it must be supposed there was a ditch without and a parrapet within, and that the wall was orig- ionally ten or twelve feet high, and that the wall has gradually sunk till the ditch and parrapet being filled up are lost to appearance, and the wall of course sunk into its present form. This is the natural operation, for I have seen this effect in respect to banks and ditches in a much shorter time.[7]

Genl. St. Clair says that there is one at Muskingum that contains 40 acres; and it is said there is another up that river that includes 600 acres; but the accounts I heard of them differed as to their size and also as to their form. They appear indeed similar in age and workmanship to those mounds in this country called Indian mounds, but are supposed by some to be the work of nations anticeedent to the present Indian tribes.[8]

Genl. St. Clair says he has seen one of these mounds 40 feet high and another 70 feet; but all I have seen are near about the same hight and none of them exceeding ten feet in hight; and all these are known to be burying places from the human bones found in them and fre- quently Indian trinkets which shews that these are the works of the Indians only, but perhaps of nations more advanced in the arts than the present tribes; but I can find no traces of those origional white inhabi- tants which I have no doubt once inhabited this country unless these works are the only remains of the extent of their knowledge and that they were buried in that distrucktion which put an end to the mamoth tribe of beasts.

Apropus, Finley told us last evening that a tusk had been lately found at Big Bonelick that measured in a straight line from the root to the point ten feet and from the root to the point tracing the middle of its circular limb 15 feet, that it is 19 inches round at the root and 23 inches round in the thickest part.[9]

We left Cincinnati at 11 o'clock.[10] Just as we set off Williams came down with his baggage and the Major brot him on board but he returned again to meet us at Louisville.

Just below the town we passed a stoney bar on Kentucky shore and rapid. A mile below this we passed another stoney bar in the river nearest to the Kentucky shore, yet the best channel tho small is next the Kentucky shore; however we passed in the middle of the river over the rapid, but the shoal is very full of wood. Just below this is Mill Creek on NW shore, a very large creek and not dry like others.[11] On the Kentucky shore just below this seat is Col. Sandfords seat who is said to be the richest man in Kentucky. We saw not any thing to denote this but a large plantation. About 6 miles below C.Cinati we passed a very large sand bar in the middle of the river, a narrow channel by it close along each shore. We passed it on the NW shore. This bar will no doubt soon be an island.

About sun down we passed Bushes Ferry and a little below it a small riffle and rapid along the old French settlement on the most northerly bend of the Ohio; and little below said settlement came to ankor at dusk in the north point of said bend 3 miles above the Great Miama, having come about [17?] miles only today.[12]

A little while after diner today we saw a large flock of wild turkies on the bank of the river. The Major and Shield went on shore with the gun; and the Major shot at two of them at 30 yds. distance but did not kill either. Our shot is too small. It require swan shot to kill them. By the information we had received set down the above distance but found in the morning that the extreme part of the N bend at the old French settlement is 5 miles above the mouth of the Miama.

⚓

Sunday, October 9th 1803, Ohio River. The fog very thick this morning. We set sail this morning at 1/2 after 6 o'clock and arrived at the mouth of the Great Miama at half after 8, so that [we] were at least 5 miles instead of three above it last night.[13] We ankord off the mouth of this river till we got breakfast that we might have a view of it, the fog being so thick we could but just see it when we came to it. There is a large sand bar a[t] the mouth, and the current or stream of it at present runs through the bar close round the uper point, the greater part of the bar being below; but when the water is up and flows over the bar the mouth of this river tends downward and is very wide; yet the stream now is but narrow. We left the mouth of the Great Miama at ten o'clock.

Our cou[r]se this morning from where we rested last night at the N. bend to the Miama and by it was WSW but soon veer'd to SW in the next reach a little below the river. Midway of this reach there is a sand bar on Kentucky shore, and a little lower a stoney bar on NW shore *[illegible]*, and just below a two story framed house with one end to the river and a brick chimny in the middle. This reach is full of wood or timber along both shores. Channel middle of the river. There is a bar indeed all the way from the Miama on the NW shore through this reach, and a 1/4 mile from the lower end a stoney bar in the river toward Kentucky shore. Just round the lower point of this reach is the largest creek we have seen on the NW shore, and at its mouth a stoney bar, and a few hundred yards below a great deel of river wood next to the NW shore. At 12 at noon we passed another large creek on NW shore about 1 1/2 mile below the last. The course through this short reach SW by W.

At half afte[r] 12 we turned the western corner of the north bend of the Ohio, about 5 or 6 miles below Miama. Here a very hansome deep creek falls in from the NW shore right on the elbow of this bend, and thence the river turns short to S by E and now our view and course is as it were for the first time directly toward our new intended home, that is southward and S westerly; for from this elbow to the mouth of the Ohio by a straight line it is nearly SW, tho the river in its course makes many windings, its whole rout being very serpentine, at least so far as we have traced it, for we have nearly met with a reach of it five miles straight, tho there is [another] one called 17 miles; yet it is not straight in any part of it more than 5 miles.

At 1/2 after I went on shore and passed 2 deserted settlements. Corn left. Saw at the first 2 flocks of patriges but coud not git a shot at them. The next there was a large flock of wild turkies round the house; and I was so near that I might have killed several of them but did not know but [if] the house was uninhabited; and soon as they got round the house they run like Indians. This was the most of a wilderness of any country I had been in. It was difficult for me to git through [the underbrush]. At 2 o'clock the boat stoped opposite a very large creek or small river on the NW shore to take me in, and I went on board coverd with little burrs.

This creek falls in about opposite the middle of a large sand bar islan[d] in the river and rather nearest to Kentucky. The channel on NW shore. This creek and barr is about half way between the last corner of the N bend and an island which will be mentioned presently now below us. Upon my coming on board at the little river before mentioned the Major and Shield denominated it *Rodneys River* and barr. This bar however will soon be an island as some bushes are already growing upon it in the highest part. We passed the lower end of the island at 4 o'clock P.M. This is the first island below Miama and about 10 miles below the W course of the N bend. It is a young island, the wood on it not appearing more than 10 or 12 years old and the wooded part is but small; but there is an extensive sand bar round it which is fast growing and will probably make it a large island in 25 years. It is a very pretty clean island and bar but the land as yet too low to be inhabited. As the Major happened to be playing on his violen as we passed this island, we called it *Violen Island*.

A mile below this island a farmer informed us we were only 12 miles above the Big Bone Lick Creek where I propose to call tomorrow. 2 miles below Violen Island the river turns short to the SW; and just after passing the turn there is a very large sand bar spreading from the Kentucky shore more than two thirds across the river, leaving only a narrow channel next the NW shore, at the head of which there is a riffle which still contracts the deep water to a narrow space; and below this is a strong whirlpool for some distance that takes great force of rowing to pass through safely.

We went about a mile or less below and cast ankor in 4 ft. water near the NW shore. The Major and I went on shore to the only cabin near. The family was from London and had lived there two years. The man was a distiller and brewer by trade and was sick and deaf. They had two daughters. The eldest was sick and had gone abroad to one of the neighbours. The youngest about 12 years old was at home and was the only one of the family in health. A nephew lived with them, 9 or 10 years old. He had the ague.

The old lady asked us for snuff. I refered her to the Major and he had left his box on board, but promisd to send some. The old lady sent her daughter with us to git her some. She came into the batteau and waited till the Major got the snuff. I stayed in the skiff and took her back again to the shore. The old lady offered us onions and sweet potatoes and cream for coffee in the morning, but I told her I would pay her for the potatoes. This is the first time I have been on shore after dark except at Cincinnati.

Ohio, Munday, October 10th 1803. Foggy as usual. Set off at 7 o'clock after having sent on shore for cream and potatoes, and they sent us a rump of fresh vinison in return for tamarinds, etc.[14] At half past 8, we passed a high rocky bar in the middle of the river but rather towards NW shore. Channel next to Kentucky about 4 miles or 5 bellow where we lay last night. Course of the river by said bar SE by E and next reach is due east and then E by N 2 miles, then veers in next reach to E by S to Gunpowder Creek.[15]

Here Shields and I landed with a man who was to guide us to the Big Bone Lick on Big Bone Creek.[16] As we went Shield shot a turkey. When we came to the lick, I measured several of the bones as follows: the face or forhead of a head bone three feet wide across the widest part which was near the uper part of the face or forhead, a thigh bone 26 inches long and very thick, one side of a gaw bone thirty inches long, and the socket of a shoulder blade six inches wide. These are the largest bones now left at the licks.

I brot away a tooth that indicates its belonging to som[e] creature superior to any of the other bones. I doubted indeed its being a tooth but the guide said he had been present and helped to dig up a gaw bone that had one just like this in it; and he took it out and gave it to Major Chambers, and that it weighed 17 lb., seventeen pounds. Captain Lewes had got the long tusk lately found and one or another has carried of[f] all the larger bones; but the situation and circumstances of these licks shew that they have been long frequented and much more formerly than latterly.[17] [I also got a small piece that had scaled off from the great tusk that Lewes had taken and some small pieces of the inner part that had dissolved and dropt off to examine its substance.][18]

There is two salt furnaces or workes at the uper licks and one large one at the lower lick. The uper lick is 3 miles from the mouth of Gunpowder Creek and 4 miles from the mouth of Big Bone Creek. The lower salt works is half way down this creek that is 2 miles, but no bones has been found at this lower lick.

The reason seems that the lower lick was most antiently used by the wild beasts and the uper one more recently; and if they be any bones at the lower lick they are deeper in the earth; yet severel pretty deep salt wells are dug there; but by the appearance of this lick it has not been much used for 200 years past. This is evidenced by the growth of trees within the border of the lick; but uper lick has been (tho used a great while) more recently used. It is probable this latter used uper one was later in bracking out, and being much salter than the lower one the creatures deserted the lower for the uper.

The uper produces one bushel of salt to 200 gallons of water, the lower one bushel of salt to 800 gallons of water. The lower lick is in the bottom ground as it were of a fork of the creek, and the uper in another fork 2 miles higher up and a mile from the mountain from which the creek decends. No doubt the mountain contains the rock salt from whence the salt springs flow. There are also rocky mountains along the creek of a soft dissolving nature in this str[et]che along its banks. We traced the creek in our return but had not time to make much examination.

They make good white salt at all the works; but they are conducted in a very slovenly and unskilful maner or they might be vastly more profitable; yet perhaps this may in time induce them to explore the mountain and find the rock salt. We visited but two of the salt [works]; one had 30 the other 42 boilers. The springs rise in mud of color and smell like salt marshland.

As to the bones found at these places most of those now there are only buffelo bones. This no doubt was there [sic] last resort when they were sick; and here they died and left their bones which sunk into the mud. The main spring at the uper salt works boiled up to the su[r]fface of the ground and fell into the salt wells they had dug around it, which were only 4 or 5 feet deep at the lower works. There was several large wells 10 or 12 feet deep.[19]

We returned to the river at three o'clock and found the batteau ankored off the creek that is Big Bone Creek. This creek snakes in from Kentucky opposite a large sand bar on the NW side the river which extends two miles up and down above and below the creek. We cross from Gunpowder Creek to this creek SW by W and several miles below there the river veers to SE in the next reach. We proceed about 6 or 7 miles and came to ankor where there was no settlements on either side.

On the Ohio, October 11th 1803, Tuesday. As the moon shone and there was little or no fogg we weighd ankor before day light and proceeded. Our first course was due west for 2 hours or better, that is for 6 or 7 miles, then changed to SW at 8 o'clock. The river full and wide. Settlement but scattering.

I imbrace a moment of lezure to make a few observation[s] on the bones of the salt lick. I have in the course of my enquieries into the opperations of nature observed that she produces boney, shelly, and other substance in imitation of those that belong to animal and vegetable nature, whenever there is a peculiar and favorable combination of the simple elements which compose those solid parts of vegetables and animals out of the natural course and unconnected with any animal or vegetable.

This has made me doubt whether the large bones called mamoth bones were not produced in this way at the salt licks, where so many animal[s] in the course of hundreds and perhaps thousands of years had perished so as to fill the earth full of those kinds of salts and other combining elements which compose the boney parts of animals. These being reduced to simple elements again by time in great abundance in time by the force of nature might be stured [stirred] up to motion again and produce massy [massive] forms of bone beyond the size of any animals existing or that ever did exist.

In this way we meet with the asbestos which looks like wood and assumes in the earth the form of trees and its texture too so as to look like petrified wood; and in the same manner I have frequently seen rocks of shells on plains and even on the tops of mountains exhibiting even a greater variet[y] of shells than are to be found in the sea or along its shore. And why may not bones be produced in the same way esspecially at a place where so many bones have been deposited and dessolved and of course supplied with so much of all that kind of matter which composes bones?

In this case it is natural to suppose that bones of a hugh and unatural size would be formed, such indeed as those which have bin found at this Big Bone Lick and have so much astonished the world, as belonging to some animal beyond the size of any ever know[n] in any part of the world. The too[t]h I have favors this conjecture, its appearing evidently at least as much of a fosil as animal production; and the greater objection to this is that guide to the lick affirmed that he took a simelar tooth that weighed 17 lb. out of the gaw bone in which it grew; but I ask why might not the gaw bone be formed in the same manner as well as a tooth, the gaw bone being naturally the fountain of teeth. Another thing is observable. These fosil teeth are of a form different from those of all known animals.

At half after nine we passed a large creek on the Kentucky shore and a small sand bar and rapid. From this our course through a short reach W by N. At ten o'clock we passed another large creek on Kentucky shore towards the lower end of this reach. There is a rocky bar runs all along the Ky. shore through this reach. Courses soon after passing creek veer to west and at half past ten to SW again. We have went hitherto at about 4 miles an hour but the wind springing up aft. Buckanan just now hoisted sale.

We have an island ahead in view, distant perhaps 4 miles at this moment. We pass a large creek on NW shore just in the elbow of the out bend of the river. The course from said creek to uper point of the island bar is exactly SW. Then in passing the island the course is WSW.

At 1/4 before 12 we passed a large creek on NW shore which falls in just at the uper end of the island bar. Here we took in the Major and Shields who had been walking on shore several miles. At 20 minutes after 12 we past the lower end of this island and the next reach varies to SW again. This is a young island, the land low and the trees but small. We call this *Flute Island* because Shields was playing on the flute as we passed by it. The channel next the NW shore is dry now.

At quarter past one we passed a riffle at the uper end of a wide sand bar spreading from the Kentucky shore more than 2/3 over the river. The channel is deep but close to the NW shore. This bar is near or quite a mile long and is about 3 miles below the said island which is the second below Miama. At 1/4 after two we passed a pretty large creek on the NW shore. This is called Indian Creek.[20] At three o'clock we passed another riffle at the uper end of a large sand bar in the middle of the river channel on the NW shore.

We over took a man, one Coulter, in a canoe who told us there was a vineyard opposite the last sand bar before this on the NW shore. This man lives on the Misouri 7 miles up that river where he says the land is very fine; and a small town at the mouth of the Misouri. He has been 50 miles up that river but saw no town. The settlements are scattering that far. Below the last bar there are pretty good settlements on the Kentucky shore. This bar is 4 or 5 miles above Kentucky River. Appropos' Coulter says, the term the Spainards granted him land on was 400 acres for a man and 100 acres a head for women and children, the purchaser paying for surveying.

1/4 after 3 the boys say we are in sight of the town at the mouth of Kentucky River. The course from the last bar to the mouth of Kentucky River is SW. At 10 minutes before 5 o'clock P.M. we passed the mouth of Kentucky River. This is a large river about the size of the Great Kanawa at *[blank]* but not so deep as there appears drift wood in it. There is a pretty little town on the uper side with 6 or 7 brick houses in it and 15 or 20 wooden ones.[21] The situation is pleasant. There is also a plantation and wooden buildings on the lower side. From the town up the Ohio for 5 or 6 miles there are good improvement[s]. We passed

2 very good brick houses 2 or 3 miles above the town. The course of the Ohio by the Kentucky River is WSW. A mile below the river there is a fine la[r]ge creek on the same shore called Little Kentucky River.[22] From Little Kentucky the Ohio runs W by N.

At 1/2 after 6 o'clock we cast ankor under the Kentucky shore. We were lucky in coming to ankor just above a dangerous riffle in the middle of the river, there being no settlement near us. The Indian land is on the NW shore from opposite the mouth of Kentucky River for 49 miles down; and there is but few settlements on the Kentucky side opposite to the Indian land.

Ohio, Wednesday, October 12th 1803. It began to rain last night at about 4 o'clock and continued raining this morning. We weighed at half after 6 o'clock A.M. We had ankord as we found in the morning just above a sand bar on the Kentucky shore and a riffle. We went over to the NW shore but found tho we got safe over that we ought to have kept close to the bar or at least between the riffle and the bar, it being very shoaly on the NW side. This we suppose about 7 miles below Kentucky River.

At ten o'clock we came to a stoney bar and riffle in the middle of the river. We passed through a narrow channel and scarce water on the NW shore but found that the right channel was on the Kentucky side of the bar round a point not keeping too near the point. There is a hansome plantation on Kentucky side opposite this bar; and the channel runs near the lower end of that settlement and then crosses obliquely down the river toward a gap in the ri[d]ge of mountain on the NW shore to avoid another stoney bar just below on the Kentucky side.

After passing these bars the wind sprung up aft; and we hoisted sail, and went, as we suppose, 6 miles an hour till one o'clock when we passed a stoney bar in the middle of the river but attached to the Kentucky shore by a flat and riffle. We took the channel next the NW shore and not far from the bar to avoid a small stoney bar on that shore. This and the last mentioned are of the most dangerous parts of the river we have passed.

After passing the last bar, the wind headed us and I took an oar with

Buckanon; and tho it blowed furiously, we rowed the boat through the reach when the wind slacked and became equinoc[ti]al among broken mountains; and we still proceeded. It has rained hard all day and still continues at 4 o'clock P.M. Our cabin leaked as before; and we could not keep even our beds dry [despite] all we could do; nor could we cook, and have been obliged to use such scraps as we had by us.

We have seen very few settlements today and those since the first but mean. Both sides of the river appeared a wilderness. We saw a flock of turkies on the NW shore; but it rained too hard for any of us to go on shore, so we passed by them. We have also seen plenty of geese today but have not passed near enough to shoot at them.

As we akord [sic] in the evening near to a settlement I went on shore while the rest were cooking. A Mr. Pryor and his wife from near Richmond, Virginia, and their nine children, 4 girls and five boys lived there; and there was a nephew to D. Boon and his wife there and several others who had come to see them. Pryor told me he had lived there five years, that it is 25 miles below Kentucky River and 35 above Louisville, and that there are but few settlements till we git within ten miles of Louisville. Boon told me that his Unkle Daniel, who is remarkable for having lived on Kentucky River long before it was settled by the whites, has removed on the west side of the Misisipi and lives 40 miles up the Misouri;[23] that he and his wife in coming here last night were belated and obliged to lodge in the wilderness all night without fire after her horse had mired by the river side and had thrown her in the river so that both had like to have been lost.

Ohio, Thursday, October the 13th 1803. The rain ceased last evening just after we came to ankor; and after we got our dinner and super altogether we went to bed about 8 o'clock in our wet clothes and wet beds; and I slept very sound and well till near 4 o'clock this morning when I got up and rouzed Buckanan to make a fire and light a candle. My cloths and bed had got dry by my sleeping in them and I felt no injury.

In passing along the Indian wilderness we saw two flocks of turkies on the shore. I went on shore with gun above [about] twelve; but they got frightend at the boat and took to the woods and run like Indians so that I could not git near them. I then went along the shore three or 4 miles and then returned to the batteau. I saw the tract of a large buck that had gone to the river and walked along it and returnd to the woods. Not long before dinner we saw a great number of geese on Kentucky shore. Major went ashore but they flew. Then Shields took the gun and went on shore.

At 4 o'clock we passed a very good settlement on the Kentucky shore where the Major went with the skiff for s[alt]. This settlement is about a mile above an island in the river, the first bellow Kentucky River and about 20 miles above the falls. The wind has been so constant and brisk ahead today that we have made but little progress. At 5 o'clock we passed the above island, it being, including the bars above and below, about two miles long; but is but a young island. The wood on it being small, we saw cattle, hogs, and turkies on it; and as the hogs were most numerous, we call it Hog Island. As it is not inhabited, we suppose these creatures foard or swim to it over the channel next to Kentucky, as it appeared small. The main river is on the NW side. The course by this island is nearly west. All day today we have been gently rounding to the west. The first musketo I have seen I killed just now. We have not been troubld on the river or on shore with insects of any kind.

Ohio, Fryday, October 14th 1803. Last evening after passing a rapid and sand bar in the middle of the river we ankord just after dusk under the Kentucky shore near a settlement. When we went to bed it was starlight and broken cloudy. In the night the wind blew fresh for awhile and a little before day we had thunder and lightning and several showers of rain; but it held up just at day light, and before six we weigh'd ankor and persued our voiage.

Immediately after breakfast the Major and Shields set down to row ten miles to forward us to Louisville; but the breaze is fresh and still head as usual, tho we expected a change yesterday and day before. I rowed myself whenever the wind was hard ahead, for they all now confess I am the best oarsman on board and the Major swares again and again that I am the *Ulysses* of the voiage. The voiage, it is true, is tedious; but we have our music and our pleasant conversation which at times woud be entertaining even to the intelligent[sia]. Buckanon our oarsman informed me last evening that he was grandson to Pearson Landrum of Maryland who had the church near Centreville in 1775, and who I remember well on acct. of his fondness for horse racing and card playing even on Sundays.[24]

We all got at the oars after breakfast and turned a point ahead and came in view of another island; but it blew so hard ahead we could not git along, and run under the NW shore and came to ankor. Then about one o'clock we moved over to the Kentucky shore; but the wind then blew so hard we could [not] move till near sundown; and then it got quiet or rather slackd very much and we got along side the island we had seen just at dark and ankored under it in 3 feet water. The evening was very threatening, the clouds dark and broken with showers and wind blustery at 8 o'clock, and our candles being out we seem to have the prospect of an uncomfortable night.

[Saturday on the Ohio, October 15, 1803.][25] But we slept well and waked in the morning at day light when the clouds had all rolld away. The wind quiet and sky serene but cooler than it has been before, wind NW, our course SSW. A little after sunrise we passed a large creek or rather a small river on the Ky. shore where the Major went on shore for fire. There were two or three trading boats laying there. This creek is half way between the last island and another now in view. The uper one Buckanon says is called Pattans Island.[26] There is a plantation on it but we did not go on shore while there. The river from the points above the first of these islands widens into a long lake as it were.

We are now at half after six o'clock along side the second of these islands keeping the channel next to the Kentucky shore; and nearly opposite the uper end of this island there is a small island in close to the Kentucky shore. We passed between these two islands. The course between these 2 islands is SW the river turning to the westward after passing Pattans Island.

We went on shore about midway of the last island to see the cane, or reed, growing, for here we met with the first of it; but it is small, growing only ten or 12 ft. high.[27] I met a man and boy on the island tho it is not now inhabited. The man told me it belonged to the heirs of Richard Terrel deceased, that it is called 6 Mile Island being 6 miles from Louisville;[28] but I shall call it Terral Island after the owner; and the little island I call Duck Island because I saw nothing there but ducks. The lower point of Terrel Island is very narrow for a good way; and as I heard geese on the other side we run the batteau on shore; and I steped out with my gun and went over the pininsula but geese were gone; and a large flock of ducks in the cove between a little willow island and the pininsula of the big island. I got [with]in about 40 yds. of them and my gun blowed in the pan, the powder being damp; and I returnd, and we went on. Primed again, and soon passed near a single grey duck. Flashed again, and then unloaded, cleaned, and reloaded my gun, and went on with batteau.

As soon as we turned the point of Terrel or Sixmile Island, we saw Louisville at six miles distance on the Kentucky shore. After passing the last island the river resumes it[s] usual form but wider than usual and is very beautiful down to Louisville. It is probably not less than half a mile wide here. The wind is steady and brisk up the river again today. Tho this is the cause of greatly delaying our journey, I rejoice in seeing the wind blowing at particular seasons so steady up the riv[er], because this will enable boats to go up as well as down; for the wind is so much stronger than the current every where but at the small rapids that I am persuaded we could have gone twice as far up the river as we have came since we have been on it if we had set out from below.

We kept the NW shore after leaving Terrels Island; and we passed a large sand bar in the middle of the river half way, rather towards Kentucky shore a mile long. As we went along the shore I shot a duck and a marsh hen. I went twice on shore with my gun. The first time I saw a small grist mill that depended on a single spring to turn it. Saw nothing to shoot. Walked quite to the point at Clarks Ville where the rocks extend along the shoar from the falls there.[29]

Got on board and crossed over to Louisville where we arrived at one o'clock.[30] Dined on board and then I went on shore and into town and to the post office, but no letters there for me, and the collector Mr. New is gone to Lexington. I then took walk through the town and to see the Court House which stands on the south side of the town and on the east side of a large square which is not yet built up. The Court House is a pretty neat small stone building with a bellfry but no bell.

A little way south of the Court House and just back of the town is a very large Indian mound. It is by appearance a hundred yards long and sixty yards wide and 20 or 30 feet high. This is much the largest I have seen; and there is a pond near each end of it where the earth was no doubt taken to raise the mound. It is still entire and unbroken. The trees were cut off but I saw many large stumps on it so that it is of long standing. As I returned I saw a smaller one at a distance in the east part of the town that was dug into; but I did not go to it as I wanted to write home.

This a hansome town and in a pleasant situation and is thriving very fast. There are already many good brick and stone houses in it and many more building. As I returned I met Shields and the Major and Williams going into town, but I came on board. There are some remains of the old fort but little worth notice now.

Louisville at the Falls of Ohio, Sunday, October the 16th 1803. Fog in the morning as usual. I wrote to Caesar my son[31] and Doctor Ham and put them in the mail at 10 o'clock. Then went to the printers and got the [news]papers.

Returned and went with Buckanan in the skiff to view the Falls. While we were there saw a canoe pass through with ease and safty. Walked a good way down on the rocks on the NW side of the shoot to look for curiosities; but only observed the rock worm, which are kind

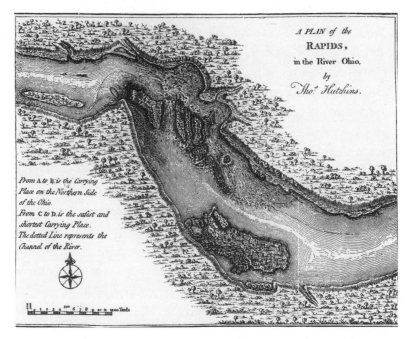

The Falls of the Ohio as sketched by Thomas Hutchins in 1778. Thomas Hutchins, *A Topographical Description of Virginia, Pennsylvania, Maryland, and North Carolina,* reprint from original edition of 1778, edited by Frederick Charles Hicks (Cleveland: Arthur H. Clark Company, 1904), facing 80. Courtesy Special Collections, Miami University Libraries.

of stoney and shelly substance in the form of large worms that grow in the rocks that forms the falls, of various [sizes], from 4 to ten inches long and some two inches diameter, the rock being sothe [softer] than the worms washes away and leaves part of them exposed so that I got several pieces but could not git a whole one.[32]

The rock that forms the great bed of the Falls is lime stone covered about 2 to 4 inches with a kind of iron stone; but [the?] iron stone is very hard and much harder than lime stone but is mostly washed off; and much of the lime stone also there worn by the smaller river stones and pebbles into sharp crags and deep holes are broken to pieces continually by the force of the water, in blocks and some times in large flakes; for the limestone rock lies bare above [its] base about a foot thick and cracks various ways, and being cut to pieces brake of[f] in block[s] and great flakes, but are first cut into deep holes and sharp and dreadful crags dangerous for vessels to touch.

This is the case mostly in the midd[l]e and towards the NW shore; but on the Kentucky shore quite to the middle channel the rock is all a flat pavement down to and round the island. The channel on the Kentucky shore however is now dry and the water all decends on that side of the island next the NW shore. This part I viewed alone in the after noon. I went in the little skiff and landed on the rocks. A flat pavement spreading over many acres cut various ways in little channels along the cracks of the rocks and waring away fast, etc.; but I saw nothing curious. There is a large creek on the Kentucky shore just above the falls, the mouth of it opposite the middle of the town of Louis Ville, with ship yard near the mouth where there is a large ship now on the stocks.[33]

Munday, October the 17th 1803, Louisville at the Falls of the Ohio. Last night the wind changed to NW and blew cold and hard so that our boat draged her ankor till got under a log which kept us from going on shore. This morning we determined to alter the cover of our boat so as to make it turn rain, and as the carpenters were extravagant Major Claybourn and Buckanan under took it and completed it before night.

In the meantime I attended to gitting necessaries and to review the town. In doing this I went to see the small mound I had noticed yesterday and then in the uper end of the town discovered three more large ones, two of them as large as the one I viewed yesterday but not quite so regular. One of them had a cellar dug for a house on the top of it; and [in] the one, largest and a little out of town to the SE near the creek, holes was dug into from one side quite to the highest part of it where the breach was 10 feet deep. I examined it attentively but there was no sign of bones. Every thing was dissolved to earth again, yet the earth itself from its feated [fetid] smell and dark redish grey clouded color evidenced its being the repository of the dead. All the ground was cleared on them but many large stumps were remaining.

There is no doubt with me now but these mounds and the old fortifications which I have before mentioned belonged to the same people, and that they were not the present race of Indians but a different people who have been distroyed by the first of the present race of Indians or by the severity of the northern himesphere at some remote period; for it must have taken a long period of time to have distroyed all the works of a people so far advanced in knowledge but these simple vestages which time can reduce no further; so that those people must have been distroyed at least 2500 or 3000 years ago for this part of the world to have been so fully restored to its natural state again.

In the evening Captain Lewis and his companion Captain Clark, son of Genl. Clark, called at our boat to see us and took a glass of wine with us and bid us adieu.[34] They do not go off till next week, yet as they have a better boat and will be strong handed they expect to overtake us tho we shall set off tomorrow.

Louisville, Falls of Ohio, Tuesday, October 18th 1803. Here we laid in stores for our future voiage. Mr. Williams lent me 3 eagles[35] and beside paid for 100 lb. of biscuit, and 10 loaves of bread, and put on board 5 gallons of brandy and several other things. I paid for qtr. of beef 18/3; a half barrel of whisky 16 dollars. Paid pilot 2 dollars; and for salt and small bowls, 3/4 of a dollar; and steering hand, 3/4 of dollar; and for gallon of whisky, 7/6 for common use; and for 2 candlesticks, 7/6, and for candles, 11/3, by Shields to whom I gave the money. Gave the Major 10 dollars to pay several things and he retur[n]ed 3 1/2 dollars and 9d. and a saw, 2 1/2 dollars. We forgot and left unpaid Mr. Hunter for carting our goods below the falls, 2 dollars.

Mr. Shields [and] the Major went with the goods and wagon down below the Falls; and I went with the batteau, with the pilot Patton and a steersman and Buckanan, through the Falls. We hung a minute on a rock above the brig and struck twice after but went through safe; and after landing below the Falls, I took my gun and walked over all the islands and streams below the falls and picked up several curiosities and then returned. Had sent Buchanan for the skiff; and some man had come off with her before he got back and lost her oars as he came through the Falls and had gone before I returned from gunining [sic].

I must now say a few words more about the Falls. They are a terrable place to pass through when the water is as low as now. For the first time I had a dread of wrecking our boat. The rocks are so cragy, the channil so crooked, and the water so furious and rapid that it requires the utmost care and dexterity to avoid the danger. There are several islands in the Falls and a large island and several sand bars below and riffles for 2 miles below, so that indeed there is 4 miles of rapid[s] and difficulty; but the pilot only conducted us the first two and we came safe over the others.[36]

We left the landing below the Falls at one o'clock P.M. It is evident that the channels now through the rocks at the Falls are 20 feet below what the rocks have been and what they are now on the islands in the Falls; and I presume the whole of them have once been at least as high as the highest now are.

On the rocks below the Falls on what is called Goose Island,[37] I saw numerous shelly and other appearances like petrefactions, and on the lowest rocks near the landing place an appearance all over the face of the rock like brush or small sticks in the rock petrified in various forms; but the substance of these appeared more like iron than any thing else or small iron rods, but fast to the rock so that I could not git any of them. I saw nothing in my guning rout but geese and woodcocks but could not git near the geese; and the woodcocks kept among the small bushes so that I did not shoot once.

The first turn of the river below all the islands and bars below the Falls is S by E then changes to S by W. We ank[or]ed just at dusk near a settlement on the Kentucky shore. A Kentucky boat that left the landing place before us and passed by us while we were dining came up again after we ankored and stoped near us till the next morning. The night was calm and clear and we saw the new moon for the first [time] and as she drooped her lower horn very much our guide prono[u]nced her a wet moon.[38]

CHAPTER SEVEN

"Nothing but wilderness"

Routine Chores and Everyday Necessities

Ohio River: Louisville to Henderson, Kentucky,
October 19–26, 1803

Other than for occasional hunting excursions and the fact that Iris once got stuck in shallows, forcing everyone to get out and push, the journey after Louisville offered little relief from routine chores and everyday necessities. Although settlements still appeared on Kentucky's side of the river, the wilderness on the Indiana shore remained practically unbroken. The weather contributed to the tedium experienced by the travelers, for winter was coming on with the nights producing "large white frosts" and cold winds making a fire feel comfortable. As Rodney predicted, this was soon to be succeeded by the South's warmer climate.

Periodic stops for provisions and attempting to pinpoint natural landmarks by questioning residents along the way helped to enliven the slow-moving days. The judge discovered there were risks in the latter practice: "Thus our information varies; and by this information the large creek we passed on the Kentucky shore was Hardens Creek, tho the foolish man that spoke [to] us *there told us it was not; but as to distances all our information seems to be erronious." Even with a guidebook, Rodney and company were often at a loss to know exactly where they were.*

On the Ohio, Wednesday, October the 19th 1803. There being very little fog this morning we set off early and a little before the Kentucky boat; but by breakfast the wind blew so hard ahead we were obliged to cast ankor and the Kentucky boat also passed us a little way and stoped also. I expect we are about ten miles below the Falls.

It is all Indian country on the NW shore and no settlement in view on the Ky. shore; of course nothing but wilderness on both sides of the river. The Major, Shields, and Williams are gone on the Indian shore to make fire as the wind is pretty cold. The last two nights produced large white frosts; but as the general drift of our course will in future be SW and, after we reach the Misisipi, near south, we shall advance as fast as the season so as not to expect colder weather; and if the northerly wind should prevail we shall outstrip the season and gain upon the warm weather.

We came to a little above a settlement on the Kentucky shore where we were told we were 12 miles above the Salt River. We were obliged to lay by till evening when the wind moderated; and we went on till after moon down, when we came to ankor near the Kentucky shore as Buchanan thinks about 4 miles above Salt River. We passed a sand bar as we suppose in the night on the Kentucky shore. We could not see it but heard a great many geese on it, and found shallow water and therefore kept away from that shore till boat got below the bar.

On the Ohio, Thur[s]day, October 20th 1803. The morning a little fogy and cloudy. Wind light and fair. At 6 o'clock we passed the mouth of the Salt River, one mile below where we lay last night.[1] There is an ugly bar on the NW shore opposite the mouth of this river. This is a fine river and a strong current out of it so as to form a smart whirlpool at its junction with the Ohio. From the mouth the course of the Ohio is west ten miles then south one mile to a creek on Kentucky shore. Then the river circles or bends a circular course 3 miles by the foot of a rocky mountain on the Kentucky shore 14 miles below Salt River round to WNW.

There is settlemen[ts] pretty frequent on Kentucky shore all the way thus far. Just below said mountain Shields we[nt] on shore for butter and eggs, etc. We soon after rounded to NW. On the lower part of this circular bend the mountain on the Ky. shore runs 3 or 4 miles, and a rock shore at the foot along the river, and opposite the lower end of this mountain a sand bar on NW shore in the uper part of the next bend where the river turn again more to the west. This bend is about 20 miles below the Salt River. We began to round the point of this bend at 11 o'clock. Just below said bar the river run by the foot of the west point of a rocky mountain on the NW shore; and after a small gap or brake the mountain stretches again along the river round said turn, the river runing along the foot of it.

At ten minutes after 12 o'clock we passed a hansome creek on Ky. shore and a good settlement close above it and another below the course of the river by these W by N. The river continued rounding to WSW forming a simecercle of 4 miles or there about. At half after one P.M. we passed a riffle or rather rapid and large sand bar on the Ky. shore. After passing said riffle the river runs SW about a mile then turns. At 1/4 after 2 o'clock we passed Buck Creek on the NW shore, our course due W.[2] At 3 o'clock we passed a large sand bar on NW shore course by it WNW. We rounded from there to NNE.

Just at sundown we were hailed and asked if we wanted fresh venison by a man on shore. We went to him and bought a hind qtr. of a fat buck for 1/6 and he gave half a fore qtr. for a handful of salt; and told us we were only 6 miles from Blew River, and that there are two islands just on this side dangerous riffles. We went 4 or 5 mile further and came to ankor under Ky. shore a little before moon down. Have come 50 miles today. By having the wind fair tho but light which that with a pressing wind our boat would easily go a hundred.

◢◣

On the Ohio, Fryday, October 21, 1803. We had no fog this morning and therefore weighed ankor a little after day light and passed Indian or Windot Creek with the nob of a rocky mountain in view at the bottom of a short bend in the river.[3]

When we arrived at the bend we saw the uper of the two islands that are in the Ohio just above the mouth of the Blew River.[4] In passing the first of those islan[d]s the course is WNW. Then the channel turns from the Kentucky shore between the islands over to the NW shore and along that to the mouth of Blew River on that shore. Then the channel turns short round the lower end of the lower island to the Kentucky shore and down that shore a little way, and then it turns short again over to the NW shore round an ugly brouken bar below the mouth of Blew River to avoid a low bar on the Kentucky shore. The Ohio from said bar winds in a regular sircle round to east, then back in the same maner to NW, then to the westward again, and so in a serpentine manner tends to the SW in its general direction or more southerly to Hardins Creek. At 1/4 before 4 P.M. we passed a large sand bar in the lower end of the third bend below the Blew River; a narrow but good channel by it next to the NW shore.

At sun down we called at a settlement on Kentucky shore and got pint of cream and 3 cabbages. The woman told us that it was 20 miles by water and only 6 by land from the house one mile above the island and only to their house and 25 miles from here to Hardens Creek and only one settlement between, 20 miles further on. A little below the house we called at the river turn to west by south. We went on 2 miles and came to ankor close to the Kentucky shore in deep water.

◢◣

On the Ohio, Saturday, October 22d 1803. No fog this morning. We weighd ankor at day light. There was a flock of turkies roosting within 30 yards of us which we discovered by their noise on being alarmd at our movement. At 8 o'clock the wind sprang up fair, and we hoisted sail, and I prisume have come all the morning to 12 o'clock at 5 miles an hour. At a qr. before 10 we passed Watrons settlement, and round a point on NW shore saw an island ahead.

The course of the river from said settlement to island SW. The course by the island west at the lower end of the island. The channel turns short across from the NW shore to the Kentucky shore between the island and the sand bar at the lower end. There it turns of[f] again between the point of the island bar and a bar on Kentucky shore, and pretty close round that bar through a narrow channel to Kentucky shore, again round a point on that shore; but notwithstanding the above direction we passed the channel across at the lower end of the island before we saw it and kept on but touchd in passing the bar which spreads quite over the river below the island.

We have not before seen a bar spread more ginerally over the river or more difficult to discover, the way over there being several channels and none good. The island that we passed is new, long, and narrow. The timber on it all young, not over 20 years growth.

We saw a settlment on Kentucky shore a little below the lower end of the island. These two are all the settlements we have seen today, to wit at 12 o'clock at noon. We have not seen Hardins Creek, yet tho we are more than 40 miles b[e]low Blew River.[5] Yet the Pilot calls it only 30 to Hardens Creek. Perhaps it come in behind the island we passed which is about 32 miles below Blew River. We passed it at eleven o'clock and are now 6 miles below it.

A little below the sand bar aforesaid, the river turn[s] to south through a long reach 8 or 10 miles. Midway of this reach there is a long narrow sand bar in the middle of the river; and a cleaver creek on the Kentucky shore falls in midway the bar channel. On the Kentucky shore, pretty close at the lower end of the bar and near the lower end of the reach, there is another bar in the river next the NW shore and a narrow channel between the lower point of that bar and a large bar on the Kentucky shore. In the next reach (which is short) and extends 3/4 across the river, there is two settlements together on Kentucky shore by this bar. This short reach turns to SE and then the river keeps rounding short to west.

At the latter part of this short round a very large fine creek falls in from Kentucky. We supposed this to be Hardins Creek at first as there is a good settlement on the lower point; but a man on shore hailed us and told us Hardins Creek was 12 or 15 miles behind us, but he did not know the name of this creek, which we now call Hallo Creek, from the circumstance before mentioned. We were pleased to hear that we were so far advanced beyond Hardins Creek and gaining on the Yellow Banks which the Pilot says are 60 miles below Hardins Creek and of course 45 miles below the creek we last passed, which we passed at 1/4 after 3 o'clock P.M.

At the lower end of the next reach below said creek is a creek on the NW shore from whence the river round pretty shortly to a short reach below the course of which is south. In this turn the river spreads into a mere lake, and there is a sand bar round the point on the Kentucky shore which spreads 3/4 across the river. The channel is on the NW shore; but we passed over the best water between that next the shore and a wide low bar in the middle of the river, yet like to have stuck. There in [sic] another creek on the NW shore just at the lower co[r]ner of this turn and just below the sand bar. The reach from Hallo Creek to said turn is NW and the one next below is south as mentioned before.

Just below this reach, in the beginning of the next which is SSW, at dusk we ankord at the settlement of Richard Stevens on the Kentucky shore, a pretty large farm and pleasant situation. We were told here that we were only 6 miles below Hardens Creek and 50 miles above the Yellow Banks. Thus our information varies; and by this information the large creek we passed on the Kentucky shore was Hardens Creek, tho the foolish man that spoke [to] us there told us it was not; but as to distances all our information seems to be erronious, for we sai[le]d 10 hours today without halting and could not have come during that time less than 4 miles an hour, and we had come 6 miles before the wind rose and three miles in the evening after it had ceased, so that we hardly came less than 50 miles today; and by this it cannot be less than 45 miles from Blew River to Hardins Creek instead of 30.

On the Ohio, Sunday, October 23d 1803. No fog this morning. We bought 4 doz. eggs for half a gallon of whisky and 4 chickens for 3/9. This pd. by Shields. We then put of[f] and rounded throu 2 turns from SSW to N by E in ten miles and 2 more same course to the next turn. In this last reach, which was 8 miles, I rowed with Buchanon, the wind being ahead, to the next turn where we hoisted sail again, this reach being west. We arrived at this place at one o'clock. At 12 we had passed a creek on the NW shore. At 2 we passed another on the same shore, both dry. The next reach below the last creek is SW.

Ther[e] is a string of large rocks on the verge of the river on the NW shore in this reach towards the uper end. They are remarkable and form in part a little kind of island as the water runs between them and the shore when the water is high, and no doubt when the river is full they are covered. There is a small knob of mountain just behind these rocks. At the lower end of the last reach the[re] is a creek on the shore and a sand bar in the river next to that shore a little below said creek and in the bottom of the next turn or bend of the river. We rounded from there to NW in a long reach of 9 or 10 miles. In this reach we left the last of the mountains on the Ky. shore behind us; thus we have accomplished this great Herculean labor of throwing the mountains all behind us, for we had left them before on the NW shore in the rocky reach before mentioned.

Nothing now but level country appears before us where we expect to be more favord by the winds than we have been, tho yesterday and today we cannot complain. Midway this long reach we passed a settlement on Kentucky shore and a long sand bar in the river before it on NW shore. Here there was a flock [of] turkies. The Major went on shore after them. We saw two flocks before but having plenty of fresh provisions passed by them as we have often done by others. We passed Andersons Creek after dark and then rounded to WSW in the next reach below;[6] and as the moon shone bright tho it was broken cloudy in the next reach below said creek the wind sprang up and we sailed hansomely for 2 hours; and the river then veered to SSW and we saw a high sand bar on our left in the middle of the river. The wind came ahead and we furld up our sail, and Williams and Shields rowed.

We keep to on the NW side the bar but not near enough to NW shore, and at leng[t]h found a sandy riffle on our right between us and NW shore, and after gitting 2/3 through the reach grounded. Got off and went forward again. Got near the lower end the riffle which was only soft sand and ground again. All hands turned out to git her off but found we could not git her over, there not being more than 3 inches water. All hands spread round to hunt a channel, and [we spent] an hour before we discoverd a passage. We had to go back about 200 yards and passed over safely into a good channel near the west shore.[7]

They all being wet returned to the cabbin; and I stood forward and let the boat drift, as there was a strong current, till moon down and then cast ank[o]r a little before 12 o'clock at midnight. After taking a round or two at the whisky we all went to bed.

On the Ohio, Munday, October 24th 1803. The morning a little cloudy and no wind. We weighd ankor a little after day light. At 7 o'clock A.M. we passed the lower end of the bar mentioned before. This bar appears to be 4 or 5 miles long and begin about 8 or ten miles below Andersons Creek and continues below the point of the reach in which it begins. The course by it is SSW as I mentioned before.

Just below the point of said reach which is on the NW shore a large sand bar spreads from the NW shore so that we had to pass over to Kty. shore between that bar and the lower point of the long bar aforesaid. The river indeed is so full of large sand bars in this wide part of it, for it has been a mile wide for 20 miles and more, that it is difficult to sail in the night, even by moon light, tho in the long reach which we were in the fore part of the evening we escaped them all. Tho we passed several towards the lower end on the NW shore we could just decern them, and heard the geese and cran[e]s numerous on them but cannot discribe them.

The next reach below the long bar above discribed is WSW and the bar before mentioned on the NW shore extends quite through it; and the channel is on the Kentucky shore. Both this and the former bar are high and will no doubt in a few years become islands. Opposite the lower point of the last bar about midway of this reach another large bar commences on the Kentucky shore and extends to the point on that shore at the lower end of the reach, so that we were obliged to cross obliquely over to NW shore again.

Frequent settlements were seen on the Kentucky shore till we reach'd the present reach but have seen none in this reach. The next reach veerd to SW. The bar on Kentucky shore continues through both. Toward the lower end we saw four deer come from the Kentucky shore across it to dring [drink] right opposite to us, and they had drank before they discovered our boat, and then they scampered off to the woods again. These were the first I have seen of these creature[s] since I left home.

The aforesaid sand bar appears to be not less than ten miles. At the lower end of this reach there is a large sand bar in the middle of the river or rather in the bottom of the bend nearest the NW shore. The river flows between this and the last over toward the Kentucky shore; but the water being shoal between them we turned into a narrow channel between the lower bar and the NW shore and preferred it; and it was very good till we got half way and then we found a riffle quite across it that we could not float over. We all turnd out and in a manner lifted the boat over and found water enough below round the bar into the river again.

A[t] the point on the NW shore where this bar ends there is a small remarkable rocky mountain in the midst of the plain country.[8] A large round stone part of the mountain has been broke off by its own weight by the rock below dissolving or moultering away, and in its fall has made a great road in the side of the rock that the mountain is composed of, which is to be seen 8 or ten miles before you git to it. The lump of rock aforesaid that rolld down persued its course to the verge of the river where it stoped and appears as you approach it like a haystack. A[s] soon as we got into the river again we cast ankor and stayed to view this rock and little mountain.

The Major and I went on shore where in the first instance we had to pass through the confused piles of massy rock that had been loosed below by the wash of the river or by dissolution and those above tumbled down one upon another in blocks as big as houses. The foundation for twenty yards had given way and all the rock above come tumbling down but broke of[f] in a smooth perpendicular manner so that it left the remaining rock and face of the mountain an even perpendicular wall a hundred feet wide and 150 ft. high.

One piece about 20 ft. square broke off and only settled a little lower so as to stand seperate from the main rock and stands alone like a massy pillar or obelisk with several small trees and bushes growing on it. The Major proceeded to examine the broaken fragments and cavities that were among them while I passed through them and went round and assended the mountain. The earth on it is very rich and abounds in vines. Among them I observed a peculiar vine with bark like an ash tree but they grew so luxurient and were so interwoved with other grape vines I could not procure a slip of them. Nothing else peculiar appeared. . . .[9]

When the Major and I returnd from the rock Shields moved for going and I granted he might try it but the wind blew so hard they were obliged to come in shore near the rock and ankor again at 4 o'clock P.M. This rock puts me in mind of Timocks discription of the first appearance of the rock at the Cape of Good Hope when Vasjo de Gama first approached it in his first voiage to India.[10] This would hardly appear less tedious in the night by moonlight or seen partially through fog. I cut the two initial letters of my name on an oak tree on the top of the mountain above the crown of this castle on that sand on the crown.

The Major has been engaged these two or three days past in composing a letter to some young lady of his acquaintance and is endeavoring to endow it as [most?] moral, sentimental, and entertaining as his mind will enable him; and from several passages which he has favord us with reading, it appears to exhibit great merits.

At five o'clock we set off again. The short turn immediately below the great rock is S by E about a mile and then the next reach below that is one south. This reach appears to be 7 or 8 miles. There is a high sand bar in the river next to the Kentucky shore *[torn]* the [said short reach?] *[illegible]* and extends a mile or two down the long reach aforesaid; thus we have not been without a large bar on one side of the river or the other for 20 miles past and in almost every reach spreading near on quite across the river thinly covered with water and frequent small ridges on spots of sand rising above it.

Our trouble last night notwithstanding we mean to try to git to the Yellow Banks tonight. It soon looked like for rain, and we pushed over to the Kentucky shore; but it growing shoal[y], we turnd over to NW shore; and finding it shoal near shore put out again till we got 4 ft. water and ankored at half 8 o'clock having just the glimps[e] of an island that began to appear round a point on the NW shore a mile or two below us.

We were told by many that when we got below this mountain we should meet with no further difficulty in the river; but in reality it is worse for altho there is generally a channel some where that woud affoard water for our boat, yet the river is so wide and so great a part of it shoal that it is difficult even in the daytime to discover where the most water or channel is. This however the current woud direct us to if it was not that the wind prevents the boat from following it; and such has been our delay that we all feel anxious now to press forward as there looks like danger of our not [arriving?] even by the first of December when the [torn] requires the commissioners to meet.

On the Ohio, Tuesday, October 25th, 1803. We set out at 6 o'clock this morning. Our course is south by the point on our right and an island runing of[f] from the point and a long sand bar next the Kentucky shore on our left. We run this course into the course of the turn in the river, then changed to WSW by a second island, runing from the first and almost united by a sand bar on our right and the settlement at the Yellow Banks on our left.[11] We past this at 9 o'clock, and from thence the river winds to WNW round the island and the point on the Kentucky shore below the island. This course is but short; and then the river veers to west by an island close to the Kentucky shore, channel on the NW shore.

At the lower end of this reach and in the turn of the river is two other islands, a large one close to NW shore, and a small one along side of it in the middle of the river. At the uper end of these islands is a vast sand bar that spreads *[torn]* the river. The channel by this bar and these islands is clear along the Kentucky shore. The river winds round the lower end of these islands to NW for 2 or 3 miles. The largest of these two islands is 3 or 4 miles long and mostly coverd with cotton wood. The cane now grows plenty on both shores.

Then WNW through a long reach. In the middle of this a large sand bar. Channel close on K. shore past said bar and near to a point on the shore. Then cross oblikely to NW shore, near to the side of a large sand bar on K. shore. Keep NW shore till you come to another island at this lower end of said long reach; then pass along south side said island. Between it and the bar on K. shore the course by this island is first west then W by S through the island reach.

We were along the middle of this island at 5 o'clock P.M. with a fine breaze from SE. This island run through this reach nearly, and the channel is along side of it to the lower end from whence a wide bar extends. The channel runs along this bar, over to a point on the Kentucky shore. Then it turn short directly across to the NW shore to avoid a bar spreading from the point of the Kentucky shore and several little bars between the two large bars; the course after crossing in the next reach is nearly SW, but the direction of a boat cannot follow the exact course of the river where there is sand bars and islands. We ankord at 7 o'clock in the evening under the uper point at the mouth of Green River.[12]

On the Ohio at the mouth of Green River, October 26th 1803, Wednesday. Green River is in appearance at the mouth the finest of all the rivers we have seen that fall into the Ohio on the same side; and the Ohio is the finest at the mouth of that river. It is deep quite across and no shoals occur, except a small sand bar just within the mouth of Green River on the lower side, which is no impediment to its navigation. There is a small island in the middle of the Ohio about 2 miles due west, below the mouth of Green River, the first reach of the Ohio below that river being due west.

I omitted yesterday to mention that both above and below the Yellow Banks there are vast ponds or little lakes a small distance from the river on both side where the wild fowl assemble *[illegible]* in vast numbers. We heard several guns fire at them and heard such a tumultious noise of the geese and cranes there, as indicated thousands and tens of thousands. The guns were numerous too in the river, on the islands and bars near those ponds; but the ponds were too distant to be seen from the river.

The river viers at the uper end of the island aforesaid to WNW, but the high sand bar from the uper part of the island runs through this reach, and the bar above it extends a great way too, and there is a large plantation opposite the uper bar, on the Kentucky shore. This island and its bars extends 6 or 7 miles. The island or wooded part not being more than a third of the distance, and but young as most or indeed all the islands are that we have seen since we left the mountains; and from the numerous sand bars in the river, the part of it below the mountains will in 20 or 30 years be full of islands, and no doubt this will improve its navigation by narrowing the channel.

In the second reach below the island the course of the river is due north. We entered this reach 1/4 before ten A.M. and conclude it to be about 10 miles below Green River. Between the island above mentiond and the NW shore, there is a large island ten miles long. It begins at the point of the uper sand bar of the former island and ends at the lower point of the last *[torn]* sand bar and near the N end of the north reach aforesaid; but there is only a sandy dry channel round this large island, which is evidently filling up and will soon unite it with the main NW shore, as the small bushes are already growing over it; yet the water still passes through it when the river is full. In this manner I presume all the bottom land on the river has been formed.

Just below this island the Major, Shields, and Williams, went on shore to walk. We took the Major in at a large creek in the bottom of the short bend called Pigeon Creek.[13]

The river makes round to the south again at the end of the north reach aforesaid on the NW shore. The first reach below this short turn is south and there is a small island close to the N shore in the uper end of it; and there seems to be a good crossing between that and the NW shore but narrow; yet we did not *[illegible]* it least there should be wood in it.

It has been cloudy and drizly all day and now at 12 o'clock when we are passing the little island aforesaid [it] almost rains, but this mist soon ceased again.

There has a good many incidents occured in respect to our crew that might have enlivend my journal if I would have taken time to have inserted them; but the river and the circumstances and incidents connected with it has demanded all my time. The favors to ladies of the Major and Mr. Shields and Mr. Williams and others are frequently mentioned, and some times I [intrude?], etc., tho seldom a reference to some of my acquaintances; yet I more frequently leave them to a more respectable notice in my correspondence, to one of whom my next letter will have the following quotation to my text:

"Such Venus shines when with a measured bound
She smoothly gliding swims the harmonious round
When with the graces in the dance she moves
And fires the gazing Gods with ardent loves."

Homer[14]

The river rounded again from E by S to a little town on the bank of the river called Henderson, within a grant of 200,000 acres made to Henderson.[15]

Here we came to ankor and the sargeant of a [surveying?] party under Lt. Hughs came down to hail us and asked who commanded the boat? Shields answered Col. Rodney. He asked if he was a Col. in the regular army. Shields answered yes. He then told that Lt. Hughs was sick on board his boat just below us, and woud be glad to see us. That they were going down to Fort Massac with recruits *[illegible]* and there is 2 boats of swine just above us probably for them. Major Claybourn, Shields, and Williams went on shore, and I suggested the Major to call on Lt. Hughs and enquire if any thing we have on board woud be good for him. It is still cloudy and misty and like to be pretty dark.

CHAPTER EIGHT

Treacherous Waters,
Salt Works, and
a Legendary Cave

Ohio River: Henderson to Cave in Rock,
Indiana Territory, October 27–31, 1803

Beyond Henderson, an almost deserted settlement which, despite its "hansome" location, appeared a "poor miserable place," the travelers relieved their tedium by simple pleasures: the notes of Shields and Williams' "fiddle and flute" often filled the autumn air, and whist games helped pass the nights. Once, too, Iris paused at what Rodney dubbed "catfish cove" where "We fished awhile but could not get a bite tho the cats were playing round us."

The company, no longer so forcibly struck by the strangeness of their surroundings, were becoming somewhat blasé about the Ohio's natural abundance. At one stop "venison as fat as mutton" was rejected, for, as the judge tersely reported, "our people are tired of fresh provision." Yet the passing landscape still held surprises intriguing enough to capture their interest. At Shawneetown, for example, Rodney and Williams walked ten miles to see the local salt works. It seemed "a woeful place, durty and filthy . . . full of fleas," but fascinating nevertheless in the way its few workers obtained, by great labor, the precious commodity from which they eked out a livelihood.

Just below the Wabash's mouth, the party viewed the remains of numerous boats strewn upon the shore, victims of the treacherous waters and a warning to all travelers. And finally, Rodney, continuing his inveterate rock climbing, was drawn to a cavern situated on a bluff near Hurricane Island, the famous Cave in Rock. Along with the valley's prehistoric Indian earthworks, the Blennerhassett mansion, and Big Bone Lick, this spectacular natural site had become, by 1803, one of the West's earliest tourist attractions. Although he eagerly explored the cave's every nook and cranny, added his name to the "thousands" past visitors had scratched on the cave's interior, and described the site at length, Rodney remained unimpressed. It was as "simple and uninteresting a cave as any one might expect to meet with in rock." He had seen many a wondrous sight since leaving home. Now, near the midpoint of his trip, some of its novelty was wearing off.

On the Ohio at the town of Henderson, Thursday, October 27th 1803. This is a poor miserable place, composed of logged huts and most of them deserted. It was first inhabited by renegads and planters and they upon governments being extended here were obliged to decamp and leave their huts, and few others are yet settled here. Nothing is to be had here. It is however a hansome cite for a town, but not favorable to business.

It rained moderately an hour or two last night and is still cloudy. We set off at 7 o'clock A.M. No wind. We passed Lt. Hughs boat for the Major to put a letter on board for Genl. Hopkins, who lives about three miles out of town on what is said to be a large settlement finely improved. Lt. Hughs is to follow us at 12 o'clock at noon today.

Our first course from Henderson is SW rounding to the westward. At half past 9 o'clock we passed on NW side a very hansome island in the middle of the river, four or five miles below Henderson Town. From here the river continues rounding to the northward. The second course below said island is NW with a small island in view, next to the NW or the east shore.

We passed the last or former island on NW side between it and a sand bar on NW shore, but crossed over a little below the island to the Kentucky shore to avoid the aforesaid bar which below the island spreads thinly almost across the river and makes a deep channel on Kentucky shore; but this channel is very full of drift wood which must be attended to. At ten o'clock we passed the little island before mention[ed], which stands over part of the sand bar which lies on the NW shore and runs along it from the point on that shore below Hendersons Town, or the Red Bank, quite round to the north turn where the river begins to round from north to west.

It has rained pretty smart since 9 o'clock. Wind NE and will be fair as soon we turn from the north to the west, that is to SW in the course above Dimond Island.[1] We reached the uper point of that island at 2 o'clock P.M. Our course by the uper part was W by S then SW by the lower end. We were on the side next NW shore where we were in the streng[t]h of the current; and a fair wind and sail up, our skiff swung on a log that the boat run very near and broke her pointer and lo[d]ged on the log. We had to down sail, row back, and cast ankor near her; and I threw her off with the setting pole.

We then went on and passed the lower point of the island at three o'clock P.M. Then we turnd W by S to the bottom of the cove on the Kentucky shore, keeping the sand bar at the lower point of the island pretty near on our left and a sand bar on the NW shore on our right, keeping after we crossed the river along to the Kentucky shore to the bottom of the cove aforesaid. Then we steered NW for the channel between the Six Mile Island and NW shore, [runing?] after crossing from the point on Kentucky shore over to the sand bar on NW shore and close by the side of said bar till we passed the island bar riffle.[2]

On our being now safe, at 5 o'clock I gave the helm to Buckanan till we dined. When diner was over I took the helm again by which time we had got below the 6 Miles Island and presently after passed between a bar on NW shore and the point on Kentucky shore and bar.

We soon after saw an island 3 miles below the former and 18 miles above Wabash River, our course being SSW from between the points above to said island. We understood that we were to go on this side of this island and run down there; but it being night we could see no channel and we [crossed] over to NW shore for [harbour?] and found a deep channel and very rapid current close to that and a sand bar runing parralel with the shore, some little distance of[f].

We did not choose to venture to run the rapid in the night and therefore cast ankor a little out of the strong current next the bar. It come on to rain and continued till all went to bed. We found however our cabbin not yet secure against heavy rain. Esspecially the e[a]ve board did not project far enough to cast the water out side the boat, so that we got our beding and births a little wet and some too seeped through the boards of our covering where they were taped one over another. The Major and Shields and Williams amuse us more or less every day with the fiddle and flute and for some nights passt, we have played a game of whist in the evening for amusement.

On the Ohio, Fryday, October the 28th 1803. We set of[f] at 6 o'clock this morning. Found we were over the riffle and in the right channel and found our course round this island from SSW to SE on the NW side of it. This last course continues 8 miles. Then the river rounds again to WSW. A large bar spreads from the point on the NW shore in this round and confines the channel close to the Kentucky shore. Then the river turns short to south directly to a settlement on the Kentucky shore near the mouth of Highland Creek and 2 miles ahead which settlement is 6 miles above the Wabash River and about 12 miles below the island we left this morning. The wind is a head today; and the cove we are now in being full of catfish as we discoverd by their swiming with fins above water, we cast ankor to fish awhile.

At 2 o'clock we passed Hig[h]land Creek.[3] Just below it is the settlement before mentioned on the Kentucky shore in a pleasant situation.[4] Here we had hard work to git from catfish cove 2 miles to said settleme[nt]. We fished awhile but could not git a bite tho the cats were playing round us.

We set of[f] again and got to the settlement where we found the best and nicest harbor we have met with in the Ohio. Two muscle bars of sand and pebbles crossed a small part of the cove of the river with a gap to go in and 6 ft. water over the bason inclosed by them. Here we rode quiet and easy close to the shore.

I went on shore and bought three cabages and went to Mr. Johnsons to git other things. There is 5 families at this place. Mr. Johnson is the princip[al] settler here and has 9 children and 2 step children. The Indians are near and supply them with venison. Here I saw venison as fat as mutton but our people are tired of fresh provision.

In the afternoon I took a walk with my gun and called at Mr. Coopers on my return where I had bought some cabbage and concluded to stay here till tomorrow when I found that she could bake us some light bread [for?] the morning. They are old people and were bred in Pensylvania near the Brandawine and her daughter a widow is [here] to help her. I come to the boat and sent up flour for her and sent her daughter a little loaf sugar for a sick child, etc.; and sent the Major up to git some short cakes baked for tea; and told him to take butter to have them made with instead of which he took some bacon greese; and I woud not touch them.

In the evening Mr. Johnson and another man came and sat with me awhile. They told me that this county (Henderson) all voted against M. Lyon for Congress but he was carried. That General Hopkins is the finest man in all the district, that he has a hundred working hands, has 4 sons and two daughters, that his daughters are accomplished girls and play on the piano; yet that the general is the greatest blackgard he knows and gave this instance of it: that he Johnson was once there when the general came in with a squirel he had killed; and while his wife and daughters were by with some young slender gentleman [who] was a visitor, the genl. cut the tisticles of the squ[i]rrel and threw them down at the door and said to the young man "he would bet that the squirrels stones were biger than his." In all other respects he is never the less a clever man.[5]

He told me the nearest way to the Saline Creek Springs is from the Shawnee Town. That it is only ten miles from there and a good road. That the said towns (not now inhabited) is where the salt is brought to from those springs. That they have only 36 kettles there now and make about 17 or 18 bushels a day that is 1/2 a bushel to a kettle which is very great. This making an allowance for accidents is 5000 bushel a year. At this rate 144 kettles would make 20 bushels. This would supply as half as many families or 50,000 people. Those springs are much richer than those at the licks I visited. I propose if possible to visit those springs, as the people along this river consider the terms of lease proposed by government are unreasonable and as I hear the [illegible] at the other salt works are but indifferently conducted.

On the Ohio at the settlement near Highland Creek, Saturday, October 29th 1803. A thick fog this morning. The bread we staid for was sent down is an ordinary kind of biscuit instead of light bread and charged 3/- for baking; and from Johnson 4 ordinary twists of tobacco for 1/10 per; and old Mrs. Cooper 3/9 for a cheese; and we put of[f], having stayed all night for nothing as the getting of light bread was my only object in staying.

Got of[f] at half after 8 o'clock. The first course this morning was SW to a short ledge of rocks running out from the Kentucky shore in a sharp point, then west from there past a second ledge that runs further still into the river. On passing the point of this the course viers to NW by W till you pass the uper end of Wabash Island, in all about 3 miles, then take the NW shore by the island first course. The second ledge of the above mentioned rocks is like a causway, long and narrow and points down the river; but the third or lower ledge spreads from a broad root and extends more than half way right across the river. These rocks indeed app[ear] as if they once extended across like those at the Falls, so as to make a falls in the river; yet there is no appearance of rocks on the NW shore.

The first course by the island is WSW. The high sand bar at the uper end of this island extends almost to the point on the Kentucky shore. Behind it are two small islands, a little child in comparison and the other a little baby. The channel round the island gradually rounds to the southward to the mouth of the Wabash River, which comes in at the low corner of the island; and then the course is south by the lower end of the island. This island is the largest in the Ohio; and is said to contain 4000 acres.[6]

The mouth of the Wabash is said to be 600 yds. wide but is shoal. A large sand bar spreads from the lower point quite across the mouth so that in passing it a boat must keep well over towards the island; and I susspect it woud be difficult for a canoe to go over it up that river now; and just within the mouth in the best water is a great deal of drift wood. We passed it at 1/4 after eleven o'clock A.M. The day having cleared up, the wind at northerly and fair but very light.

There is a French family settled just above the mouth of the Wabash. We saw the wrecks of a great number of arks there and like to have run on one in the middle of the river below the mouth of Wabash.

The sand bar at the lower point of Wabash Island as well as the uper extends to the Kentucky shore, so that not more than the water of a spring passes through; and we may expect this island will soon unite with the mainland and become a part of Kentucky. The first reach below the island is SSW by two small islands on the right next the NW shore.

Note. I omitted to mention that yesterday afternoon three Muscogee Indian hunters came along the shore and stopped and lookd at our boat a good while and then went up to Coopers and stayed all night; but we did not understand their language or they ours, so that we could not converse with them.[7]

We passed the first of the two islands before mentioned at one o'clock P.M. It is about two miles below Wabash Island. There is a small settlement opposite to it on the Kentucky shore behind a large sand bar along that shore. There is also a long sand bar in the river from the first point below Wabash River quite down to the island aforesaid after passing which the river viers to SW. The second island is partly behind the other of these two small island[s].

Here we discover a great error in the Ohio Pilot. He places these two islands as 18 miles above the Wabash and 27 below Diamond Island, that is neither one place or the other suits them and there is no channel by them on the NW side; tho perhaps when the Pilot wrote, the channel as he says was on the NW shore by the first and then across between the two to the Kentucky shore. They look as if the channel had run so but it is now filled with sand, and a good and wide channel on Kentucky side. The sand bar continues a great way below them on NW shore.

About 2 miles below those two islands there is a third on the same sand bar. We past the latter at 2 o'clock P.M. The bar end at a point on NW shore a little below the last island; and the channel turns short round it over to the NW shore, and runs along it a very little way, and then turns to the middle of the river between a large bar spreading out from a point on Kentucky shore and another bar on the NW shore. On leaving the NW shore at said turn the course is south SW through the next reach.

Shawnese Towns, that is a ledge of rocks on NW shore 12 miles below Wabash and 7 above the Saline Creek.[8] Here we came to and at 1/4 pas[t] 4 o'clock P.M.

Mr. Williams and myself set of[f] on foot to the salt works at the great spring on said creek 10 miles from said towns. We arrived at the works at 8 o'clock. Found no house or settlement there and no body but those engaged at the works and 4 other men who came for salt.

The works are carried on by a Mr. Fleharty and he has 34 kettles which make when kept busy 15 bushel a day. He says it takes 300 gals. of water to make a bushel of salt. His kettles hold 28 gals. each. He got them from Cumberland River. He says when he keeps all his kettles at work the water is some times deficient tho the spring is very flowing. It is 14 feet deep[9] and whenever they rest a day it flows over the top of the well before next day; yet it will not allow works to be increasd; yet one of his workmen told me there was great plenty of water and the works might be increasd to make as much again.

He told us the little hole on which the salt works stand is full of the broken kettles of former workers from 3 to 10 feet deep, and that kettles were much larger than those now used; that he dug up the skelliton of a large man and his pipe 14 feet under ground; that the pipe was of the same kind of stone ware as the salt kettles were made of which appeared to be a mixture of earth and muscle shells burnt into lime or pounded; that on the border of the hills or mountains just below the works, in diging to find salt springs, they dug up great quantaties of human bones in piles.[10] This is similar to the mounds that are not too antient for the bones to be disolved to earth again, etc., but that they had not yet found any bones of beasts there. The reason may be that they have yet dug but few pits.

⚜

Sunday, October the 30th 1803. There is nothing at the salt works but a large shed cover over the salt works and under this all the workmen lodge and cook, etc.[11] There is no woman among them and not but wilderness around them. It is indeed a woeful place, durty and filthy, [completely?] full of fleas; yet here we had to rest last night. Williams indeed slept but I could not sleep tho exceding tired with a walk of ten miles to see this spring.

I laid down awhile and rested but I got up and sat by the fire and conversed with one or another of the people there till day. Then I turnd out and viewed the spring and circumstances around it.

There is but one spring there. They have sunk a logged frame round this, ten feet square and 14 feet deep. The spring when left a day, flows over the top of this and runs of[f] to the creek about 200 yds. from it. It is in the bottom of a small pebbly or stoney bason with the mountain behind it and partly round it are the uper side and the high hole on which the works stand below it. This nole appears to be mostly made land and much higher than the bason in which the spring rises; and the spring is 20 or 30 ft. higher than the creek; yet even this nole is some times overflowd. After circling and viewing the spring I assended the mountain and viewed the country round, for here below this creek the mountains begin again.

I obtained some pieces of the stone ware before mentioned; and Mr. Williams set of[f] on foot back; and I waited to ride on horse back with one of the workers, behind him on a poor dull beast that was almost tiresome as walking. Flaharty him self came to the boat too and I presented him a gallon of whisky and 2 pieces of beef as they had no meat of any kind; and then we set sail with fair wind.

[At these works there was nothing to eat or drink but we had carried a bottle of whisky which was very comfortable. They had a little flour, only with which they made a cake in the morning; but Fleharty was very kind to us and told us how he had been misused.]¹²

[NB This was the first place where I saw parakeets and Fleharty killed 6 for me with his rifle.]¹³

The course of the river is nearly SW but winding to the south to the Saline Creek; and the channel is along the N shore till you come to a large sand bar on that shore at a point above Saline. Then it crosses to Kentucky shore but returns round said bar to NW shore again and continues along it to near the point below Saline. A little below Saline we came to ankor in the evening; but soon after leaving the Shawnese Towns we passed an island, to wit one o'clock P.M., on the Kentucky shore.

On the Ohio, Munday, October 31st 1803. It rained very heavy last night so that the water was over the floor of my cabbin in the morning. This first reach of the river after turning the point below Saline. The course of the river is E by S.

I now return to say some thing more about the Saline. They told us there that the uper lick, called by them the Half Moon Lick, is three miles above the one we were at. That it is also called the Dry Lick because there is no salt spring there, but the lick is very large. The ground being clay it is licked in the form of a half moon 4 or 5 acres round. Lately five or six holes had been bored in it with an augur 6 inches diameter, 21 feet deep, and the water now flows over the top of them so that is supposed that when a well is sunk it will afoard a plenty of water; and Fleharty who works the lower spring says he thinks the water of the uper lick is a third stronger than the lower, so that he supposes 200 gallons of it would make a bushel of salt or in other words the same quanty of water would make one third more salt.

But he said there was lately discovered on the Highland Creek a lick which affoards salt in far greater proportion than this and that a tusk was found there that weighed 172 lbs. That they were obliged to brake it in two to move it. That he saw half of it and run his arm up the hollow of the centre of [it]. That it was a[s] thick as his thigh, which perhaps was 8 or 9 inches diameter.

Another person present veryfied this and said he saw it when whole; and both said it was round and simecircular in form, something like a boar's tusk only round, so that they would have supposed it to be a horn. This man said he saw a large gaw also at the same place that was intire and full of teeth; and that the grinders were like those of other animalls and rooted in the gaw in the same manner; but that this gaw was not in proportion in size to the tusk aforesaid; yet we stayed all night at the settlement near Highland Creek and heard nothing of this before.

The mountains since we passed the Saline appear again on our right on the NW shore but it is still a level country on the Kentucky side the river. At the second point on the NW about 3 or 4 miles below the Saline, the mountain runs down to the river and presents a wall of solid stone 20 ft. or more high. We went up to this to view some thing like a cavern in the face of it; but it was only a small concave and we turnd on our way again. Near shore the face of the rock continued a little way then presented numerous broken fragments. Then it retired and formed a cimecirclle of 150 yards diameter.

Here we land and Mr. Williams and myself traced the circle round. In the centre the durt covering the piles of broken rock had risin into high ground like a mound and covered with trees and undergrowth; but next to the uper side, and indeed all round, the ground decended to the root of the rocks, and a stream runs along it that falls over the top of the rock at the bottom of the simecircle and formd the most delightfull shower bath I ever beheld; and here I received the shower on my head for some time; but we walked round under the rock far behind it for all round this simecircle you may walk round with the rock juting out over you 20 feet and in some parts a great deal more.

This circle is large enoug[h] to form a delightful garden or vineyard.

The rock is mostly limestone, but is interlarded with thin clusters or bundles, if I may so express myself, of a kind of ironish shell stone very hard, and will strike fire as we found by trying to break of[f] some of it. Indeed it runs thro the main rock in various forms, but some parts of the rock are clear of it.[14]

A little way lower the face of the rock rises higher and retires gradually from the river. Here it exhibits its most romantick appearance. Here I went on shore myself and viewed it alone. Such rude piles and massy fragments of broken rock I hardly ever beheld before. Many of the blocks as big as a House yea indeed like little mountains, in some places piled one on another to the top of the mountain 200 ft. above the river, in others hurld at random and scatterd over the space between the mountain and river. Just above these rocks the mountains rise again on the Kentucky shore.

From the rocks too or rather a mile below, we crossed with the channel over to a small island next to the Kentucky shore. We passed this at eleven o'clock. The course of the Kentucky shore of the river from said island is SSW one mile and then veers westward round a sand bar on NW shore. Indeed there are sand bars now continually and have been since we pass'd Green River on one shore or the other and some times on both shores, so that we are obliged to follow the channel on. They make our course more crooked than the river itself which indeed is crooked enough.

A mile below the last island we come to the foot of a rock on the Kentucky shore, at the foot of the first of the lower range of mountains on that shore that come down to the river. On the lower side of this mountain there is a hansome settlement; and from here we have a hansome island in view in a WSW direction standing nearly in the middle of the river. Just below the plantation aforesaid a very cleaver [cleaving] creek falls in so that the plantation extends from the mountain to the creek; and little below this is a bar we had to go round then back to Kentucky shore, which we found rock all the way to the next point.

As the wind blew hard I took my gun and went on shore while the boat lay at ankor. I spied a hill or low mountain and traveled on downward. The side and top of the hill was broken stoney land. Here I found the prickly pair growing on the flat massy rocks and the cane in the lower land. I turnd down to the river shore, and hallo'd to the boat to come on as the wind had ceased, and went on board near the point just below which is another farm below another large creek, which falls in behind the point of rocks. We then steer oblikely across toward the NW shore between that and the island last mentioned, which is united as it were to Kentucky by a sand bar.

Opposite to the uper end of this island on the NW shore begins a formadable wall of rocks which appear like a regular wall from 10 to 60 ft. high. This ledge runs along that shore the whole length of the island; and some distance below at the tip end of this ledge it gradually recedes from the river and returns to it again; and then there is severe brakes and distinct piles of rock, some thing like large stone houses.

Then we come to a regular wall along the brink of the river continuing perpendicular and perhaps mostly 15 ft. high, quite below the lower end of the island aforesaid; and there we came to the Cave in Rock as it is stiled.[15] Here we came to at 3 o'clock P.M. and then dined opposite to the mouth of the cave; and then I went up to the cave which I found far inferior to the report of it.

The mouth of the cave is 12 yds. wide. The length 60 yds. The hight perhaps about 20 feet. The arch gradually decends and the floor of it gradually rises till they meet at the far end. The arch is pretty regular and on each side stands on shoulders that decend inward to the center from each side; and at the entrance a passage of [a] path 3 or 4 feet wide between them is left at the bottom, as it were, for a path to assend into the cave. This continues about a 3d of the length of the cave and thence to the far end. The floor is even.

When you git half way there is a crack in the rock quite across the arch and an aperture in the top of the arch through which it is said a stream of water decends, but it does not run now. There is a tree step ladder placed there by some body to assend up through that apperture. Shields and the Major assended through to hunt for another chamber but found none. It is indeed only the outlet of water that in wet seasons

Interior of Cave in Rock as sketched by Charles Alexander Lesueur in 1825. Otto O. Rothert, *The Outlaws of Cave-in-Rock* (Cleveland: Arthur H. Clark Company, 1924), 299. To many early river travelers, Cave in Rock was just another geological curiosity to visit en route. If it did indeed serve as a focal point for outlaws, Thomas Rodney was not aware of it.

finds its way through the cracks of the rock and by time has increased the outlet at that particular place to which it most tended; but it is now dry and all the floor of the cave is perfectly dry; and indeed this is a simple and uni[n]teresting a cave as any one might expect to meet with in rock. It woud however answer very well for the residence of a varmit or a flock of sheep yet I do not think it would always be safe from the pieces of rock that are often falling off even inside the cave for some of them are heavy enough to crush a man or sheep.

The front, sides, and top of the cavern as high as people can reach are full of names. I believe there is thousands of them. All who visit it no doubt leave their names there and so did we.

The Ohio Pilot discribes this cave 4 miles below the Saline Creek in which he is mistaken, it being rather ten miles. The author also who he quotes says there is a fine cypress grove before the mouth of the cave. There is no such thing. There are a few trees such as are common along the bank of the river and nothing peculiar. The cave, however, is easily discovered, as no one can well pass it by day light without seing it if they look that way, the trees before it being too few and small to interupt the view. The stupendious wall of rocks which appear to be chiefly limestone ends a little below the cave.

From here the course of the river is nearly SW and from the cave Hurricane Island is in view;[16] but between the cave and said island about 2 miles below the cave is a large sand bar in the middle of the river. The channel is along the Kentucky shore from the cave to the lower end of said bar, then it crosses round the bar over to the Kentucky shore and rises between that shore and Hurrycane Island aforesaid. This is a rocky and long narrow island. We arrived at the uper end just as the moon rose at the ending of day light.

Opposite to the middle [of the island], or rather above the middle falls, is a large creek from the Kentucky shore which Buckanan says is Tradwater Creek.[17] There is a settlement at the mouth of this creek and one above and several below it. They hailed us and told us the passage was very full of drift wood at the lower end; and so we found it; and it was with great attention that we got through safe; but the moon got bright and we pushed on and got clear below. They told us also that three boats for Natches passd there at one o'clock today. We are just now passing them a mile below island where they are encamped on the NW shore for the night.

The first reach below the island aforesaid is SW by S. This we are runing by moon light. We went on till we came in sight of an island, and found the water shoal turned under the Kentucky shore, and came to at 10 o'clock P.M.

I find by Carys map that Tradewater is laid down about half way between the Saline and the cave.[18] I was writing when we passed that part of the river. Some of our people observed it.

CHAPTER NINE

The Last of the Ohio

Ohio River: Cave in Rock to Mouth of the Ohio,
November 1–8, 1803

After Cave in Rock, Iris *entered the final stretch of the Ohio, with each passing day bringing it closer to the broad reaches of the Mississippi. Rodney's absorption in his books and papers continued unabated, his classical allusions proving him very much an eighteenth-century gentleman. This was most evident on those occasions when he was moved to renew his habit of rechristening local landmarks — once inflicting the names Tumora, Trathal, Comhal, Fingal, Ossyan, and Oscar on a succession of islands he passed.*

Nor did he lose, despite the party's shrinking travel time, his fascination for geology and for scaling promontories along the way. At one point he explored a "mountain of rock 400 ft. high" which "presented romantic and curious appearances." Here he described, in one gloriously vivid and tightly packed sentence, his exhilaration at dislodging a "vast" rock which "passd and dashd and smoked and knocked down all the trees before it rolld near the brink of the river."

The judge's detailed and interesting narratives of Indians he encountered and of a United States Army outpost, Fort Massac, bring the frontier indelibly to life, a frontier that would become progressively wilder and less settled once the Ohio was left behind.

On the Ohio, Tuesday, November 1, 1803. A thick fog this morning. We let our boat go with the current and it took us over to the NW shore where I thought last night the channel was. After gitting on the NW shore our course is the same it was last night, to wit SW by S; but the fog is too thick for us to see the river round us.

Haricane Island is about 8 miles below the cave; and they told us at said island it was 35 miles from there to Cumberland River. About ten miles below Huricane is a large sand bar on NW shore extending from a point on that shore where the river makes a short turn. The channel is on the Kentucky shore. We got on the bar in the fog, and turn back a little way and followed the current to Kentucky shore, and were rounding the bar when the fog rolld off. In the bottom of this turn a large creek falls in on Kentucky shore and a settlement on the point below the mouth from this creek. The course is NW one mile along the side of a stupendious rocky mountain. Then the river veers to west round the end of the mountain and still round.

While we were on our west course and passing a settlement on Kentucky shore three Cherekee Indians in a canoe come on board from the NW shore. They had venison but we did not want any. We gave them a dram of whisky and some buiscuit and they went off to the settlement on the Kentucky shore. The chief had a peice of flowerd cut tin in his nose and a crisent of tin such as the Masons wore hung round his neck with a buffello ingraved on it. He could talk and understand a little American but very little. I invited him in the cabbin; and seing my scisors hanging up he took them down and asked for them; but I told him I could not spare them, and he put them back again.

Our west course runs over to the NW shore, round a large sand bar spreading out from the Kentucky shore, to the uper end of a stupendious ridge of mountain rocks that appear like a high wall a little distant from the verge of the water. Then our course veers to WSW along those rocks, the uper end of them being about 6 miles below the last mentioned creek. These rocks are much higher than those above the cave.

I went on shore to examine these rocks and found them of various composition between the bottom and top as the mountain had been composed of various soils or stratas of earth; but they were fast decomposing at bottom so that [viscosities?] are seen here and there in them. They dissolve to a kind of redish clay colord dust full of salt petre in some places and allum in others. Where the allum is, the rock is dark colord; thus they git under mined and the weight above brings them tumbling down. The foot of these rocks are 150 or 200 ft. above the water, and the space between composed of the broken rocks that have fallen from the mountain. The top of the perpindicular wall is not less than 400 ft. above the water in appearance, but I had no instrument to take hights with.

A little way below this ledge of rocks a hansome creek falls in on the NW shore near the end in the bottom of the lower corner of the WSW reach. The river thence rounds to SW. At one o'clock P.M., when we were as we suppose about 15 miles bello Hurricane and about one above the next island bellow, the wind was a head again so that we are making slow progress; but as Carey has marked ten islands between us and Cumberland River, we expect it [will be] a rapid [progress] all the way from the first of them now in view.

At half after one the wind blew so hard we were obliged to come too. I went on shore and at a broken gap assended the mountain of rock 400 ft. high. The face of the rock presented romantic and curious appearances, salt peter and allum covering. After walking from the spot where I assended which was almost perpendicular, I could not find another place where I could decend again till I reached the end of the mountain; but half way, finding a large rock at the brow of the precipice a little loose and cackling [cracking], I got a prize and threw it off; and it hurld down the steep knocking down all the trees in its way and made a tremendious noise; so that they heard the cruss [crush] to the boat, and they were fearful I had fallen with it; but it was done to give them notice of my advance and to see the simely that Homer gives of Hectors progress when he was driving the whole Grecian army before him.[1]

Such was the vast size of the rock I cast off that it being thrown from an emminence of 400 ft. it passd and dashd and smoked and knocked down all the trees before it till it rolld near the brink of the river. On this mountain I had an extensive view of the Ohio up and down, but was obliged to proceed to the end of the mountain before I could decend to the river again. The chief wood on this mountain is black oak, white oak, and hickory and some ash. The soil is fine but in the hands of Indians who only live by hunting. I saw no living animal while on this mountain which I traced to the uper end of the island before mentiond.

There I came to the shore and hoisted my han[d]k[erchie]f on a tall cane as a signal for the boat. It was about 4 o'clock when I got on board; and as the wind lulled soon after, we proceeded by the island and passed the lower end at half past 5 o'clock. Just below it there is a large plantation on the Kentucky shore. Our course is S by E.

The next island in view below baring due south, but several sand bars between which make the channel very crooked, as these oblige us to pass from one side of the river to the other. There is indeed a little island by the side of the one we have passed, and the sand bar extends quite from the island to the Kentucky shore, so that there is no passage on that side at this time. Our gentleman agreed to row on till 9 or 10.

We went on for the 2d island, but a little before we got to it we easy [eased] on a sand bar in the middle of the river. By steering for the right side of the island I turnd out in the skiff, and soon found we were close to the channel, and that it was on Kentucky side the island. We pushed of[f] into the current and went with it to the island where it was deep and then rowed again.

Passed the island at half after 7, and at 8 passed an Indian camp on Kentucky shore. We could only see their fire but as they haild us we answerd them but could not be understood and passed on. Soon after the water shoaled and we ankord.

At 9 o'clock P.M. we passed the third island by moon light, having passed the 2d on Kentucky shore half way below it. We let the boat go with the curren[t] and it carried her in towards the NW shore; and we passed on that side the third island which we call Rag[g]ed Island from the raged appearance of the woods on it. The two last are but smaller ones.

We went on till ten o'clock and then ank'd close under the Kentucky shore in 6 ft. water where the river turns to SE by E with 2 more islands in view.

On the Ohio, Wednesday, November 2d 1803. The morning cloudy. Wind SE and of course right ahead. We weighd ankor before sun rise but went but a little way before the wind was so hard we were obliged to cast ankor again.

Opposite to where we lay last night there was an Indian hunters camp on the NW shore. We saw their fire and heard their noise. They had a dog and were hunting and shooting till twelve o'clock when I went to sleep. Soon after we cast ankor an old Indian man and his wife and two girls and a boy came on board of us. They were very modest and wanted several things we could not spare; but I gave one of the girls, the youngest of the two and a hansome girl, some flour in the sleave of an old clean shirt, and she returnd me a fine ham of venison, and gave each of them a biscuit and the old man a twist of tobacco.

The old man and woman had no ornaments. The eldest girl had a necklace of glass purple beads and a half a dozen ringlets of tin bobs in each ear. The youngest girl, which was the hansomest of the two tho both likely [i.e., comely], had similar bobs and [illegible] of tin round her neck and bracelets of the same [illegible] wrists that were kept bright and neat and looked very well. The boy had a tin flower [illegible] in his nose. They had some durty rag[g]ed linnen and calico beside their blankets around them. They, I presume, however, were not of much distinction; nor could we learn of what nation they were as they could not talk our language or we theirs; only the old woman on seeing a cheese pronounced the name very distinctly.

As they were going of[f] we gave them each a wine glass of whisky. The old man and woman drank theirs; but the girls to whom I handed it myself tasted it and made wry faces and woud not drink it. They then went off quietly; but the old man first offered me a ham of vinison for the twist of tobacco I gave him, but I by signs let him know we had enough. The girl that got the flour was greatly pleased with it and in her way discovered [i.e., exhibited] her pleasure.

The half naked appearance of these beings indeed looks to us miserable; but I was well acquainted with Indians who were plenty among us when I was young and therefore know they enjoy a great degree of tranquility; yet those who then remained among the white people enjoyed great advantages which these do not, for they could always purchase with their wares and skins, etc., plenty of bread and cloathing of the white people and therefore never suffered for want of either; but they always preferred their bark cabbins in the woods to living in houses which they might have had.

I took walk with my gun, and when I returnd there was a flock of turkies near to the boat. I went and shot at the old cock about 40 yds. distant and did not seem to have hurt him as he walkd off without alarm. We then went over to the foot of a nob of mountain on the NW shore. The wind being too hard to row against I went up and viewed the mountain. It had been cleared and the country round as far as I could see at least some hundred acres and has been some time but not long deserted for, tho it was covered with small growth of hickory, oaks, sassafras, and poplar, it was none of it thicker than a mans arms but so crouded I could hardly git through it beyond the mountain. Seemed little more recently cleared and deserted as many old trees and stumps were remaining and the growth from stumps but few but I had not time to travel to the large clearing. Could see no vestige of any house or cabbin. I returned and dined and then we went off again.

Being near to it we set off round the sixth island next to the Kentucky shore. Our first course was east by south. Our last, passing it was S by E and the 7 island now in view baring SSE. There is a new settlement on the Kentucky shore just below this island.

These islands it seems have no names and in honor of Caledonia I mean to name the principal ones Tumora, Trathal, Comhal, Fingal, Ossyan, and Oscar noticing those only which stand as it were in the middle of the river, omitting the 2 and 5th which is small and in the NW corner of the river opposite to where we lay last night. These then I name them No. 1 Tumor, No. 3 Trathal, No. 4 Comhal, No. 6 Fingal, which is the one we have just past, and the 7th which we are now approaching Ossian. The next one is great Caledonian chief of the roial [royal] line remembered by Ossian.[2] We observd 2 or three other settlements on the Kentucky shore below the 6th island.

At 4 o'clock we arrived at the 7th island. Our first course round this was SE rounding to S by E. The channel runs between this island and Cumberland Island which is next to the Kentucky shore.

Cumberland Island covers the mouth of Cumberland River so that you cannot see the river till you git below it.[3] Cumberland Island is the 8th island in this chain between Hurrican and Cumberland. Tho the 2 small ones diserve not mention, yet Carry has 2 more; but we have not seen [them?]. The Cumberland Island begins just below the lower end of the 7th island but the sand bar from the uper end of Cumberland reaches several miles up the river opposite to the 7th island so that the channel runs between for there is no channel next to the NW shore round the 7th island at this time because the sand bar of that island spreads to the NW shore and over the river above for several miles up so that the whole water of the river now is confined between these two islands and their bars.

We found as we went on that the sand bar from the lower end of the 8th island extends down to another island which appeared to be chiefly ceadars but as it was growing dark when we passed this we could not distinguish the wood on it; and altho Buchanan said Cumber[land] River came in behind the eigth island, it seemed evident from the appearance and opening of this woods behind the last island that the river of Cumberland comes in behind that island; but it was growing dark. We could not certainly assertain that fact. We went on a little below said island which makes the 9th in the last chain and came to under the NW shore just at dark. Thus [after] a long progress we have arrived within 60 miles of the mouth of the Ohio.

On the Ohio, Thursday, November 3d 1803. We ran at one o'clock this morning and went about 4 or 5 miles; and then as we were on a lee shore and wind hard we run out into shoaler water and ankord till day, and lay down again to sleep. It rained very hard in the night and continues raining on to morn moderately.

At nine o'clock we arrived on the NW shore opposite the mouth of Tenessee River, and the wind being a head we come to ankor.[4] After passing the island at the mouth of Cumberland the channel runs over to the NW shore and runs along it a mile or two. Then it runs oblikely to the Kentucky shore and along it several miles, and then over again to the NW shore, and along that shore to a point opposite the mouth of Tenessee where we now are.[5]

We set off again and at two o'clock passed the mouth of the Tenesse River. It is covered by two small long islands, so that you cannot see the mouth till you git below the lower island where it open with great dignity, being half as wide as the Ohio itself and by far superior to every other branch of it. The rain and head wind obliged us to ankor in the mouth of the river.

[While the boat lay here I took the skiff and went up that river a little way to git a more perfect view of its mouth.][6]

The wind slackd a little and we proceed. After passing a point below Tenessee, the river veers to WNW quite to Fort Massac. We got in sight of the fort, but it rained and blowed so that we were obliged to cast ankor under the NW shore. No more sand bars have appeared since we left the Tenesse.

On the Ohio, Fryday, November 4th 1803. The morning still cloudy but not raining tho it had rained hard great part of the night. Wind still a head; but we pushed on and got down to Fort Massac at half after nine and cast ankor near the landing;[7] and Williams went to getting breakfast. Every thing being so wet we could not kindle our fire before. This morning is as cool as any we have had.

The Major and Shields went up, and Captain Bissell who commands here a company of 63 men sent us sergeant to invite us to dine; but I was busy and sent my compliments that I could not dine with him.

Williams did the same and we dined on board then walked up to see the captain.[8]

Sat there awhile. He told me that Lyons was contracted for the garrison, but that he had been electioneering and had neglected the supplies, and that he, [Captain Bissell,] was obliged to purchase flour and venison, and the garrison had suffered by being on short [rations?] a good while and had been [illegible] this without [illegible] etc.; but he understood a new person was appointed. He says there is a good deal of the intermittent [fever] here; but from the attention of Doctor [blank] they have not lost a soldier for a year past. After this I bid him adieu and Williams and myself walked round and viewed the garrison.

It appears to be in good order and the soldiers on duty. It is a small fort stockaded round, with 6 or 9 inch pointed posts ten or 12 feet high, with a shallow ditch and bank, and is supplied with several pieces of brass cannon beside musquitry and other guns. The soldiers we saw appeared well dressed and neat and clean. The fort stands on high bank on a point of the NW shore in a pleasant situation; but the land seem sterile tho a strong clay. There is a little subburb or a collection of buildings bellow the garrison; but I saw no cultivation of any kind, tho there is 40 or 50 acres of land cleared and fenced and some lots which I suppose are pasture grounds.

There is ten or a doz. houses beside those of the garrison and a store kept here. We had to give a qtr. dollar a lb. for 10 lb. of maple sugar here; and they sold whisky at 2 dollars, but we did not want any. I borrowed an eagle of Mr. Williams here, which makes four I have had of him. The sugar cost 2 1/2 dollars, and Mr. Shields had 1 1/2 dollars out of it; and Buchanan returned me 6 dollars in round silver change. Shields is to pay for some lard out of what he had. There is no white inhabitants nearer than Cumberland to this fort except those around it. What a solatary situation. Shields came on board and returned the 1 1/2 dollars he had as the lard was furnished by Captain Bissell and he woud not take any pay.

The wind having fallen [a] little, we put off again at 4 o'clock P.M. The wind moderated and we got about six miles and ankord at dusk under the Kentucky shore, being now about 30 miles from the mouth of the Ohio. The river here assumes a dignified and beautiful appearance being a mile and a half or 2 miles over without bars. Captain Bissell presented the Major and Shields soap, vinegar, and 2 or 3 lb. of lard for the use of the boat.[9]

On the Ohio, Saturday, November 5th 1803. In the night it cleard up and the wind increased about 2 o'clock so that the boat draged her ankor and got her stern closer shore, when I got up and rouzed all hands and rowed her further of[f] shore, where the ankor held her till day[break]; but being exposed to the wind I did not go to sleep again. After, we found that our situation was not so bad as at first expected for the wind increased. She rode tolerable easy. It became also very cold in the night; and this also increased after day[break], so that the Major, Shields, and Williams went on shore and made a fire to keep them warm. I stayed on board with Buchanan [and] took care of the boat.

Here we were wind bound till evening, and wind blew so hard we dared not to raise the ankor; but in the afternoon I went on shore and saw a very safe harbour in a cove near at hand, and we waited till evening and then got into it and laid quiet there all night; but the wind blew so hard in going the[re] Williams broke another of our oars.

On the Ohio, Sunday, November 6th 1803. The wind being quiet in the morning and clear, we put of[f] and got into the great turn of the river below Massac 9 miles to what is called the Little Chain of Rocks; and the wind being so hard up the river that we could not go on, we ankord under the NW shore just above the rocks so that they diffended us in part from the wind.[10] Just before we got to the rocks three large deer came down to the river to drink, but seeing us took to the woods again. I went on shore to examine these rocks to see where we might pass them, and saw about them the track of hunters feet and shod horses feet where they had gone this morning or last night; and wherever we go on shore the tracks of deer are to be seen. Much do I now begin to feel this desperate opposition of the winds when our time has got so scant.

The pican (or as it is spoken here the pc caun) nut tree has appear'd for some days past on the shore, but no nuts as the late frost last spring distroyed most of the fruit in this country. This nut is known in Dalaware by the name of the Illinois nut.

Munday, November 7th 1803, on the Ohio. The morning being mild and clear we put and reachd Wilkinson Ville on the NW shore by 12 o'clock.[11] The Major had gone on shore some time before and met us there and hailed the boat to let us know we could git butter, vinison, and potatoes there; and the wind blowing hard we cast ankor, and I went on shore where several Indians were waiting.

One of them who was half Spainard could talk pritty good American. I went on shore with him. He had plenty of vinison, and I took a ham that was very fine, etc. He took me next to the chief, Captain *Flea*, who is about 65 years old. I bought a lb. of butter of him and 4 cabages and a bushel of potatoes for one dollar and 3/8. He told he did not know his age but shewed me how old he was at the commencement of Bradocks war and thereby I assertained his age.[12] He shewed me his crop of corn and beans he had plant[ed] in his house and in a large field they were gathering. The Spainard Indian whose name is *Tom Brown* interpt what we said.[13]

I went to the corn field to see it. There is 20 or 30 acres in it and the corn very fine. I went to see the potatoes dug also. They had a large patch, and appeared to have been well tended and were fine. He sent his Negro man Billy who talks quite plain;[14] and his wife was already there to help dig them, scratch them up with their hands.

They got [some?] for me and when measured I paid the chief [with?] one dolar; and they observed if we woud let them have ploughs and a white family to shew them how to cultivate the ground, they woud sell much cheaper. Butter however was only the 1/8 of a dolar per pound. He had two very good horses and among them was a hundred head of cattle. The one we got 8 lb. butter of had 8 fine calves; and what we got was all churned while I stayed. Paid her 1 1/2 dollars for or one dollar in cash and 1/2 a dollar in flour.

There is 2 or 3 hundred logged houses in this town, built for our army in regular streets as a post or place of arms; but they are all but a few uninhabited now and none occupied but by Indians. There is about 200 of them here but most of them hunting. We saw however 8 or 10 families and of the Cherikies and one Cherokies own chief Captain Coldwell. I shook hands with him but had no dealing with him. He was only here hunting and was incamped near the river; but the rest lived in the best of the houses our army left. There was one white woman among them with 2 white children. She had an Indian husband and lived in the Negroe house; and he told me he wanted her but she woud not have any but an Indian husband. She is a pretty likely woman.

Tuesday, November 8th 1803, on the Ohio. We left Wilkinson Ville in the evening to cross the lower ledge of rocks; but the wind was so hard we were obliged to come to under a ledge of rock on NW shore a mile below this Ville.[15]

[I must not omit here that while we were at the Ville yesterday, the Major, Shields, and Williams had made an assignation with the white woman and some of the Indian women to have a frolic with them at night, and they pressed me much not to leave the Ville that night; but I thought it best to go on, at which they were much vexed; and as we got only a mile below the town they all proposed to return by land and got out on shore for that purpose, and then asked if I wou'd wait for their return. To which I replied that I could not wait if the wind ceased so that we could proceed; and if this happened they must travel by land till they over took the boat, for time wou'd not allow me to wait; beside[s] I expected they wou'd cause a rumpus among the Indians and perhaps might git massacered. Shield[s] remembered his former difficulties and wou'd not go. Then Williams returnd, and last the Major, but with great reluctance and grumbled at me violently.][16]

This morning we set off again and wondered through shoals and rocks till we got over to Kentucky shore, and then passed the great ledge on the Kentucky side of all the rocks tho the boat channel was between the rocks; but as there was water, we prefered going between the rocks and sand bar, and then crossed over to NW shore where there was plenty of water; but must here observe that tho the violence of the NW wind obliged us to keep the NW shore; yet is a bed of rocks half way over the river along that shore, from the uper or Small Chain down to the lower or Great Chain from Wilkinson Ville to the gap of the lower chain, the straight course to the gap through the Great Chain is SW; but this course cannot be kept for the channel is on the Kentucky shore, or rather next to the sand bar on Kentucky shore, from the Small Chain to the Great one.

After being 2 miles below the rocks on NW shore, the river opened to us between the points below quite to the mouth SSW; yet there were 2 points on Kentucky shore below us and one on NW shore. The shore is so verry rocky opposite to Wilkinson Ville that we found it difficult to git through among the rocks to the shore there.

I omitted to mention that the chiefs Negro man, who is not a black man but of the Indian born, gave me several pieces of oar *[sic]* of a stoney *[blotted]* mixed with shining appearances of gold *[blotted]* silver. He said he got this at the foot of a *[blotted]* on the NW shore about 8 miles below Wilkinson Ville and about a mile from the river *[blotted]* there was great plenty of it; and that [which?] appeared most metalic he got deepest [in the?] ground. I tried a small piece of it in the fire. Found it was mostly sulpher, but left, when burned, a kind of red earth in the basson. In spreading this then on a smooth board numerous particles of metals appeared very shining among it like gold or silver; but the quantity was so small that I did not take pains to wash it to see what the metal was; but intend to examine this ore more fully when at lazure. Not improbable to be the vane of a gold or silver mine.

The SSW course I find did not reach mouth of the Ohio but the lower point on Kentucky shore. There observed was the lower end of an island next to that shore, 7 miles above the mouth of the Ohio. There is a large

sand island on the NW shore opposite to said island. The channel is
between them but very rock[y] and dangerous. From this island the river
rounds from SSW to SE, which is the last course of the Ohio on its
entrance into the Misisipi. We went 3 miles below said island and ankd
und[er] NW shore.

CHAPTER TEN

Southward Bound on "The Prince of Rivers"

Mississippi River: Mouth of the Ohio to St. Francis River,
Louisiana Territory, November 9–21, 1803

Rodney reached a significant milestone in his journey through the West when on November 9th "we entered the Misisipi with great joy." Now the change in surroundings became increasingly greater as Iris was carried farther and farther south into the great wilderness valley. The western side of the Mississippi still lay under the jurisdiction of Spain and foreign soldiers at one point were spotted. Indians occasionally came on board, but American settlers were few. Aspects of the flora and fauna appeared strange, while the river at times seemed more like "a vast lake" than a stream with discernible banks.

The Mississippi itself remained the most awe-inspiring feature in the near-exotic landscape. It was, to use Rodney's phrase, truly "the Prince of Rivers." Its muddy yet majestic waters, which lacked the clear Ohio's rapids and only occasionally produced sandbars, were swift moving. The judge and his friends found themselves propelled along at five miles per hour, seven if oar and sail were applied. This was fortunate as by now the December 1 deadline for Rodney's arrival in the Mississippi Territory was fast hoving into view, filling him with apprehension as to whether he could get there on time.

Wednesday, November 9th 1803, on the Ohio. The morning clear and cold, only a little smoky. We put of[f] early, and having no further interruption we went on and entered the Great River or Misisipi at 9 o'clock A.M. with a SE course.[1] The banks on both sides the Ohio appear high quite to the points but fall back. A long bar runs from the fork points half a [mile] beyond the woods. Having been so long in the Ohio we entered the Misisipi with great joy.

Here two things were instantly observable: the great increase of the current and the great difference of the water, the Ohio being clear and pelucid, the Misisipi thick and tergid. We found now that we went with force of the current alone more rapid than we had sailed at any time in the Ohio. At 12 o'clock, we came to 2 islands on the same bar next to the east shore 15 miles bellow the Ohio,[2] and passed them rapidly.

We were visited by 4 Indian canoes this morning; but none of them could talk American; and we did not want any thing they had, and got clear of them as soon as possible, as they impeded our way.

This is the Prince of Rivers; and tho it appears not wider than the lower part of the Ohio, yet it is a far more majestic river, no rushes, no riffles, only planter[s] and sawyers and bars here and there always visible to avoid, and this current five miles an hour. The bar before mentioned continuing on ten miles down the river, and instead of 2 contains a chain of 4 or 5 islands which reach nearly to the Iron Banks 17 miles below the mouth of the Ohio; and so rapid was our progress, tho the wind was a head, that we reached these banks at half past 2 P.M.[3] The course of the Misisipi, from the point above the uper island to the Iron Banks crossing this bar on which islands are, is SE. Then the next course is S by W from the turn at the Iron Banks downward.

I omitted to mention that we observed a large island in the Misisipi just above the mouth of the Ohio.

About a mile below the Iron Banks we come to a very large island with large sand bar united to it. On the eastern side this island and bar is not less than ten miles long and 4 or 5 wide, so that the river bows off round it both to the east and west.[4] We come on the east side. The

Thomas Rodney's Mississippi River Journey. November 9– December 1, 1803

Iron Banks are high bank[s] of earth. The lower part of them appeared to be a kind of fullers earth and the uper part a redish clay; but we only viewed them as we passed and nothing like iron appeared to us; yet perhaps if we had gone on shore we might have seen some thing of that sort that gave them the name Iron Banks.

We went on till after sundown having passed a long bar and small island laying on the east shore; and ankord on the side of a sand bar under a point on the west shore about 40 or 30 or 35 miles, as we guess, below the mouth of the Ohio. We think indeed we must, by the time we were coming (to wit 3 hours), be 15 miles below the Iron Banks which are said to be 17 miles below the mouth of Ohio, and 6 miles an hour all the way, that is from 9 A.M. to 5 P.M. We have come 35 miles and I hardly think we have come less. We found upon inspection that we had ankord at the uper end of the bar of an island that extends more than ten miles down the river; but no *[illegible]* channel round the island now on the west side, the bar spreading quite to that shore and is only covered when the river is full.

⚛

Thursday, November 10th 1803, on the Misisipi. The morning cool and clear, only smoky. We took up our inkor *[sic]* at 7 o'clock A.M. and at ten had rounded from S by W to NW, having an island and bar on our left, the bar extending to the east shore. We rounded this island on the west side.[5] This island, or rather the bar on which it stands, commences on the east shore presently after the one last menti'd ends on the west shore, and thus we have an island on one hand or the other almost continually; but the bars on which the islands stand are generally more extensive than the islands and generally spreading to the shore, so that the river, now the water is low, is confined to one side of the island and of course compressed in a bed often not so wide or thick as the Ohio. This occasions the current to be quite as rapid now as when the river is full, which is about 5 miles an hour; so that if the wind was not continually a head, with the help of our oars we shoud make good 7 miles an hour. Our NW course is only *[sic]*.

⚛

Misisipi, Fryday, November 11th 1803. The morning clear and wind light and sharp. We found this morning that we had ankord opposite to New Madrid or Sans Le Grass rather below the chief part of the town and fort.[6] It stands on a fine bank and the clearing exten[d]s 5 or 6 miles along the river; but we saw none but logged houses on the shore. We left our station at 7 o'clock and proceeded on our voiage, the river being quite smooth.

At half after 10 o'clock we passed the lower end of a large island on the eastern shore and a river coming in from that shore which we suppose to be the Obian.[7] Course SE. A short turn next more to the south then to SSE. The river then rounds to SW. A deep cove and sand bar in it. We cut across between sand bar and point on the west shore. Run SW in the next reach some miles. Then the river round again to S by E with a group of islands on an extensive bar on our right and several ragged island [joining?] the point of the bend on eastern shore. Run several miles SSE. Then the river rounds to west with a large group of islands on the right and extending along the west shore to the next turn when the river turns to the southward again.

A settlement on the west shore in the bottom of this bend and cattle on the shore. When we draw near the settlement, the owner was on the shore and told us he came there last March. That it is called 120 miles from the mouth of the Ohio to Sans Le Grass, 30 from there to this place, six from here to the Little Prarie, and 130 from there to the Chicasaw Bluffs. Williams says it is 90 from Ohio to Sans Le Grass, which makes the whole 246.

[The River Pilot calls it 45 miles Ohio to Sans Legrass, but when the river is low it is much more, say 1/3.][8]

We passed the Little Prarie just at dusk and intended staying there all night;[9] but the shore was too steep and water too deep for a harbour; and therefore we went on to the next point about 2 miles below and ankord under the point just above a long narrow island that seems to have been cut off from the point. The night was clear and quiet, and we all went to bed early. The Major, Shields, and Williams not liking our not stoping at the Little Prarie where they expected some girls.

Misisipi, Saturday, November 12th 1803. The morning being fine but wind a head. To avoid round an extensive cove on the east shore and avoid the wind, we took through the island channel, which continued 6 or 7 miles and then opend into a part of the river that spread out into a great lake, to appearance no less than 15 miles over one way and 8 or 10 the other, with a large wooded island on the right and an extensive sand island on the left. Our courses through the island channel was south and after we entered the river SSW through said lake between the island and sand island aforesaid.

Here the wind met us so hard that we had to put in to a small cove on the sand island at ten o'clock; and Shields and Wms. took the skiff and went on shore; and soon as Shield jumped on shore, a large racoon sprung out of a hole in the sand and run on board the skiff; but seeing Williams then jumpt on the land again. We hallowed to Shields to kill him, and he took after him with a skiff oar in his hand; but the racoon turnd on him and Shields fled. Then we call'd to William[s] to run, and he jumpt out of the boat and persued with the other skiff oar; and the racoon now seing the odds of two to one against him took to the river; and Williams got one stroke at him but did not hurt him; and the racoon was soon out of their reach. I then sent Buchanan after him in the skiff, and he took him and brot him on board. Williams and Shields walked on the sand bar to the eastern shore and met with two young deer; and the bank being so high the deer could hardly git up, Williams was near taking one of them. In the mean time the Major and Buchanan skind the racoon and it was very fat.

At 12 at noon we set of[f] again; and after passing the points of the river below the lake aforesaid we enterd into another great lake containing several islands. At one o'clock we saw a great wind coming from the SW, and we put over to a cove in the great bar on the east shore. We had scarcely got to shore before the storm darkened the atmosphere with dust off the sand bars.

Two peroges and a family from Kentucky landed a little below us on the same bar.[10] They are going to Natchez. Came away from a little below the Falls of Ohio the 18th of September and entered the Misisipi the second of this instant;[11] but Shield[s] who I sent to enquire did not learn his name. There is another white man and a Negro man and woman and 2 Negro boys.

The wind soon brot rain with it and both continued till night so that we kept our station. We spent the evening as usual by a few games of whist and ending with music. The Major and myself did not go to bed till near midnight.

⚛

Misisipi, Sunday, November 13th 1803. It rained great part of the night and is still cloudy. Wind easterly. Our course this morning rounded from S by W to NE. This last course took us to the lower end of the second lake which is full of islands. We wanderd through them, following the strongest current till we got below all on the right hand, and then kept the west shore to the lower end of the lake. This lake in the widest part appears not less than ten miles across and more than that in length. At the bottom or rather lower end of the lake the river turn southward again.

At ten o'clock we passed the lower end of said lake and immediately entered into a third full of islands; but these, as is usual at the common turn of the river, are disposed in a group on the convex part of the turn while the river runs along the cove or concave side. Yet when full of water it runs in many streams among the islands. At one o'clock P.M. we reached the lower end of this third lake. The last course was west; and then the river rounded to the southward again with a group of islands round and adjoining the convex point, the channel runing as usual round the cove or concave side of the bend. In these turns of the river the concave side is generally almost perfectly circular. We presume we have come 30 miles today.

At one o'clock aforesaid the river rounded to SSW. A str[a]ight reach this course for 20 miles. At 2 o'clock P.M., we came to a small island in the middle of the river and passed it on the eastern side. At two we were passing between a large island on the eastern side of us with the appearan[ce] of a river falling in behind it which we suppose the Forked Deer or Catchey.[12] The peroge that was near us yesterday has been about 5 miles ahead. The wind has been fair since one o'clock but mostly light so that the peroge keep nearly her distance. It is still cloudy.

Wind northerly and now at 1/2 past 3 begins to blow fresh; but soon learnd we passed 2 boats loaded with French or Spaniard going up the river. One was a keel boat and the other a mast boat. They were under the west shore and too far off for us to hear where from or bound. They were firing a number of guns before we got near them, by which we guessed they were soldiers perhaps French going to take possession of those posts which are to be delivered to us.

Just at dusk we passed the perouge who had encamped on the lower part of the first island in WSW bend but went on to find a better harbour.

On the Misisipi, Munday, November 14th 1803. The morning foggy and cloudy. We lay by the side of the lower bar of the great island on the east side and at the lower end of the WSW reach. We set of[f] early and rounded in our course to ENE. The wind being hard ahead, we came to ankor near the western shore under a sand bar in a safe situation at 10 o'clock. Soon after, the perogue over took us and passed by before we had got done breakfast; however we immediately set off after them.

We soon passed the point on the western shore below us; and then went about east over to the eastern shore, with a large sand bar and two islands on our left and a small island and sand bar on our right, with one large island on the same side in the hollow of the bend. We rounded this on the east side and rounded to SW in passing said island, and soon after came to a long island that extends on our right 7 or 8 miles along the west shore. The course along the lower end of this island W by S. In the last course we passed the perouge and in this course she over took us again.

We rounded then to east a short turn, and then round to south by west; and this course brought us to the uper end of the first high bluffs which we reached at 4 o'clock P.M.; and here we saw the river assume its own form without interuption, flowing from bank to bank, having these bluffs on our side, that is on the east side the river. These bluffs are a kind of mountain of earth without rocks about 200 ft. high; and, being undermined by the river, have caved in so as to leave a perpendicular face exhibiting a great variety of strata, viz., dark brown, light brown, orange, red, or brick dust color, bright yellow, and pale yellow, which is the uniform color of the uper stratum. The face of these bluffs exhibit various romantic figures as pillars, crescents, amphitheatres, etc.[13]

Our course along these in the first reach where we met with them rounded gradually to NW, forming a regular segment of a circle. Immediately on passing these great bluffs the course varies to W by N and round a island on the co[n]vex part of a bend to S by E. We came to ankor on the west side said island; and the peroge stoped on the west side the river nearly opposite to us.

Misisipi, Tuesday, November 15th 1803. The morning cloudy but signs of clearing. We set out at day light in a strong current and fair wind but light. We set of[f] before the perouge; but she, being in shore where the strength of the current was, soon over took us; but as we just then reached that side of the river then kept way with her; for we found yesterday when there was no wind that we could pass her in the same current. Wind we find of little service on this river, for when it is fair it is seldom as swift as the current. We can hardly give the wind credit for 5 miles on this river but have been hindred many [times] by it. Yet it has been more favorable today.

Our first turn was round to the eastward the[n] turned round in a pretty wide circuit, having on our left a large island below the one we ankord at last night; then a turn in arm of the river [and] past between the second island aforesaid and a large island below it; and run round said third island and two others still below; and [in] another arm of the river passed across to said eastern channel between the two lower islands; but we kept the channel that run on the western shore, leaving all those islands on our left hand; and after passing the lower island and meet[ing] the other stream of the river, it rounded to NN west till we returned within a few miles from where we set out [as] if a str[a]ight line had been struck across the land; and we saw that the river had made some attempt to cross.

Then we rounded again to SSW till we reached a new vagary of the river where it divided into three branches forming a new figured group of islands at this place. We took the middle channel leaving the most western island on our right and two others on our left, one of them formed by a subdivision of the left hand stream of the river in rounding these islands. We varied first to SW then round to ENE when the river assumd its own form. Then we round gradually to WNW again, and then round a point and island to east again, and ankord at the lower point of said island where the river begins to turn again to the southward.

The soil on both sides the Misisipi is generally very good, but [for] the tract on the western shore round the east turn of the river that we passed this evening, which tract I presume is part of or a little below the tract given by Spain to a tribe of the Dalaware Indians.[14] Two of these came on board of us today about 12 o'clock at noon and brot us some fine venison for which we gave them salt. They cou[ld] speak sufficient for us to understand them. I felt a favor [toward] them merely from their name on the denomination of their tribe; but when they came on board we were under full sail and in a rapid current that we could not stop.

The Major, Shields, and Williams took a walk on the bar and then we had music and a few games of whist; and they all went to bed. We had a few pics [or nips] to the flask.

Misisipi, Wednesday, November 16th 1803. A thick fog this morning. We set off early and kept the shore. Rounded from east to west, then back to east again, and then to south.

At ten o'clock reached the Spanish settlement and garrison on the west side the river[15] and an old settlement [on] the east side[16] just below Wolf River;[17] and soon after, to wit at eleven o'clock, reached Fort Pickering at the Chicasaw Bluffs.[18] This is a hansome picketted fort with very comfortable accomodations for both officers and soldiers. There is a company here commanded by Captain Carmical with Lt. Many of Dalaware and Lt. Strong of Tenesse.[19]

The officers came on board and invited us to dine with them which we did and had a very good dinner of pork, venison, and duck and spent a pleasant afternoon and stayed to coffee. The young officers were all very friendly and polite. Finding they had no dish at dinner, I made them a present of a hansome pewter dish and they sent me a fine quarter of venison. We got our cloaths washed and got some paper and a loaf of sugar which we paid for; and I made a present to Peterkin, the store keeper, of a viol of perfumed oil to rubb with when he baths in the river, for a weakness he complained of. When I returned on board my leg hurt me; and I felt in some degree unwell, but not sick from this degression from our common *[illegible]* of living.

Misisipi, Chicasaw Bluffs, Thursday, November 17, 1803. A fine morning but wind west and of course a head in the first reach. Having left a letter for my son[20] and another for Fisher with officers to be forwarded to the nearest Post Office, we set of[f] a little after 7 o'clock, and turned first to the westward, and then round eastward again, and then rounded to SW for about 30 miles, varying a little at different points more to the westward and southward; but the str[a]ight course was nearly SW; and just at sundown the wind being a head as we were turning to NW, we came to ankor in a cove of a sand bar on the south side. The bar is we suppose 45 or 50 miles below Chicasaw Bluffs.[21] We saw the perogue a little ahead of us on the other shore; so that tho we spent yesterday at the Bluffs while she came on, yet we have overtaken her in one day. This was by having a good wind most of the day.

Buchanan went out on the bar [and?] pickt up a good deal of coal that looks like a mongrel breed of charcoal and sea coal; and I must here observe that coal has not been k[n]own on the Misisipi heretofore. Yet this burns very fine and has a sulpherous smell but not so much as stone coal. We tried this coal and found it excellent to keep fire all night, but made too much sulpherous smoke to cook with or *[illegible]* in our cabbin.

[At ten o'clock today crossed the line of the 35th degree of N lat. which is the division between Tenessee and Misisipi Territory.][22]

Misisipi, November 18th 1803, Fryday. A large white frost and beautiful clear morning and cool air. We set off at sunrise and went 2 hours, nearly NW ward and rounding to east, till breakfast. Two keel boats now passed us on the opposite shore going up the river. We went on 15 miles east and east by north then rounding to south to west and to NW, then between 12 and one round again to west, going all this day at the rate of about 5 miles an hour. We must be now about 30 miles on our way. There is 3 or 4 cuts across the point of this bend, which makes 4 or 5 islands on our left, which we are now rounding in this bend. We rounded to east and went on shore on the west side of the river at 2 o'clock post miredian. Here the river assumed her own form and presented both her shores which she seldom does.

We then rounded to south east, and saw Dalaware Indians on them, but did not stop. They had piles of skins on an island in the bend of the river on our left. We went on to near the lower end of this reach and ankord on the east shore by the sand bar at a little before moon down, which we suppose [is] a hundred miles below the Bluffs.

Misisipi, Saturday, November 19th 1803. Morning broken cloudy and a little foggy. Upon turning out we saw a settlement on the west shore. We soon after called there and found 6 American families settled there and got turnips and potatoes. Then rounded the island and cove in to the reach below; and found another American settlement of two families; and called and got 2 lb. of butter @ half a dollar, turnips and potatoes cost one dollar, all which I paid myself. They told us we were 120 miles below the Bluffs and 250 miles above the Walnut Hills, and that the perogue passed here this morning. These people say that the Americans on the west side the Misisipi are all anxious to be under the American government; but that the French and Spainards are uneasy and, they said, the Indians. The Americans are mostly settled under Spanish grants as they say.

From this settlement we went south an hour, then rounded to SW, and then gradually to SE, then round to SW by W, then round to SE, then made a short circle round to NNW in this course.

At 4 o'clock 4 Dalaware Indians came on board with 4 dead beavers they had just caug[ht] in traps. I gave the chief a twist of tobacco and

6 turnips. They wanted flour, corn, salt, and whisky, but we had none to spare. We have seen no Indians along the river from 20 miles above the Chicasaw Bluffs to this place but Dalawares; and here were many of them on shore beside those that came along side.

We then circled round from NNW to the eastward and ankored on the SW side the island bar, just at dusk, in a small cove. I went out for the first time on the island bar on the Misisipi Teratory in which my jurisdiction as a judge extends, and also as a comissioner along the river, it being part of the Western District. On the western shore of the river round this turn is some of the finest looking land we have seen on that shore below the Bluffs, and the banks look high too. The evening is cloudy so that we cannot go on by moon light; and we now have but eleven days left to git to Natches before the first of December, the day the commissioners are to meet.

Misisipi, Sunday, November 20th 1803. The morning soft, cloudy, and mild. No frost the two last nights. We are crossing the 33d degree of latitude.[23] In about an hour we enterd in a south course into one of those places where the river when full spreads into a vast lake full of large islands; and now her main channel passed through among the island, tho a less channel passed round a large old island on our left and between that and a bar in the bottom of the bend on the east shore. In passing among the island we also had a large low island on our right, great part of it sand bar, and then wood and below it another wooded island and sand bar. Our course rounded first to west then to south and then to west again in passing *[illegible]* the lower end of the last mentioned island.

Indeed there is such groups of islands laying this lake, some old and some young. There is no distinguishing all of them as we pass. Some times 3 or 4 are standing on the same bar and no doubt appear much more distinct when the river is full and the bars all covered.

We passed the lower end of the last island at ten o'clock. Having come about 5 miles, ankord. This is a long island and stands single below all the rest that form the groups before mentioned. In passing the lower end of this island, our course being on the east side of it was west and immediately after veered to SW. Just into the lower end of the last island commences another more close to the western shore, and extends several miles lower down the river when it veers southward again and so on quite roun[d] to east and then rounds again to west.

All round this bend on the east shore is very excellent land. Here bank 40 or 50 [ft?] high bordered with cane and green rushes, the canes 15 or 20 ft. high, the rushes 4 or 5. I wanted to land here but the bank was so steep there was no place to assend it. Then we had a large round to the east again and very fine land all round it on the west side, with banks of about the same height as on the eastern side. In short, the land is as rich as can well be on both sides the river, and the woods much alike. Near the bottom of this bend there is two small creeks falls in half a mile apart which is an unusual thing to see a creek along this river.

At the point below this turn we stoped in the evening but went on again after night till after 9 o'clock. 15 miles through the two next turns below, the first rounded from eastward round to west by north, in the convex part of which we passed the [first?] of the perogues. The next turn rounded back to SSE, and near the bottom we ankord on the east shore, a little above the point of the next turn on the opposite.

Misisipi, Munday, November 21, 1803. The morning clear and a great white frost. The air quiet but in our favor. We set off at day light. The air sharp.

Our first course SE, then round to SW, then round to SE again, then round to SSW and WSW, then a stretching round to E by N. Then round to WSW, a short turn the lower point of which we passed at 12 o'clock. A group or cluster of 7 or 8 small young islands on one bar on the lower part of this bend. At 10 o'clock we saw a lone wolf runing on a sand bar. This is the first of them we have seen.

At half past 12 we passed a large river falling in on the western side which our rowman supposed the River St. Francois of Louisiana;[24] yet after passing a large island which we took before to be part of the main land which seems to make it doubtful whether this be a river or only a *[illegible]* of the Misisipi, yet we noticed no *[illegible]* of that sort above; yet she so hides her pranks with islands that her pranks can not be always seen in passing up or down.

Directly SW of the mouth of this river there is a large island in the middle of the Misisipi 2 miles below. We rounded said island and continued about 9 or 10 miles eastward then rounded westward nearly or quite as far leaving as it were a narrow peninsula between the easterly and westerly reaches of the river. Then we round short to the south and rounding back easterly again as far as before or nearly making another peninsula connected with the eastern side of the river. This last reach we are now in and runing by moon light. We went on and passed one island. Rounded the second to WSW at 9 o'clock P.M., our course being WSW. We went on to a point on the eastern shore and ankord just below it at ten o'clock P.M. 60 miles today.

CHAPTER ELEVEN

A Near Disaster and
Journey's End

*Mississippi River: St. Francis River to Washington,
Mississippi Territory, November 22–December 1, 1803*

In their journey's last days, the judge and his companions met with challenges
and adventures never faced before. Perhaps they should have been warned of
impending disaster by a landscape grown rather sinister. Jungle-like growth of
cane bordered the river. Long strands of moss "which the watermen call
Spanish hair," hung down from and darkly veiled the trees. And banks,
towering above passing vessels, frequently caved into the turbulent stream, trees
and all, "with terrible crushes and noise."

Most frightening of all was the river itself. Despite its conveniently rapid
current, it was replete with dangers, mainly the sawyers and planters. Rodney
called them "snags"; they were tree limbs or logs with one end stuck in the
river bottom or free-floating. Either partially or totally hidden from view, they
could make a boatman's life a nightmare, for avoiding them was comparable
on land to running through a field strewn with mines. A snag could sink a
boat within minutes of penetrating its bottom.

Except for the earlier accident at Amberson's Island, the party, thanks to its caution, skill, and luck, had navigated the western waters unscathed. Luck ran out on the afternoon of November 23rd.

Because Rodney's orders as to an anchoring place were disobeyed, Iris hit a snag. Even though the boat and most of its contents were saved, the travelers were stranded for two days on a mudbank while they made repairs. Enhanced by his moving style and attention to detail, Rodney's description of the incident, which climaxed both the journey and his journal-keeping, remains one of the most valuable firsthand accounts we have of a riverboat sinking during this period.

On the voyagers went, ever conscious of the deadline closing in, their progress frustratingly slowed by heavy winds and rain, their taut nerves frayed even further by Buchanan's crazed antics one night, the cause of which Rodney laid to either "brandy or opium or both." On December 1, 1803, with only hours to spare, Iris docked at Natchez from which, on hastily borrowed horses, Rodney and the Major departed for the territorial capital only ten miles away. Against mountains, flea-infested taverns, bad roads, drunken crew members, wood nymphs, wind, rain and treacherous waters, the intrepid Rodney had persevered; and the journal which he had begun so many weeks before came to a close at last.

Misisipi, Tuesday, November 22d 1803. The morning broken cloudy but mild, and air not quite so sharp as yesterday morning. Set off just after day light.

Yesterday the western shore below the River St. Francois presented a redish brown paint colord soil below the first black mould down to the water. But this morning below the island we passed last night presents a solid clay soil below the black mould which [is] 3 or 4 feet thick quite down to the water, say 30 [to 40?] ft. deep. The land too is covered with lofty trees chiefly conton [cotton] wood but mixed with [blotted] and hickory; yet the bank is bordered with cane as usual. I have little [doubt?] however but this is fine wheat land [fully?] of the first quality. It is the most substantial land in appearance that we have seen on the western [rivers], most of the land on both sides the river being of ash or sandy color and loose soil; but this below the mould exhibits a wheet clay soil; but soil continues only 2 or 3 miles.

The last settlements we have seen on the Misisipi were the two American settlements where we got turnips and butter. A mile back from those settlements is a large pond or small lake, 2 miles over and verry deep, and abounds in fish of several sorts. We take buffilo fish in it of a hundred weight, large catfish, carp, and pike. The wild fouls also abound in it. This lake has a large outlet which falls in 2 miles below the settlements. There are many of those ponds or lakes in all the lower country both on the Ohio and Misisipi which abound with fish and wild foul and most of them with beavers.

We rounded first to the eastward, then to the westward, then again to the eastward quite to NE. Then round to SW, west round Horseshoe Island and cove.[1] Passed the lower end of said island at one o'clock P.M. Soon after met a boat from New Orleans with a sail and 8 oars going up the river to [illegible]. We enquired the distance to the Walnut Hills. They said 150 miles. They enquired for the river called Noahs Ark or Oas Ark.[2] We told them we passed a river yesterday at half after 12 which we took to be the River St. Francois; but they said it was Noahs Ark, that the River St. Francois is farther up. If so, it comes in behind some island where we did not observe it, or we must have passed it in the night; but Carey and Scott are poor directors on this river, so that we in fact have no guide below the Horse Shoe.[3]

We round again to the east; and in this bend we see the long moss hanging from the trees which the watermen call Spanish Hair.[4]

The next bend below the Horse Shoe in which [we] met the boat aforesaid I call the quoit bend because it comes nearer to a circle than the Horse Shoe and is in the form of a quoit.[5] In the bottom of this bend is the finest cypress land on the western shore that we have seen. The bank is about 30 ft. high and bordered with rushes. The soil of the color of moist ashes and covered with straight tall cypress trees but not large, few of them being more than 2 ft. diameter; and this is generally the kind of cypress that grows along the Misisipi. Excellent for rails and planks but too small for shingles unless it be 18 inch shingles.

We observe acres of this bank that had lately sunk into the river with all its timber on it, hurld into the most disorderly confusion, many of the trees standing upright, and others stooping every way, and a third broken and hurld about in every direction. Where the cypress and rushes end, the cane and cotton wood begin and display a more cultivatable soil, having above the ashes bank 4 or 5 ft. of grayish clay soil, which continues on the western shore to the lower point of the quoit bend.

We then turned to the westward again round a circling bend, and ankord on the convex bar of said round, 2 thirds round, in the night. It thundered and rained from 2 o'clock till morning; and the wind blew at SW, but not hard, being in a cove of the bar and in shoaly water. We rode very quiet; but I got up and sat up till the wind and rain was ceased. It was ten o'clock when we came too.

Misisipi, Wednesday, November 23d 1803. The morning cloudy, wind a head but does not blow much. Set off at day light. After passing the first bend below the one we rested in all night, we stoped on the western shore to git wood.

All the crew but myself went on; and the Major and Buchanon brot me several rush, some of which were six feet high, tho as we pass in common they do not seem to be above three. One of them had been broken off at a joint towards the top and branched out from the same joint into four small sprangles; yet they all grow when uninjured with a single stock and jointed like the cane [but?] do not like the cane put out branches from the joints. They produce no leave[s], flower, or seed. How then are they propogated? Nature produces them wherever the soil is sutable, as she does other plants that have no other means of fruitifaction. These rushes are always green and tender and are said to be excellent food for cattle and horses and equal to the best grass.

They have no resemblance to what we call rushes in Dalaware but are somewh[at] like cane [so] that I at first mistook them for young cane. They grow with a tap root having numerous small branches runing from it near the surface. The cane is also an ever green, and the leaves of it also is food for cattle and horses and the buffilos, etc. The cane from half way up the stalk to the top has one branch from every joint, which immediately sprangles out into numerous smaller branches, which are full of leaves that easily bend their heads down with their weight where they do not support each other by growing in thick clusters; and this is generally the case, for they generally stand on the ground as thick as wheat, and so do the rushes and so support one another.[6] Both these plants perhaps might grow in Dalaware; and the rushes if they could bare our winter would be very valuable for stock; but I presume they would not grow anywhere but in our meadows.

As to the course of the river today, I must refer to my map of the river; but have to observe that on account of the wind, we ankord on a sand bar below part of an island which heretofore has been in a large lake now grown up with sand bars and islands, all united except a small lake or large pond left in the NE corner of what was once the great lake and still has an outlet towards the lower end at what was once the great lake. On said bar I went on shore and walked a while. Shields and Williams also went on shore and took the gun with a view to meet us below the bar.

When I returned the wind had slacked and we went on. I rowed my self till we got near below the bar, and then laid down to rest a while it being calm and pleasant, and left the oars to Buchanan, directing him where to go on shore to take in Williams and Shields. They soon after called; and the Major, who was looking, shew them where to meet us only a little further on below a corner of the large old island in the bed of the old lake.

Buchan[an] rowed on; but instead of going up at the spot I directed in a little cove where the shore was shelving and clean, he was rowing to a small cove just bellow where a point of sunken shore run out between them and was full of snags. In crossing this first without those that appeared above water, he run the boat on coverd snag which run through bottom and made whole [hole] more than 6 inches square.

Buchanan immediately stoped a blanket in it; but, the snag remaining in the whole, the water poured in rapidly. I jumpd into the skiff, and got all our trunks in it, and went on shore with them; but my small trunk was afloat first and got all my papers wet. By this time Shields and Williams came, and we got all we could out; but she filled so fast that even our provision chest floated away off our quarter, and we had to take it after gitting the flour bbls. a shore and our meat, so that we lost most of our sugar which was in the chest.

The Major acted heroically and stayed by the boat while Buchanan left her and swam on shore; and till he was waste deep in water then we took him off, and went to taking up such things as had floated away, and presently after our boat, with the weight of the current, over set and releaved herself from the snag; and, in her oversetting, she dropped the ankor over board which took the bottom and held her fast.[7]

Finding this, Buchanan and Williams went to bring her on shore; but they could not raise the ankor, and I ordered them to tie it to a stick and loose it from the boat; and then they toed her on shore. We had landed our things at the nearest point but was obliged to move them across a small cove in the skiff to where the batteau had been got on shore; and this took all the rest of day light; and by the time we got a fire made and our tent spread, that is our sail, it was night; and none of us got any dinner, for dinner was ready and waiting for takeing the boys on board when the boat got snaged at half after 3 or 4 P.M.

We however got our dish of coffee[8] and after a little of the flute and violin by way of consolation, we prepard our camp on a mud bank where there was but a small cover of dry sandy earth. All the ground on the shore was so muddy and soft that our situation was much imbittered by this circumstance; however fastened the drowned batteau to shore, and all rested tolerable well.[9]

Thursday, November 24th 1803. The morning cloudy and like for rain. All our thoughts now respected our situation. Shipwrecked in a Wilderness 150 miles from any settlement, we had no resorce but in ourselves and our own materials. We had however yesterday seen a good looking perogue on shore not long before we got wreckd, and I sent W. and B.

to see what she was; but she was also wrecked, and we had no resorce but in mending our own boat.

We therefore went to work to try to raise her side so as to git at the breach without over setting her; but finding this could not be done we striped her and took out her mast and turned her bottom upwards; and then the Major cut up our table and made a plank to cover the breach which was not so bad as I expected; and I cut up one of my shirts to spread a double piece of it under the plank which was placed and well nailed by way of patch on her bottom. This being done, the Major who had long been naked in the water was taken with so great a chill he could do no more. We gave him plenty of whisky and rapped him up in several blankets with a large fire at his feet; but finding he still could not be warmed, I advised him to git up and run all he could; and this soon warmed him.

By this time it began to rain; and in the meantime S., W., and B. turned the boat over again on her bottom and got her to shore and bailed her; and we found her as tight as ever again; and just as we had done this and was moving our things on board again, the perogue of a Mr. Rice from Kentucky came to us and enca[m]ped with us.

We stayed at our camp till evening; and having got all on board but our sail which formed our camp, we all went on board and took a supper of chocolate and left our tent to the perogue people. Our boat, and most of our things [were wet]; yet by warming the cabbin with the stove we felt much better off than at the tent as it continued to rain hard all night.[10]

Fryday, November 25th 1803. Still cloudy and wind NE. I had spoken in the evening to Rice for some meat and peach brandy. We got 2 gallon and one qt. of brandy, one flitch of bacon, and three pieces of dried beef, all of which came to 7 1/2 dollars and a fippenny bit the brandy, 15/ Virginia money for bacon, and 6d. for beef.

Immediately on gitting this we sat of[f] again on our journey; but at 12 o'clock ankord under a point on the eastern shore, the wind being off that shore and too heavy for us to proceed. The perogue however which had followed us went on. We rested a while and went on again but was soon obliged to rest again. The clouds all rolled away and the wind settled at NW.

I went ashore and took a long walk; and when I returned diner was ready; and by the time it was over about 4 o'clock we went on again, rounding by the east to quite to NW to the lower point of the bar and convex point of sand; and here we ankor just at dusk under the NW shore, which we call the eastern shore because it belongs to the eastern side of the river; but this is the first time that we have rounded on the left hand or by the east to NW. Indeed this is an extraordinary turn in the river and such an one as I did dream of meeting with.

We have made but poor progress today as the wind has been high, for tho it was fair in the early part of the day as our cabin was wet and heavy I did not venture to raise the sail; and as we had suffered so great a disaster and the boat but newly repaired, we kept near the bar where we were most safe; but we find she is as tight as ever and hope to make better progress tomorrow. The man that pilots the perogue told us at the place where we were wrecked that we were then 150 miles from the Walnut Hills; and we have not come over 20 miles today.

The Major has been so unwel today that he has not done any thing but row about an hour and took a short walk where we first rested.

Misisipi, Saturday, November the 26th 1803. The morning cloudy, wind NE but light. We set off at sun rise and rounded a large island from NW by the east to south, then rounded a point to SE, then rounded a large island by the south to west, then at a[bout] 11 o'clock entered a long reach of the river SSW; and here the wind being fair we raised our sail; and having a strong current went on rapid and passed the Little Lonely Isle which stands in the middle of the river on the centre of a large sand bar, at 1/4 after 12; this small island being SSW about 8 miles below the last mentioned large island which also stands in the middle the river.[11]

There being a channel on both side each of them, we came on the east side the large on[e] and on the west side the small one. This last has about 50 large trees on it in a group and no bushes and has perhaps half an acre of high land on the centre of a large sand bar. From the large island to this, the river flows from shore to shore, which she seldom does for such a distance.

After leaving this long reach we round by the south to NE, then rounded again by the south to west, then back by the south eastward; and in this round below two outer island in a deep narrow cove, cut through the lower part of the bar by the current between the two islands aforesaid and an inner island next to the east shore; and here we took our place of rest the night of the 26th of November, by informant about 70 miles or less above the Yazoo River and 84 above the Walnut Hills; but this we shall k[no]w more of when we reach those places, for our informants generally differ widely in their distances, and this I do not wonder at since it depends on the hight of the water.

For I am sure our distance now is fully double what it would be if the river is full; for we have often indeed at almost every turn of the river to go from 5 to ten miles round, where if the river was full we could cut across behind the islands and bars between them and the main land and reach the same point in two or three miles; and thus our voiage has been rendered much more lengthy and tedious than we expected; but even after all, if we should be favord by the Most High God who alone I adore and trust in, I may yet arrive by the first day of December after all our disasters, and to Him I this night present my humble thank[s], devout adoration, and sincere praise, and to Him I submit as the God and guardian of my life.

Misisipi, Sunday, November 27th 1803. The morning cold and cloudy. Wind east and our course east. All night the banks of the river in the cove opposite to us were falling in with terrible crushes and noise.

In the night before I got sound asleep, I heard the stove burning vehemently and called to our rowman, who I found up by a great fire complaining much of the cold, tho he slept in the cabbin. Major Claybourn waked up on my calling and he immediately began to talk with the Major; and when the Majo[r] got silent, he B. went out of the cabbin and had a great many antic actions like a crazy man, so that I discovered that he was greatly intoxicated either with Brandy or Opium or both; and therefore I kept awake untill he laid down again. The Major also noticed his conduct and mentioned it to Wms. this morning. But after resting, B. has got to his business again this morning; yet his countenace is still wild.

Soon after we set of[f] we saw an old bare and her young cub going up the hill on bank on the western shore. This is the first we have seen on the river.

At 12 o'clock we were passing the 4th turn of the river from our last nights station, and count on having advanced 20 miles this morning down the river, and hope to reach near the Yazoo by night; yet we have but just breakfasted. Our boat still keep[s] dry and comfortable; but the weather is cloudy, raw, and uncomfortable. The last or fourth I call the first circle and the next turn the second circle. At the entrance of the second circle we stoped to git wood, and I went across the point while the boat went round. They in going round met a French boat whose hands told them that it was then 10 leagues from the [Walnut] hills.

We went on about ten miles further, and ankord on the bar in the next round to the westward, a little above the lower point in a cove of the bar, expecting to pass the Yazoo and the Walnut Hills tomorrow. Shields got in a pett and went to bed early and the Major and Wms. and myself had coffee at 9 o'clock and music and sat up till after ten. The night soft, cloudy, and wind SE.

Misisipi, Munday, November 28th 1803. C[l]oudy and rainy, wind east. We set off at 7 o'clock but were obliged to ankor in the next round, the wind and rain being too hard for us to go on. At 11 o'clock we went on again, and at half after 12 at noon passed the mouth of the Yazoo River.[12]

This river come[s] in at an eastern bend of the Misisipi, which bend is nearly filled with two islands between which the Yazoo pours in its waters directly opposite to the point on the western shore; and it runs in with such force that it presses or drives the waters of the Misisipi so hard against the point on the west shore that a large cimecircle is cut out of that point, presenting a kind of cresent formed gulf.

[At this time however there was hardly water in the Yazoo to float our boat.][13]

The course to the mouth of the Yazoo is east, then from it the first short course of the Misisipi is SE and to S by E, then turns eastward again.

At half after one the wind and rain obliged us to ankor again in the second turn and about two miles below the Yazoo River. Thus the elements oppose at a time when we have not a moment to spare and when 3 days favorable weather wou'd enable us to reach the Natchez, the place of our distination, and in time to commence our business on the day the law contemplates; but when I look at this late period of life for aid or special favor, the Most High in whom I trust renders my life as usual a life of ardor and difficulties. Thus like Moses and David, He leaves no alternative but to work my way through adversaty and affliction; but since I have been struggling with these till the vigor and prime of life has rolld away, why will He not at this yield a little to common lot of human nature and render my course more easy and pleasant or renew that prime and vigor of body and mind which may be superior to all difficulties that He throws in my way; for surely the God of the universe means not to punish but enlighten those who He afflicts, for the tract of enlightend minds has ever been through the paths of affliction and wilderness of adversaty, and even this wilderness has now become pleasant to me.

After awhile the wind ceased a little, and Williams and Buchanan went to the oars and rowed us through the long round NE round we were in; and when we ankord a little beyond the point, we saw the Walnut Hills ahead at 4 or 5 miles distance. We came too just before dark and dinner being ready dined; and all hands agreed to go on to the Hills. A light soon appeared there, and having been up in the rain till dark I laid down to rest; and when the boys reached the Hills they could find no place to ankor, the shore being steep till they passed them. I then looked out; and seeing a fine str[a]ight river ahead baring S by W and the wind from NE being now fair, they went on till 9 o'clock and then ankord on the western shore near a bar, 6 or 7 miles below the Hills.[14]

After resting a little while I got up; and finding the wind fair and a fine river I rouzed Williams and proceeded first S by W then S by E to the upper end of the island above the Yankee settlements, where we found the perogue, and turned to shore and rested with her till we took a dish of coffee; and at 2 o'clock past midnight set out again, rounding the island and bar from SW, rounding to the southward towards the Yankee settlements.

We left the perogue and passed the *[illegible]* island behind which the Yankee settlements are said to be, and then rounded to SW and went on. The wind being fair and the rain over tho cloudy but moon light and the river open and clear, all agreed to go on so as to git to Judge Bruins in the morning.

Buchanan made a mistake about the Yankee settlements being behind the former island. At 5 o'clock after midnight we came to another island at the uper end of which the Yankee settlements begin. Here Williams struck up the tune of Yankee Doodle, and Shields sang to the fiddle. At half after six we passed the lower end of Yankee Island. Course is west. Shields and Williams at the oars and the Major at the fiddle. At 5 o'clock in the morning[15] we ankord on the west side of the river opposite the island; but the cable broke, and we run to the shore and went to bed. We kept up a round of [festivity?] all night.

[During this nights voiage have no wood on board. The Major first split up his own bed board then Williams, then Shields's to cook.][16]

Misisipi, Tuesday, November 29th 1803. We row at 8 o'clock this morning. We got up and found our ankor, and then went on rounding to the south round a third island in the same bar which we rested on last night below the Yankee settlements. I having been up most the night have not had time today to mention the courses of the river but refer to my map.

At 3 o'clock I noticed however our passing the sudden turn in the river called the Grand Gulph.[17] It at this turn that the river appears narrower than any where else, I turn of[f] short round from the eastward to SW; and untill you git close to the river [it] seems to end and then breaks off as it were from one side through narrow pass aforesaid. On the east side of this narrow pass, the[re] is a high hill or little mountain which confines the river. At this turn there is a house on the point on the western side and a house just below the hill aforesaid and the east side; and on each shore below this turn there are several settlements.

Judge Bruin lives as we were told nine miles below this turn. We arrived at Judge Bruins 48 miles above Natchez about sun down. I sent Major Claybourn up to see the judge; and he returned with Negro boy and 2 bottles of claret and a bottle of whisky for us and an invitation to me and the other gentlemen to go up and drink tea and lodge there. The Major and myself went and drink tea but declined lodging. We had to move on.

The judge is an old soldier and was Major in Genl. Morgans corps, and is no lawyer, but a very talkative robust man and a moderate Fed.[18] He was very hospitable and friendly and invited me to spend Christmas with him. Had some bread baked for us and sent us some fresh beef and told us I could git down sooner by water than by land. Car [Ker] the other judge he says was a schoolmaster who took to reading law;[19] and he hoped I was to be the Chief Justice of the Court; and that there is 20 lawyers at Natchez but some of them do not practice; that it is a genteel place, etc.; and that the country is not very unhealthy, etc.; that he has lived here 16 years and has not lost one [slave] by [much?] sickness out of 50 or 60. He has a wife and six children and two of them married.

After we got our bread baked and on board, etc., etc., we moved over to the sand bar on the other side the river, and ankord in a small cove in the bar, and all went to rest. I awoke about 3 or 4 o'clock; and finding that the wind was rising, I dressed and sat on my bed watching boats.

A little before day, the wind increased so furious that the boat parted from her ankor; and I call up Buchanan to pole her on the beach just behind us where the wind indeed too carried her for we were very near it before. Here I had a stern and bow fast made to stakes drove in the sand where she could not move much.

This accident rouzed all the crew; but when they saw the boat safe they laid down again [except for] only Buchanan and myself; but the wind rose presently, as day appeared, to a desperate degree so that our cabbin seemed to be in danger of being injured; and at the same time it rained very hard, so that it was difficult to keep safe; but after an hour the wind and rain subsided, and as soon as Buchanan recovered our ankor we set off again.

Misisipi, Wednesday, November 30th 1803. While the wind lulled, we put off to try to git round the first point below Judge Bruins, to git near the woods for a better harbour in case if the wind should blow again, for tho there was appearances of its clearing in the west the flying clouds looked squ[a]lly; and we had hardly reached the point before the wind increased, so that we could not but just turn the point and run to the shore just where the bar begins to run off from it and put our ankor on the shore. Here we seemed to lay pretty quiet and secure while the wind greatly increased again.

By this time B. had breakfast ready, and we enjoyed a comfortable meal; and then the Major, Shields, and Wms. went on shore to walk. The Major, who had steped on shore while breakfast was setting, brot wild water mellons on board which he found growing on the bank. One of them tho small they all said was very good, but I did not taste them. I suppose the seed had been cast there by water being thrown over by some vessel on the river.

Apropos, there was a river sloop laying at Judge Bruins when we went there named the Industry of Natchez, navigated by French and Spaniard, collecting bails of cotton.

This being the last day of November, tomorrow being the first day of December is the day that our board is to meet. At present there seems little prospect tho now so near of my gitting there in time; however I trust that the Most High who rules the winds and waves will be pleased to still them so that I may reach there in time, as we are now not more than ten hours quick progress from Natchez; and if we can arrive by 12 o'clock tomorrow, I shall have time to go out to Washington, which is only 6 miles, to call the board.

Judge Bruin informed the Major last evening after I left him that Turner the register of our board is quite a boy and not distinguished for talents or integrity, and is so far from being approved by the inhabitants that they had presented a petition to the legislature to interpose and if possible to git him removed, and that West, the Secretary of the Terratory, is susspected of having procured the appointment for him, yet that Governor C. had been susspected to have recommended him, but he had been told the governor denied it.[20]

The judge is one of those settlers who hold under the Spainards but has an incomplete title; and so far as we have yet heard any thing of claims, it seems as if they would include all the land within the Terratory; but it is said many of them are very wild, and particularly the claim of one Green and Co. called the Burbon Claim. At any rate, the great variety of claims talked off bid fair to find us much business.

The Judge told the Major that having heard my carractor every body approved of my appointment; and most of them have confidence in Mr. Williams,[21] but that all object to Turner. How this may be will be better known; but however it may be I shall proceed with that impartial integrity which has been the rule of my life in the discharge of public duties.

We put of[f] from the point below Judge Bruins in the evening and rounded the barr eastward; and turned a point that stretches several miles to the eastward; and then rounded to the westward and run down a large island that lies along and below said points, the river baring SW for 8 or ten miles. Then we rounded again to the eastward passing in the bend two or three large islands, from whence the river bare near SE to Coles Creek.[22] Then the river rounded to near SW 8 or 10 miles, passing two or three islands; and then it rounded again to the SE; and we passed 2 or 3 islands in the bend; and at the lower end of the last of these we came in sight of Natchez when the river rounded to the south and SSW; and we went on under easy sail to the landing at Natchez where we arrived at 5 o'clock P.M.

"Natchez Under-the-Hill depicted by the artist [Edouard de] Montule, about 1800."
David G. Sansing, Sim C. Callon, and Carolyn Vance Smith, *Natchez: An Illustrated History* (Natchez, Mississippi: Plantation Publishing Company, 1992), 34. Courtesy Carolyn Vance Smith.

The Major and Shields went up immediately into the city to git horses for the Major and myself to ride out to Washington. Robert Williams had arrived the day before and was at Washington.[23] It was near sun down when the Major and I set off. He had got a horse of Major F. L. Claiborne, and Garret and Wood sent me their horse.[24] We arrived at Washington[25] a little after night and found Williams and the Register there.[26]

They had called and adjourned the board; but as we were now all together we repeated the ceremony and made a formal entry of our meeting; and I gave notice of this by the next mail to the President.[27]

Thus having left Dover the 14th of August 1803, I arrved at Natchez the 1st day of December following,[28] having been on the road from Dalaware to the Ohio and at Wheeling till the 21st of September and the rest of the time on the Ohio and Misisipi—in all three months and 17 days; 71 days of the time on the rivers.[29]

NOTES

Introduction

1. This is the date of Rodney's birth under the Julian calendar (Old Style). Great Britain and the colonies converted to the Gregorian calendar (New Style) in 1752. Under the present calendar, therefore, Rodney's birth date is June 15, 1744. Frank Freidel, ed., *Harvard Guide to American History*, 2 vols. (Cambridge, Mass.: Belknap Press of Harvard University Press, 1974), 1: 23-25.

2. Under its constitution of 1776-1793, Delaware's chief executive officer was designated as "president." Caesar Rodney served in that capacity, 1778-1782. John A. Munroe, *Federalist Delaware, 1775-1815* (New Brunswick, N.J.: Rutgers University Press, 1954), 85-86, 265.

3. Hamilton, *Anglo-American Law*, 7.

4. Clarence Edwin Carter, "The Transit of Law to the Frontier: A Review Article," *Journal of Mississippi History* 16 (July 1954): 183-192.

5. This biographical sketch is derived principally from William Baskerville Hamilton, *Thomas Rodney, Revolutionary & Builder of the West* (Durham, N.C.: Duke University Press, 1953), which is a reprint of the biographical chapters of Hamilton's *Anglo-American Law*.

For convenient biographical sketches and information see *Dictionary of American Biography*, s.v. "Rodney, Thomas," by George H. Ryden; "Rodney, Thomas," in Dunbar Rowland, ed. *Encyclopedia of Mississippi History: Comprising Sketches of Counties, Towns, Events, Institutions and Persons*, 2 vols. (Madison, Wis.: Selwyn A. Brant, 1907), 2: 547-575; *Biographical Directory of the United States Congress, 1734-1989*, Bicentennial Edition, s.v. "Rodney,

Thomas;" Dunbar Rowland, *Courts, Judges, and Lawyers of Mississippi, 1798-1935* (Jackson, Miss.: Press of Hederman Bros., 1935), 19-20.

These same sources may be referenced for his brother, Caesar Rodney. See also *Dictionary of American Biography*, s.v. "Rodney, Caesar," by George H. Ryden; William P. Frank and Harold B. Hancock, "Caesar Rodney's Two Hundred and Fiftieth Anniversary: An Evaluation," *Delaware History* 18 (fall-winter 1978): 63-74.

6. For two perspectives on Rodney's Mississippi years see Hamilton, *Anglo-American Law;* John Carroll Eudy, "Thomas Rodney, 1744-1811: Patriot in the Mississippi Territory," in Dean Faulkner Wells and Hunter Cole, eds., *Mississippi Heroes* (Jackson: University Press of Mississippi, 1980), 2-26; John Carroll Eudy, "The Political Intrigues of Thomas Rodney: Territorial Politics, 1807-1809," *Journal of Mississippi History* 40 (November 1978): 329-339.

Rodney's name was given to a town first laid out and settled about 1826 on the Mississippi in northwestern Jefferson County. A bar was formed in the river in 1864 and this river port changed to a landlocked, virtual ghost town. Present-day maps include Rodney Cutoff, Rodney LDG (Landing), Rodney Island (Island No. 111), Rodney Bend (or Rodney Lake), and BM (Bench Mark) Rodney, as well as the town itself. Howard Mitcham, "Old Rodney: A Mississippi Ghost Town," *Journal of Mississippi History* 15 (October 1953): 242-251; Marion Bragg, *Historic Names and Places on the Lower Mississippi River* (Vicksburg: Mississippi River Commission, 1977), 178-180; U.S. Army Corps of Engineers, Mississippi River Commission, *Flood Control and Navigation Maps of the Mississippi River, Cairo, Illinois, to the Gulf of Mexico . . .* , 29th ed. (Vicksburg, Miss.: U.S. Army Corps of Engineers, 1961), map 36.

7. Simon Gratz, "Thomas Rodney," *Pennsylvania Magazine of Biography and History* 43.2 (1919): 117-142; 43.3 (1919): 208-209.

8. Christian Schultz, Jr., *Travels on an Inland Voyage through the States of New-York, Pennsylvania, Virginia, Ohio, Kentucky and Tennessee, and through the Territories of Indiana, Louisiana, Mississippi and New Orleans. . .* , 2 vols. (New York: Isaac Riley, 1810; reprint ed., 2 vols. in 1, Ridgewood, N.J.: Gregg Press, 1968). While there were, to be sure, other American travelers in this pre-1810 period who wrote lengthy, insightful accounts of their journeys in Western America, most limited their voyages and perambulations to the Ohio and upper Mississippi valleys. The few who persevered to the lower Mississippi, and left descriptions of their travels, wrote with far less breadth and detail than Rodney and Schultz.

Schultz was born in 1774 in New York City and died in Wood County,

(West) Virginia, in 1830. For additional biographical information see Thomas D. Clark's Introduction to the 1968 reprint edition of Schultz's *Travels on an Inland Voyage*, and Robert L. Pemberton, *A History of Pleasants County, West Virginia* (St. Marys, W.Va.: Oracle Press, 1929), 33-36. For an excellent overview of early Ohio River travelers, see Michael Allen, "Beyond the 'Endless Mountains': The View from the Ohio River," *Queen City Heritage* 53 (fall 1995): 33-39.

9. Its complete title page reveals why it was considered indispensable to western river travelers: A New And Corrected Edition. / The / Ohio and Mississippi / Navigator / Comprising / An Ample Account Of Those / Beautiful Rivers, From The Head Of / The Former, To The Mouth Of The / Latter. / A particular description of the several / Towns, Posts, Caves, Ports, Harbours / &c. on their banks, and accurate directions / How to Navigate them, / As well in times of high Freshes, as when the / water is low. / A Description Of Its / Rocks, Riffles, Shoals, Channels, / And The / Distances From Place To Place. / Together with a description / Of Monongahela And Allegheny / Rivers. / First taken from the Journals of Gentlemen of obser- / vation, and now minutely corrected by several / persons who have navigated those rivers for / fifteen and twenty years. / Third Corrected Edition. / Pittsburgh: / Printed By John Scull, / For Zadok Cramer, Bookseller & Stationer, / 1802. /

Both the third and the fourth editions are available in a reprint edition: Zadok Cramer, *The Ohio and Mississippi Navigator of Zadok Cramer.* (Morrison, Ill.: Karl Yost, 1987). For a bibliographic discussion of the several editions see Yost's Introduction, pp. xi-xxxiii. For a commentary on Cramer's methodology and principal thrust see John Seelye, *Beautiful Machine: Rivers and the Republican Plan, 1755-1825* (New York: Oxford University Press, 1991), 242-247.

10. See chapter 8, note 18 below.

1. "All my friends lamented"

1. Thomas Jefferson to Thomas Rodney, June 17, 1803; An act providing for the disposal of public land south of the state of Tennessee; Seth Lewis to James Madison, April 16, 1803; all in Clarence Edwin Carter, comp. and ed., *The Territorial Papers of the United States*, vol. 5: *The Territory of Mississippi, 1798-1817 [sic]* (Washington: Government Printing Office, 1937), 218-219, 192-205, 215.

2. An entry dated August 13, 1803, concerning a financial matter unrelated to the journey, has been omitted.

3. Charles, Ann, and Dr. John Hamm were children of John Hamm, a Little Creek Hundred, Kent County, Delaware, farmer. The Hamm and Rodney families were friends. Marie Windell, ed., "James Van Dyke Moore's Trip to the West, 1826-1828," *Delaware History* 4 (September 1950): 71 and n. 10, 99.

4. Duck Creek Cross Roads at the northern tip of Kent County, Delaware, was renamed Smyrna in 1806. Wilson Lloyd Bevan and E. Melvin Williams, eds., *History of Delaware Past and Present,* 4 vols. (New York: Lewis Historical Publishing Co., 1929), 2: 851; Jeannette Eckman, *Delaware: A Guide to the First State,* 2d ed. (New York: Hastings House, 1955), 346.

5. Brick Tavern or Brick Hotel was located at Brick Store Landing which is today designated Brick Store. Eckman, *Delaware,* 346.

6. Iron Hill is three miles to the south of Newark, Delaware. Grays Hill, Maryland, is some three and a half miles southwest of Iron Hill and a mile to the east of Elkton, Maryland. Newark West (Maryland-Delaware-Pennsylvania) Quadrangle; Elkton (Maryland-Delaware) Quadrangle. Unless otherwise noted, the U.S. Geological Survey maps cited in documentation are 1:24 000 scale maps.

7. Washington, D.C., was popularly called Federal City in the late eighteenth and early nineteenth centuries.

8. William Bayard Shields (1780-1823), a Delaware native related to the Rodney family, had studied law under Rodney's son. Shields was to play a prominent role in the legislative and judicial history of Mississippi, his initial appointment coming as an assistant clerk to the Board of Land Commissioners. He was appointed to the governor's staff in 1805. He became a district attorney general three years later and also served in the General Assembly, 1808, 1813-1814. His election as a judge to the state supreme court in 1818 was superseded in the same year when he was commissioned the first federal judge for the district of Mississippi, an office he held until his death. Shields was characterized as "a man of popular qualities, a leader of the Jeffersonian party throughout his career, and as a judge, 'patient, laborious, discriminating and scrupulously impartial.'" Rowland, *Encyclopedia of Mississippi History,* 2: 660; Rowland, *Courts, Judges, and Lawyers,* 10, 68-69; Albert Gallatin to William B. Shields, June 2, 1804, in Carter, *Territorial Papers, Territory of Mississippi,* 5: 327-328, 327 n. 55, et passim; 6 (1938): passim; Hamilton, *Anglo-American Law,* 62-67; Gary E. Moulton, ed., *The Journals of the Lewis & Clark Expedition* (Lincoln: University of Nebraska Press, 1983—), 2: 74, 75 n. 6; Richard Aubrey McLemore, ed., *A History of Mississippi,* 2 vols. (Hattiesburg: University & College Press of Mississippi,

1973), 1: 205-206, 210, et passim; Thomas Rodney to William C. C. Claiborne, August 7, 1803, Historical Society of Delaware, Wilmington, Delaware.

9. The balance of the manuscript page, here omitted, notes the purchase of sundry items.

10. Chestnut Hill, Delaware, is adjacent and to the northwest of Iron Hill. See note 6 above. Newark West (Maryland-Delaware-Pennsylvania) Quadrangle.

11. Phillip Lewes.

12. This and the succeeding paragraph were added at a later date or dates.

13. Three manuscript pages, here omitted, note the purchase of sundry items and business transactions.

14. John Fisher, Rodney's brother-in-law, was secretary of state for Governor David Hall. Munroe, *Federalist Delaware,* 213, 265; John A. H. Sweeney, ed., "The Norris-Fisher Correspondence: A Circle of Friends, 1779-82," *Delaware History* 6 (March 1955): 212 n. 62.

John Hunn served as a privateer captain in the American Revolution. In addition to his daughter Susan being married to Rodney's son, the two families were also otherwise related. Munroe, *Federalist Delaware,* 154, 244; George Valentine Massey, II, "Priscilla Kitchen, Quakeress, of Salem, Mass., and Kent County, Del., and Her Family," *New England Historical and Genealogical Register* 106 (January 1952): 46-47; William Henry Egle, "The Federal Constitution of 1787: Sketches of the Members of the Pennsylvania Convention," *Pennsylvania Magazine of History and Biography* 11 (1887): 218-219.

James Wilson was the publisher of the *Wilmington (Del.) Mirror of the Times, & General Advertiser.* Clarence S. Brigham, *History and Bibliography of American Newspapers, 1690-1820,* 2 vols. (Worcester, Mass.: American Antiquarian Society, 1947), 1: 84-85.

John Warner and William Warner were Brandywine (Wilmington) merchants. Munroe, *Federalist Delaware,* 213; George H. Gibson, ed., "William P. Brobson Diary, 1825-1828," *Delaware History* 15 (April 1972): 60 n. 8, 65 n. 23.

15. By Rodney's calculations, this was twelve miles from Wilmington. See entry for August 25, 1803, below.

16. In all likelihood, this refers to the stream rather than to the settlement bearing the same name. Doe Run is a tributary of Buck Run which in turn is a tributary of West Branch of Brandywine Creek. Rodney possibly was traveling near the source of Doe Run, near Cochranville, five miles to the west of the village of Doe Run. Wilmington (Delaware-New Jersey-Pennsylvania-Maryland) 1:100 000 Quadrangle.

According to Rodney, Lilleys Tavern was twenty-six miles out of Wilmington. See entry for August 25, 1803, below.

The Lancaster and Wilmington turnpike road, sometimes called the Gap and Newport (Delaware) Road, entered Lancaster County, Pennsylvania, through Mine Hill Gap where it terminated at the Philadelphia and Lancaster turnpike road. J. I. Mombert, *An Authentic History of Lancaster County in the State of Pennsylvania* (Lancaster, Penn.: J. E. Barr & Co., 1869), 347; W. W. Thomson, ed., *Chester County and Its People* (Chicago: Union History Company, 1898), 494. See also Charles I. Landis, "History of the Philadelphia and Lancaster Turnpike. The First Long Turnpike in the United States," *Pennsylvania Magazine of History and Biography* 42 (1918): 1-28, 127-140, 235-258, 358-360; 43 (1919): 84-90, 182-190.

17. On this first day from Wilmington, Rodney's party had traveled forty-eight miles. See entry for August 25, 1803, below.

18. This visit may have been in connection with his 1778-79 service as clothier to the Delaware Regiment. Hamilton, *Anglo-American Law,* 32-33. The reference to the Dutch is a common mistake which arose from the confusion of "Deutsch" for "Dutch," a mistake frequently made by eighteenth- and nineteenth-century travelers and other writers when describing Pennsylvanians of German blood.

19. Little Conestoga Creek flows into Conestoga Creek, a tributary of Susquehanna River. Conestoga (Pennsylvania) Quadrangle; Safe Harbor (Pennsylvania) Quadrangle.

20. Among the names it bore in its early years, York was called York Town and Town of York as well as Little York. W. C. Carter and A. J. Glossbrenner, *History of York County from Its Erection to the Present Time; (1729-1834),* new ed. by A. Monroe Aurand, Jr. (Harrisburg: Aurand Press, 1930), 19-27.

21. Thaddeus Harris, visiting York in June, noted it also contained Presbyterian, Roman Catholic, and Moravian churches, a Quaker meeting-house, and an academy. Thaddeus Mason Harris, *The Journal of a Tour into the Territory Northwest of the Alleghany Mountains. . . .* (Boston: Manning & Loring, 1805), 74.

22. Codorus Creek is a tributary of Susquehanna River. York Haven (Pennsylvania) Quadrangle.

23. They had traveled seventy-three miles together from Wilmington. See entry for August 25, 1803, below.

24. According to Thaddeus Harris, "Abbot's town [was a] pretty flourishing village, the chief town of Adams Country." Harris, *Journal of a Tour,* 74. Abbottstown is on highway U.S. 30, midway between York and Gettysburg.

Heroutford ("Hartford") or Pigeon Hills settlement was named for Joseph Herout, a Sulpician friar and early settler. *History of Cumberland and Adams Counties, Pennsylvania. . . .* (Chicago: Warner, Beers & Co., 1886), part III, pp. 322-324.

25. This is probably South Branch Conewago Creek, which flows into Conewago Creek, a tributary of Susquehanna River. Gettysburg 1:50 000 Army Map Service; York Haven (Pennsylvania) Quadrangle.

26. Hunterstown is situated on road Pennsylvania 394, five miles northeast of Gettysburg.

27. South Mountain ridge, as do successive ridges to the west, runs in a north-by-northeasterly-south-by-southwesterly direction. This is depicted graphically on Samuel Lewis, "The State of Pennsylvania Reduced with Permission from Reding Howell's Map," in Mathew Carey, *Carey's General Atlas* (Philadelphia: Mathew Carey, [1810]), map 33. Rodney's description of Black Gap in this entry suggests that it may have been what is designated as Locust Gap, to the northeast of today's placement of Black Gap at the intersection of road Pennsylvania 997 and highway U.S. 30. Scotland (Pennsylvania) Quadrangle.

28. Rodney uses "entertained" in its eighteenth-century sense of hospitality which provides for a guest's needs, especially in regard to food.

29. Rodney's employment of this spelling of Natchez exemplifies the curious eighteenth- and early nineteenth-century practice of occasionally writing the name in the plural. Another example of this custom at work is the ancient French settlement of Kaskaskia, part of Indiana Territory during Rodney's journey but subsequently capital of Illinois Territory (1809) and of the state of Illinois (1818). It was variously identified as "Kaskasias," "the Kaskaskies," and "the Cascaskies." John D. Barnhart, *Henry Hamilton and George Rogers Clark in the American Revolution with the Unpublished Journal of Lieut. Gov. Henry Hamilton* (Crawfordsville, Ind.: R. E. Banta, 1951), 192; Dudley Woodbridge, Sr., to James Backus, October 26, 1811, Backus-Woodbridge Papers, Collection 128, Box 2, Folder 2, Ohio Historical Society, Columbus; Prescott Hildreth to Samuel P. Hildreth, April 23, 1846 (transcription of personal interview of Major John James, Jr.), Samuel P. Hildreth Papers, I: 94, Marietta College Library, Marietta, Ohio.

30. When Christian Schultz visited Natchez a few years later, "a married gentleman of the town" characterized the married ladies there as "indulgent as the Cyprian goddess." Schultz protested, however, that it was unfair to generalize from what "may be applicable to a few." Christian Schultz, Jr., *Travels on an Inland Voyage through the States of New-York, Pennsylvania,*

Virginia, Ohio, Kentucky and Tennessee, and through the Territories of Indiana, Louisiana, Mississippi and New-Orleans. . . . 2 vols. in 1 (New York: Isaac Riley, 1810), 2: 134. This 1810 edition of Schultz, *Travels on an Inland Voyage* will be cited henceforth rather than the 1968 reprint edition used in Introduction note 9 above.

31. Conococheague Creek is a tributary of the Potomac River. Scotland (Pennsylvania) Quadrangle; Williamsport (Maryland-West Virginia) Quadrangle.

32. See entry for August 24, 1803, above.

33. Thaddeus Harris gave a more detailed description of Chambersburg when passing through it in June: "This is a fine town, situated on Conogocheague Creek, through which might be opened an easy communication with the Potomack. It is a post-town, and the capital of Franklin County, . . . and is principally built on two large streets which intersect each other at right angles, leaving a public square in the centre. It contains about two hundred and fifty houses, handsomely built of brick or stone; two Presbyterian churches; a Court-house of brick, and a stone Gaol. There is a printing-office in the place, and a paper-mill in the vicinity. It is a situation favourable to trade and manufactures, and every thing looks lively and thriving. The land in the neighbourhood appears rich and fertile, and is highly cultivated." Harris, *Journal of a Tour,* 73.

34. As Rodney is not consistent in the matter of points of compass direction abbreviations, the preferred style of eliminating periods is used herein. See chapter 2, note 21 below.

35. Rodney's reference here is probably to Parnell's (Parnel) Knob and Jordan's Knob to the north and northeast of Fort Loudon. D. G. Beers, *Atlas of Franklin County, Pennsylvania, from Actual Surveys under the Direction of D. G. Beers* (Philadelphia: Pomeroy & Beers, 1868), 43, 49.

36. "Taverns or inns are very numerous throughout the United States," noted Francois Andre Michaux while traveling through Pennsylvania in 1802, "but particularly in the small towns: every where however, except in the large towns and their environs, they are of a wretched description. . . . There are always several beds in one chamber; clean sheets are a great rarity, and fortunate is the traveller who arrives on the day when they are changed; but this is a point on which an American gives himself little concern." Francois Andre Michaux, *Travels to the Westward of the Allegany Mountains.* . . . (London: Richard Phillips, 1805), 18-19.

37. MConnells Town is now McConnellsburg. N. Mountain is North Mountain ridge. See note 27 above for South Mountain ridge.

38. Thaddeus Harris described it the previous June simply as "a delightful, well-watered village in Bedford Country." Harris, *Journal of a Tour,* 70-71.

39. Sideling Hill is another of the mountain ridges. See notes 27 and 37 above.

40. Caesar Rodney, who had been recruiting men in his county when George Washington went into winter quarters at Morristown, New Jersey, in January 1777, was put in command at the post in Trenton for a few weeks. He served as president of Delaware, 1778-1781. *Dictionary of American Biography,* s.v. "Rodney, Caesar," by George H. Ryden.

2. "Grand and beautiful scenes"

1. Juniata Crossing is situated where highway U.S. 30 crosses Raystown Branch Juniata River. Mench (Pennsylvania) Quadrangle. One nineteenth-century Ohio historian wrote of the difficulties experienced by late eighteenth- early nineteenth-century travelers crossing Pennsylvania: "The roads, at that day, across the mountains were the worst we can possibly imagine—cut into deep gullies on one side by mountain rains, while the other was filled with blocks of sand-stone. The descents were abrupt, and often resembled the breaks in a flight of stone stairs. . . . As few of the emigrant wagons were provided with lock-chains for the wheels, the downward impetus was checked by a large log, or broken tree top, tied with a rope to the back of the wagon and dragged along on the ground. In other places, the road was so sideling [i.e., slanting] that all the men who could be spared were required to pull at the side stays, or short ropes attached to the upper side of the wagons, to prevent their upsetting." Samuel P. Hildreth, "Early Emigration, Or, The Journal of Some Emigrant Families 'across the Mountains,' from New England to Muskingum, in 1788," *American Pioneer* 2 (March 1843): 121.

See also Max Farrand, ed., *A Journey to Ohio in 1810 as Recorded in the Journal of Margaret Van Horn Dwight* (New Haven: Yale University Press, 1913), 32-33, 35-37, 44, 46-47, 55-57, 60-61. Miss Dwight's narrative provides as vivid a picture of the road horrors of traveling west as any firsthand account from the frontier period.

2. Waynesboro, usually called Bloody Run at the time, lay eight miles east of Bedford. It is today called Everett. I. Daniel Rupp, *The History and Topography of Dauphin, Cumberland, Franklin, Bedford, Adams, and Perry Counties. . . .* (Lancaster City, Pa.: Gilbert Hills, 1846), 512; *County Atlas of Bedford, Pennsylvania, from Recent and Actual Surveys and Records under the Superintendence of F. W. Beers* (New York: F. W. Beers & Co., 1877), 65; Everett East (Pennsylvania) Quadrangle.

3. Fort Raystown, built in 1757 and renamed Fort Bedford in 1758, when Raystown became Bedford, was in ruins by the time of the Revolution. Pennsylvania Writers' Project, *Pennsylvania: A Guide to the Keystone State* (New York: Oxford University Press, 1940), 449-450.

4. Warrior Mountain is today designated as Warrior Ridge. Everett East (Pennsylvania) Quadrangle; Carey, *Carey's General Atlas,* map 33. And what Rodney calls Bedford Mountain is probably Evitts Mountain. Everett West (Pennsylvania) Quadrangle; Carey, *Carey's General Atlas,* map 33.

5. "The first judge 'learned in the law' appears to have been James Riddle, who died in Chambersburg in 1838, leaving an honorable record." He was the "first law judge of the county." William H. Egle, *History of the Commonwealth of Pennsylvania, Civil, Political, and Military . . . ,* 3d ed. (Philadelphia: E. M. Gardner, 1883), 367, 369.

6. The year before Rodney passed through Bedford, François André Michaux commented that "there are scarcely more than a hundred and twenty houses, of which some are constructed of brick, and others of shingles." François André Michaux, *Travels to the Westward,* 22.

7. Thomas Rodney to Caesar A. Rodney, August 30, 1803, in Gratz, "Thomas Rodney," 43.2 (1919): 119-120.

8. The Allegheny Mountain range approximately parallels the ridges mentioned above. Carey, *Carey's General Atlas,* map 33. See also chapter 1, notes 27, 37, and 39, and note 4, above.

9. Glades Valley of Stony Creek, to the northeast of Berlin. "The Glades" is a high tableland between the Great Allegheny Mountain and Laurel Hill Mountain in what is now Somerset County, Pennsylvania. In the late eighteenth and early nineteenth centuries, it was a region of well watered grassland. Pennsylvania and Virginia cattlemen at this time were in the habit of driving their stock to the Glades each summer and pasturing them on its lush grasses. Berlin (Pennsylvania) Quadrangle; Sherman Day, *Historical Collections of the State of Pennsylvania. . . .* (Philadelphia: George W. Gorton, 1843), 615-616; Hildreth, "Early Emigration," 125; Paul A. W. Wallace, ed., *Thirty Thousand Miles with John Heckewelder* (Pittsburgh: University of Pittsburgh Press, 1958), 239, 410.

10. Probably East Branch Coxes Creek, a branch of Coxes Creek that flows into Casselman River. Murdock (Pennsylvania) Quadrangle; Somerset (Pennsylvania) Quadrangle; Rockwood (Pennsylvania) Quadrangle; see note 13 below.

11. Laurel Hill ridge was "so named from the profusion of Rhododendron, or Rosebay, and Kalmia latifolia, or Laurel, which clusters along its

rocky sides." Carey, *Carey's General Atlas,* map 33; Hildreth, "Early Emigration," 125.

Bremers Tavern. Thaddeus Harris, who had lodged there in the spring, recorded the tavern owner's name as Behmer. Harris, *Journal of a Tour,* 22.

12. While passing through this area the year before Rodney, François André Michaux noted, "In this mountainous part of Pennsylvania, there are great numbers of rattle-snakes; many of which we found killed on the road. In hot and dry weather, they come from beneath the rocks, and conceal themselves in places which contain water." François André Michaux, *Travels to the Westward,* 23.

13. Laurel Hill Creek converges with Casselman River to enter Youghiogheny River at Confluence. Bakersville (Pennsylvania) Quadrangle; Confluence (Pennsylvania) Quadrangle.

14. Called "Jones' mill" by Thaddeus Harris a few months earlier, it was the site of a grist mill and other Jones enterprises. Today called Jones Mills, it is situated in southeastern Westmoreland County. Harris, *Journal of a Tour,* 23; George Dallas Albert, *History of the County of Westmoreland, Pennsylvania, with Biographical Sketches of Many of Its Pioneers and Prominent Men* (Philadelphia: L. H. Everts & Co., 1882), 173; S. N. Beers and D. G. Beers, *Atlas of Westmoreland County, Pennsylvania, from Actual Surveys* (Philadelphia: A. Pomeroy, 1867), 21.

15. Chestnut Ridge. "This chain [of mountains] is so named from the immense forests of chestnut trees that clothe its sides and summit, for nearly the whole extent in Pennsylvania and part of Virginia. The soil is sandy and rocky; and so exactly adapted to the growth of this tree, that no part of the world produces it more abundantly. In fruitful years, hogs, from a distance of twenty or thirty miles, were driven by the inhabitants, every autumn, to fatten on its fruit. Bears, wild turkies, elk and deer, traveled from afar to this nut-producing region, and luxuriated on its bountiful crop. The congregation of wild animals, on this favored tract, made it one of the most celebrated hunting grounds, not only for the Indians, but also for the white man, who succeeded him in the possession of these mountain regions." Hildreth, "Early Emigration," 126; see also Carey, *Carey's General Atlas,* map 33.

The Youhagana is probably Indian Creek which enters Youghiogheny River some five miles upstream from South Connellsville. Seven Springs (Pennsylvania) Quadrangle; South Connellsville (Pennsylvania) Quadrangle.

16. Jacobs Creek enters Youghiogheny River at the village of Jacobs Creek as the Westmoreland County–Fayette County boundary. Mount Pleasant (Pennsylvania) Quadrangle; Smithton (Pennsylvania) Quadrangle. Mount

Pleasant is in south central Westmoreland County, ten miles to the south of Greensburg.

17. Parkinson's Ferry, today's Monongahela, was subsequently renamed Williamsport, and Monongahela City. Alfred Creigh, *History of Washington County from Its First Settlement to the Present Time . . .* , 2d ed. (Harrisburg, Penn.: B. Singerly, Printer, 1871), 241, 243-244.

18. W.b.N. or WbN denotes west by north, the compass direction halfway between due west and west by northwest; or 11°15' north of due west. Rodney employs this kind of abbreviation from time to time. For the sake of clarity, the preferred style W by N is used herein.

19. Rodney employs the eighteenth-century definition of "spunk" as "spirit" or "passion."

20. A chief notary or clerk or a register of a county court.

21. Previously called Alexander and Alexandria, it is today named West Alexander. Boyd Crumrine, ed., *History of Washington County, Pennsylvania, with Biographical Sketches of Many of Its Pioneers and Prominent Men* (Philadelphia: L. H. Everts & Co., 1882), 747-748. Interestingly, Thaddeus Harris, in passing through the town in April, reported that it "contains between fifty and sixty dwelling-houses." The only explanation of the discrepancy between these two observations may be in Harris's method of delayed journal entries. These he "first sketched down, as opportunity presented, in a pocket-book with a lead pencil," but did not transfer them to his journal until evening. Harris, *Journal of a Tour,* vi, 48.

22. For other comments on the Ohio Valley's large number of children see John Francis McDermott, ed., "The Western Journals of Dr. George Hunter, 1796-1805," *Transactions of the American Philosophical Society* n.s. 53 (July 1963): 40; Dwight L. Smith, ed., "The Ohio River in 1801: Letters of Jonathan Williams, Junior," *Filson Club History Quarterly* 27 (July 1953): 206-207, 209; Francois Andre Michaux, *Travels to the Westward,* 51. The enormous families prevalent in the West at the time of Rodney's journey was still a phenomenon two decades later: James Hall, when traveling through the Ohio Valley in 1820 noted with astonishment how "the number of children there was surpassed only by the squirrels of the surrounding forests." Quoted in Charles Henry Ambler, *A History of Transportation in the Ohio Valley with Special Reference to Its Waterways, Trade, and Commerce from the Earliest Period to the Present Time* (Glendale, Cal.: Arthur H. Clark Co., 1932), 79.

3. A Sojourn on the Ohio

1. Delf Norona, *Wheeling: A West Virginia Place-Name of Indian Origin*

(Moundsville, W.Va.: West Virginia Archeological Society, 1958), 21; J. H. Newton, G. G. Nichols, and A. G. Sprankle, *History of the Pan-Handle: Being Historical Collections of the Counties of Ohio, Brooke, Marshall and Hancock, West Virginia* (Wheeling, W.Va.: J. A. Caldwell, 1879), 127-131; John Gerald Patterson, "Ebenezer Zane, Frontiersman," *West Virginia History* 12 (October 1950): 15-16.

2. Nathaniel W. Little, Journal, September 6, 1802, William L. Clements Library, University of Michigan, Ann Arbor.

3. Literally, in childbed; or giving birth. The term originated during the Middle Ages, when "a woman in childbirth was said to be 'in the straw' since this was the type of mattress used. The phrase lingered on long after its origin had been forgotten." Phillis Cunnington and Catherine Lucas, *Costume for Births, Marriages & Deaths* (New York: Barnes & Noble Books, 1972), 16.

4. The berths were to be equipped "with curtains to roll up occasionally like the Stages." Local opinion held that the journey to Natchez could be completed in four weeks. Rodney planned to engage two men "used to the River . . . to row us down when we cannot sail—and we carry 4 oars that two of us may assist at Times our Selves and our boat will be so Constructed as to sell more down there than she will Cost here." Thomas Rodney to Caesar A. Rodney, September 7, 1803, in Gratz, "Thomas Rodney," 43.2 (1919): 122.

5. Richard Claiborne (1755-1819), of Virginia planter aristocracy, had served in the American Revolution as a Virginia officer and as an aide-de-camp to General Nathanael Greene. Unsuccessful in promoting himself at home or abroad as a speculator in western Virginia lands, his acquaintance with Thomas Jefferson and the influence of the governor of Mississippi Territory, his cousin William Charles Cole Claiborne, secured him appointment as clerk to the Board of Land Commissioners in Mississippi Territory.

Months later, when his cousin became governor of Orleans Territory, Major Claiborne went along. Rising steadily, in a few years he became a territorial parish judge. Although acquitted of corruption charges, his judgeship terminated when Orleans Territory became the state of Louisiana. For the remainder of his days, he practiced law in New Orleans.

Indenture, July 5, 1798, between Richard Claiborne and John Hopkins and George Pickett, Deed Book I: 453-458, Monongalia County Courthouse, Morgantown, West Virginia; Richard Claiborne, genealogical notes and manuscripts, Lolita H. Bissell, Nashville, Tennessee; Lolita H. Bissell, *Cliborn-Claiborne Records* (Nashville, Tenn.: Williams Printing Company, 1986), 202-209, 219; John Frederick Dorman, comp., in collaboration with

Claiborne T. Smith, Jr., *Claiborne of Virginia: Descendants of Colonel William Claiborne: The First Eight Generations,* (Baltimore, Md.: Gateway Press, 1995), 732-738.

6. Meriwether Lewis (1774-1809), soon to be joined by William Clark, had departed Pittsburgh August 30, 1803, on the expedition that would raise the two to historical immortality. A veteran of the Indian wars in the Old Northwest, Lewis had become the private secretary to President Jefferson. Upon his return from the Pacific Northwest in 1806, Lewis was appointed governor of Upper Louisiana Territory. His competent administration was fraught with political infighting, leading to his return to Washington. En route he died mysteriously. The latest theory is that his mind was deranged by syphilis contracted during the expedition and that he died by his own hand. *Dictionary of American Biography,* s.v. "Lewis, Meriwether," by Louise Phelps Kellogg; Richard Dillon, *Meriwether Lewis: A Biography* (New York: Coward-McCann, 1965); Reimert Thorolf Ravenholt, "Triumph Then Despair: The Tragic Death of Meriwether Lewis," *Epidemiology* 5 (May 1994): 366-379; John L. Loos, "Lewis, Meriwether," in *Dictionary of American Military Biography,* ed. Roger J. Spiller, 3 vols. (Westport, Conn.: Greenwood Press, 1984), 2: 635-638; Moulton, *Journals of the Lewis & Clark Expedition,* 2: 65.

7. One of the most remarkable characteristics of the frontier Ohio Valley forest was its phenomenal growth of grapevines, which in many places formed a crown canopy that darkened the space beneath it year-round. The historian Hulbert wrote, "The most impressive characteristic of the old forest was this absence of undergrowth; this could not live without sunlight, and the sunlight could not pierce through the dense overgrowth. This density of the tree tops was, also, an impressive feature of the old forests, since almost every tree was loaded with vines, especially those of the wild grape; these vines revelled in the sunshine found at the tree tops and ran riot from one tree to another binding them together with cords as strong as steel hawsers. In hundreds of cases, before the pioneers could cut down the trees, boys were sent up to cut away the vines which attached each tree to its neighbor." Archer Butler Hulbert, *The Ohio River: A Course of Empire* (New York: G. P. Putnam's Sons, 1906), 71-72. See also Winthrop Sargent, Journal, July 20, 1786, Massachusetts Historical Society, Boston; Solomon Drowne, Journal, May 11, 1789, Brown University, Providence, Rhode Island; Ray Swick, "'The Smoky Time': Ohio Frontier Valley," *History Today* 27 (April 1977): 236-237.

8. Thomas Rodney to Caesar A. Rodney, September 7, 1803, in Gratz, "Thomas Rodney," 43.2 (1919): 120-122.

9. Thomas Rodney to Caesar A. Rodney, September 8, 1803, ibid., 43.2 (1919): 123-124.

10. Meriwether Lewis had arrived in Wheeling the day before "in his Barge . . . and Canoos which he had to draw by Horse or Oxen over several riffs in the Ohio before he got here. . . . he Dines with us today—his Barge draws 2-1/2 feet water but our Batteau will draw only 8 Inches So that there is no riff below this that will stop us. . . . Lewes offered me a berth in his Barge but as he goes only to the mouth of the Ohio and then turns up the Misisipi it would not sute us—and our Boat will be Equally Comfortable." Thomas Rodney to Caesar A. Rodney, September 8, 1803, ibid., 43.2 (1919): 124. See also entry for September 9, 1803, below. Lewis and Rodney, according to the former, had first met the day before at Caldwell's store. Moulton, *Journals of the Lewis & Clark Expedition,* 2: 74-75. For more on the air gun, see Moulton, *Journals of the Lewis & Clark Expedition,* 2: 65, 66 n. 5.

11. Rodney's reference is most likely to Ebenezer Zane, who operated a tavern. Patterson, "Ebenezer Zane."

12. Publication of Alexander Mackenzie's account of his 1792-1793 transcontinental journey was probably the catalyst of Thomas Jefferson's decision to launch the Lewis and Clark expedition. He had been pursuing the idea for several years, since at least 1783 when he asked George Rogers Clark to consider leading a privately sponsored expedition to explore the West. Moulton, *Journals of the Lewis & Clark Expedition,* 2: 3.

13. Consin: Wisconsin. River St. Pear or St. Peter: Minnesota River.

14. Thomas Rodney's description of Lewis and Clark's mission is further confirmation of Thomas Jefferson's intention to keep its real destination a secret. Donald Jackson, ed., *Letters of the Lewis and Clark Expedition with Related Documents, 1783-1854* (Urbana: University of Illinois Press, 1962), 14n.

15. Rodney is mistaken about the relationship of the two men. William Clark (1770-1838) was the younger brother of George Rogers Clark, who had been prominent in the Old Northwest campaigns of the American Revolution. William Clark achieved his own fame in American history as the partner of Meriwether Lewis in the 1803-1806 Pacific Northwest expedition which bears their names. Born in Virginia, he moved with his family to Kentucky in 1785 and fought in the Ohio Valley Indian wars of the 1780s and 1790s, both in the Kentucky militia and the United States Army. After returning from the Pacific exploration, he moved to St. Louis where he was appointed brigadier general of militia for Louisiana Territory and principal Indian agent. While governor of Missouri Territory, 1813-1820, he fought in the War of 1812. Thereafter, except for an 1824-1825 term as surveyor general

for Illinois, Missouri, and Arkansas, Clark devoted his career to his duties as superintendent of Indian affairs. *Dictionary of American Biography,* s.v. "Clark, William," by Louise Phelps Kellogg; Moulton, *Journals of the Lewis & Clark Expedition,* 2: 513; John L. Loos, "Clark, William," in *Dictionary of American Military Biography,* 1: 182-185.

16. For more details and a sketch of the keelboat, see Moulton, *Journals of the Lewis & Clark Expedition,* 2: 65, 66 n. 7, 162.

17. Loose bowels or diarrhea.

18. This is possibly the letter published under the date line of the next day. Thomas Rodney to Caesar A. Rodney, September 12, 1803, in Gratz, "Thomas Rodney," 43.2 (1919): 124-125.

19. Moses Shepherd (1763-1832), one of Wheeling's wealthiest and most prominent citizens: chiefly remembered today as the first husband of Lydia Boggs Shepherd Cruger, a woman famous in Ohio Valley history as a frontier heroine and later as a political hostess. The couple's home, Shepherd Hall, a Federal style stone mansion constructed in 1798, ranked as one of the Ohio Valley's finest homes. Christin L. Stein, *Monument Place: A Palace for Lydia, June 29-October 11, 1992,* Oglebay Institute Exhibit Catalogue (Wheeling: n.p., 1992), 1, 3, 7, 14.

20. Thomas Rodney to Thomas Jefferson, September 12, 1803, Historical Society of Delaware. In this letter Rodney tells of the progress of his journey so far and speculates on the rest of the route. The letter to Gallatin is an abridged version of his letter to Jefferson. Thomas Rodney to Albert Gallatin, September 12, 1803, Historical Society of Delaware.

21. Rodney's probable reference here is to Vivant Denon, *Travels in Upper and Lower Egypt, During the Campaigns of General Bonaparte . . . ,* 2 vols. (London: F. Cundee, 1802). Rodney's baggage included Alexander Pope's translation of Homer's *Iliad* and *Odyssey.* See chapter 1, note 9 above. Rodney gives no indication as to which edition he was carrying.

22. Another natural phenomenon of the frontier Ohio Valley forest was its great hollow sycamores. Most of these trees, called the buttonwood by New Englanders, became hollow past the age of one hundred years, a fact which did not prevent them from continuing to grow. The valley's first white settlers, when hard-pressed for shelter, used the giant cavities as temporary homes for themselves and as stables for livestock. Large sycamores also were converted into boats, grain bins, troughs, barrels, and trunks. Donald Culross Peattie, *A Natural History of Trees of Eastern and Central North America* (Boston: Houghton Mifflin Company, 1950), 318-319; James Nourse, "Journey to Kentucky in 1775, Diary of James Nourse, Describing

His Trip from Virginia to Kentucky One Hundred and Fifty Years Ago," *Journal of American History* 19 (April-May-June 1925): 126; Winthrop Sargent, Journal, July 21, 28, 1786; Peter Haward, Journal, June 2, 1804, Hunterdon County Historical Society, Flemington, New Jersey.

23. Mad River is a tributary of Miami River in southwestern Ohio. Dayton North (Ohio) Quadrangle.

24. Tower Rock is at Grand Tower, Illinois, some fifty miles up the Mississippi River from the mouth of the Ohio River. Paul M. Angle, ed., *Illinois: Guide & Gazetteer* (Chicago: Rand McNally & Company, 1969), 284-285; Federal Writers' Project, *The WPA Guide to Illinois: The Federal Writers' Project Guide to 1930s Illinois*, rev. ed. (New York: Pantheon Books, 1983), 499-500.

25. The letters mentioned here are probably the ones he had written the day before. See entry for September 14, 1803, above. Thomas Rodney to Caesar A. Rodney, September 14, 1803, in Gratz, "Thomas Rodney," 43.2 (1919): 125-127. Thomas Rodney to John Dickinson, September 15, 1803, Historical Society of Delaware. This last is a general letter promising an account of his journey when he settled into his new responsibilities in the Territory of Mississippi.

26. Rodney had once owned a sloop of the same name. Hamilton, *Thomas Rodney*, 51.

27. Thomas Rodney to Caesar A. Rodney, September 17, 1803, in Gratz "Thomas Rodney," 43.2 (1919): 127.

28. Late eighteenth- and early nineteenth-century Americans apparently believed that the color green repelled insects. An explanation for this may be found in the high arsenic content of green paints and cloth dyes of the period, making them poisonous to bugs. Mary Butler, interview, by Ray Swick, Homewood House Museum, Johns Hopkins University, Baltimore, Maryland, June 26, 1992.

29. A statement with which Christian Schultz agreed: "The inhabitants of the Ohio country in general have very little of that unmeaning politeness, which we so much praise and admire in the Atlantic States. They are as yet the mere children of nature, and neither their virtues nor their vices are calculated to please refined tastes." Schultz, *Travels on an Inland Voyage*, 2: 20.

30. Dr. Gideon C. Forsyth was a prominent Wheeling physician and author of an important scientifically descriptive article about the Wheeling area, "Geological, Topographical and Medical Information Concerning the Eastern Part of the State of Ohio," *Medical Repository, Comprehending Original Essays and Intelligence Relative to Medicine, Chemistry, Natural History,*

Agriculture, Geography, and the Arts . . . , 2d hexade, 6 (February, March, April 1809): 350-358.

4. The Launching of the *Iris*

1. A coarse sieve.

2. Grave Creek enters the Ohio River on the West Virginia shore at Moundsville. Moundsville (West Virginia-Ohio) Quadrangle; Cramer, *The Navigator,* 3d ed., 24.

3. See chapter 6, note 24.

4. Captina Island lies over a mile upstream from Powhatan Point. Powhatan Point (West Virginia-Ohio) Quadrangle; Businessburg (Ohio-West Virginia) Quadrangle.

5. During the eighteenth and early nineteenth centuries, the word "plantation" frequently was employed in the Ohio Valley, as it traditionally had been for hundreds of years in England and America, in the same sense that "farm" is used today. The term had not yet attained, as it would later in the nineteenth century, its modern agricultural definition of a large piece of land in the American South or West Indies devoted to a single cash crop. Although by 1800 "farm" was rapidly surpassing "plantation" in popularity, the latter survived in the valley's personal writings and official records as late as the 1850s. Mary Helen Dohan, *Our Own Words* (New York: Alfred A. Knopf, 1974), 102-103.

6. Rodney's Statton Island is probably present-day Fish Creek Island near the mouth of Fish Creek. Powhatan Point (West Virginia-Ohio) Quadrangle; Cramer, *The Navigator,* 3d ed., 24.

7. Fish Creek flows into Ohio River on the West Virginia shore at Woodlands. Powhatan Point (West Virginia-Ohio) Quadrangle; Cramer, *The Navigator,* 3d ed., 24.

8. Logically this sentence belongs to the first paragraph of this entry, above. Captina Creek joins the Ohio River on the Ohio shore at Powhatan Point. In 1794, it was the scene of the "Battle of Captina," a skirmish with Shawnee Indians. Powhatan Point (West Virginia-Ohio) Quadrangle; Cramer, *The Navigator,* 3d ed., 24. See note 4 above.

9. A few months earlier, Thaddeus Harris noted them as "the islands called 'The Three Brothers.'" Harris, *Journal of a Tour,* 51. Shadrach, Meshach, and Abednego are the names of Daniel's companions who, with him, played dramatic roles in the Babylonian captivity of the Jews. Daniel 1-3.

The presently named Broadback (Middle Brother) Island at Belmont, West Virginia, and Eureka (Lower Brother) Island at Eureka, West Virginia, are the two remaining islands of the original "Three Brothers." French (Upper Brother) Island was joined to the mainland when its West Virginia channel silted in early in the twentieth century. Belmont (Ohio-West Virginia) Quadrangle; Willow Island (West Virginia-Ohio) Quadrangle; *Ohio River Navigation Charts: Foster, Ky., to New Martinsville, W. Va.* (Huntington, W.Va.: U.S. Army Engineer District, 1970), chart no. 165; Helen M. White, "Seven Islands Dot Pleasants County's River Frontage," *Parkersburg (W.Va.) News,* November 22, 1962.

10. Little Muskingum River flows into Ohio River on the Ohio shore four miles upstream from Marietta. Marietta (Ohio-West Virginia) Quadrangle. Here and again later in this entry, Rodney mistakenly calls this Muskingum Island. Later he corrects himself in a margin-located sentence, designating it "Duvalls Island," as it was indicated in Cramer. Duvall's Island, modern-day Buckley Island, lies between the mouth of Little Muskingum River and Muskingum River, adjacent to Marietta. Muskingum Island, which he correctly names in the next day's entry, is three miles downstream from Marietta. Marietta (Ohio-West Virginia) Quadrangle; Parkersburg (West Virginia-Ohio) Quadrangle; Cramer, *The Navigator,* 3d ed., 26. See also Samuel P. Hildreth, "History of a Voyage from Marietta to New Orleans in 1805," *American Pioneer* 1 (March 1842): 92.

11. Marietta was founded in 1788 by the New England-based Ohio Company of Associates, and named in honor of the Queen of France, Marie Antoinette. Samuel P. Hildreth, *Pioneer History: Being an Account of the First Examinations of the Ohio Valley, and the Early Settlement of the Northwest Territory.* . . . (Cincinnati: H. W. Derby & Co., 1848); Andrew R. L. Cayton, *The Frontier Republic: Ideology and Politics in the Ohio Country, 1780-1825* (Kent, Oh.: Kent State University Press, 1986); Andrew R. L. Cayton and Paula R. Riggs, *City into Town: The City of Marietta, Ohio, 1788-1988* (Marietta, Oh.: Dawes Memorial Library, Marietta College, 1991).

12. This sentence has been inserted here from its margin location in Rodney's manuscript. See note 8 above.

13. Muskingum River comes into Ohio River on the Ohio shore at Marietta. Marietta (Ohio-West Virginia) Quadrangle.

14. See note 10 above.

15. Griffin Greene (1749-1804), a native of Rhode Island, settled in Marietta in 1788. He was appointed a judge in the quarter sessions court of Washington County. His cousin, Nathanael Greene (1742-1786) served as a general and as a quartermaster general in the American Revolution, eventually becoming the commander of the southern theater. Hildreth, *Memoirs*

of the Early Pioneer Settlers of Ohio, with Narratives of Incidents and Occurrences in 1775 (Cincinnati, Oh.: H. W. Derby, 1854; reprint ed., Baltimore, Md.: Clearfield Company, 1995), 279-290; Richard K. Showman, ed., *The Papers of General Nathanael Greene* (Chapel Hill: University of North Carolina Press, 1976—), I: 107; *Dictionary of American Biography*, s.v. "Greene, Nathaniel," by Randolph G. Adams.

16. As no person of this name or any related spelling appears in the voluminous records of early Marietta or Washington County, including the census of 1803, Judge Pigot may have been a visitor to the area or a transient resident.

17. Rufus Putnam (1738-1824), a Revolutionary War general and leader of the New England settlers who founded Marietta. As he had no grandson in 1803 old enough for such a responsibility, Rodney is mistaken here. The general's son, Edwin Putnam (1776-1844) taught school. A graduate of Pennsylvania's Carlisle College, he had served in the Indian wars of the 1790s and had been a private secretary to Arthur St. Clair, governor of the Northwest Territory. Later, he was admitted to the bar and became a judge of common pleas in Zanesville, Ohio. Eben Putnam, comp., *A History of the Putnam Family in England and America: Recording the Ancestry and Descendants of John Putnam of Danvers, Mass., Jan Poutman of Albany, N.Y., Thomas Putnam of Hartford, Conn.* (Salem, Mass.: Salem Press Publishing and Printing Co., 1891), 287-288; Robert E. Putnam, editor of the occasional *Bulletin of the American Friends of Puttenham,* interview by Ray Swick, November 24, 1996; *Dictionary of American Biography*, s.v. "Putnam, Rufus," by Beverley W. Bond, Jr.; James Lawton Memoirs, 1878-1879, Ruth Lawton Lee (Mrs. Robert E. Lee), Belpre, Ohio.

18. Marietta was the West's chief center of shipbuilding, an industry that began in 1801 and declined rapidly after President Jefferson's 1807 embargo that forbade export of all goods from the United States. Using the region's abundant supply of virgin timber, the town's New England shipwrights and seamen built ocean-going vessels that shipped the valley's farm produce to New Orleans and the West Indies. Archer Butler Hulbert, "Western Ship-Building," *American Historical Review* 21 (July 1916): 720-733; Leland D. Baldwin, *The Keelboat Age on Western Waters* (Pittsburgh: University of Pittsburgh Press, 1941), 166-173.

In early May 1803, Thaddeus Harris recorded the river traffic at Marietta to include: the schooner *Dorcas and Sally,* 70 tons, built at Wheeling and rigged at Marietta; the schooner *Amity,* 103 tons from Pittsburgh; the ship *Pittsburgh,* 275 tons, from Pittsburgh, with a cargo of 1700 barrels of flour and "with the rest of her cargo in flat-bottomed boats"; and the brig *Mary Avery*, 130 tons, built at Marietta. Harris, *Journal of a Tour*, 52-53.

19. Colonel Ebenezer Sproat (1752-1805), a native of Massachusetts, was a Revolutionary War veteran and a surveyor by profession. Settling in Marietta in 1788, Sproat served for many years as one of the Northwest Territory's first sheriffs. Samuel P. Hildreth, *Memoirs of the Early Pioneer Settlers of Ohio*, 230-240.

20. This sentence has been inserted here from its margin location in the manuscript.

21. This is an example that further confirms Rodney was using Cramer. See Cramer, *The Navigator*, 3d ed., 26.

22. Known at various times in its history as Briscoe Island, Little Island, Middle Island, Halfway Island, Bailey Island, and Upper James Island, it is today called Vienna Island. Albert J. Woofter [and Ray Swick], "All Ohio's Islands Have Special Place in History," *Parkersburg (W.Va.) News*, June 14, 1987.

23. Designated James Island at the time of Rodney's visit, it is today called Neale Island. In the 1830s and early 1840s, it was one of the homes of the orphaned Thomas Jonathan (later "Stonewall") Jackson, a grandson and nephew of the Neale family. H. E. Matheny, *Wood County, West Virginia, in Civil War Times with an Account of the Guerrilla Warfare in the Little Kanawha Valley* (Parkersburg, W.Va.: Trans-Allegheny Books, 1987), 568-569.

24. Little Kanawha River flows into the Ohio River at Parkersburg. Parkersburg, founded in 1785, was in Rodney's time known as Newport; it is today the seat of Wood County, West Virginia. Parkersburg (West Virginia-Ohio) Quadrangle; Alvaro F. Gibbens, *Wood County Formation: A Century of Progress: History of Divisions, Courts, Buildings, Past and Present, and Engravings of the Same* (Morgantown, W.Va.: Acme Press, 1899), 15-17.

25. Belpre, Ohio, is situated on the Ohio River opposite the mouth of Little Kanawha River and Parkersburg, West Virginia. Belpre, established in 1789 as an offshoot of Marietta, derives its name from a contraction of Belle Prairie, French for beautiful meadow. Parkersburg (West Virginia-Ohio) Quadrangle; Hildreth, *Pioneer History*, 349-418.

26. For Blennerhassett Island see Parkersburg (West Virginia-Ohio) Quadrangle; Little Hocking (Ohio-West Virginia) Quadrangle.

27. Harman (1764-1831) and Margaret Agnew (1771-1842) Blennerhassett, well-to-do members of the Irish gentry, emigrated to the United States in 1796. It was a move prompted by their marriage—which was incestuous, Mrs. Blennerhassett being her husband's niece—and by his involvement

with the subversive Society of United Irishmen. The Blennerhassetts' huge Palladian mansion, completed in 1800 on the Ohio River island two miles below the mouth of the Little Kanawha, was considered the Ohio Valley's most beautiful home. Blennerhassett Island became nationally famous in 1806-1807 as the center of Aaron Burr's "conspiracy." It is today a West Virginia state park. Hildreth, *Memoirs*, 491-528; William H. Safford, *The Blennerhassett Papers. . . .* (Cincinnati: Moore, Wilstach, Keys & Co., 1861); Milton Lomask, *Aaron Burr*, vol. 2: *The Conspiracy and Years of Exile, 1805-1836* (New York: Farrar, Straus, Giroux, 1982), 58-64, 127-133, 186-192, 259-293; Fortescue Cuming, *Sketches of a Tour to the Western Country. . . .* (Pittsburgh: Cramer, Spear & Eichbaum, Franklin Head Bookstore, 1810), 109-111; Ray Swick, "Aaron Burr's Visit to Blennerhassett Island," *West Virginia History* 35 (April 1974): 205-219.

28. When the Blennerhassetts purchased the upper part of the island in 1799, it was owned by Elijah Backus (1759-1811), a Marietta lawyer and land speculator. Hildreth, "History of a Voyage," 92; Reno W. Backus, comp., *The Backus Families of Early New England* (Duluth, Minn.: Service Printers, 1966), 44.

29. Little Hockhocking Creek is Little Hocking River, which enters the Ohio River on the Ohio shore at Little Hocking. Little Hocking (Ohio-West Virginia) Quadrangle; Cramer, *The Navigator*, 3d ed., 27.

30. Rodney's "Newberry" was Newbury, so named after Newburyport, Massachusetts. The settlement died out in the nineteenth century but the misspelling by Rodney and others is perpetuated on today's maps in the name of a cemetery and an island. This is not to be confused with present-day Newbury, a town due east of Cleveland. Lubeck (West Virginia-Ohio) Quadrangle; Cramer, *The Navigator*, 3d ed., 27; Laura Curtis Preston, *History and Some Anecdotes of the Settlement of Newbury, Washington County, Ohio* (Marietta, Oh.: Marietta Journal Print, 1909).

Mustapha Island (Mustaphy Island in Cramer) is situated opposite the terminus of the Athens County, Ohio-Washington County boundary. Lubeck (West Virginia-Ohio) Quadrangle; Cramer, *The Navigator*, 3d ed., 27.

31. Big Hockhocking River is today's Hocking River, which flows into the Ohio River at Hockingport, Ohio. Coolville (Ohio-West Virginia) Quadrangle. Lee Creek falls into Ohio River on the West Virginia shore at Lee Creek. Lubeck (West Virginia-Ohio) Quadrangle. The final sentence of this paragraph has been inserted here from its margin location in the manuscript.

32. One of the earliest white settlements on the Upper Ohio, Belleville was founded in 1785 by a group of Philadelphia merchants who owned a

tract of 91,000 acres in the vicinity. Lubeck (West Virginia-Ohio) Quadrangle; Pond Creek (West Virginia-Ohio) Quadrangle; Samuel P. Hildreth, "A Brief History of the Settlement at Belville, in Western Virginia . . . ," *The Hesperian; A Monthly Miscellany of General Literature, Original and Select* 3 (June 1839): 25-34; (July 1839): 109-115; (August 1839): 194-199; (September 1839): 269-277; (October 1839): 352-354; (November 1839): 431-435; Roy Bird Cook, "Fort Belleville, A Forgotten Frontier Post," *West Virginia History* 9 (October 1947): 57-69.

Belleville Island, adjacent to Belleville, was joined to the mainland in 1968 when its West Virginia channel was filled in during the construction of the Belleville Dam. Cramer, *The Navigator*, 3d ed., 27; Pond Creek (West Virginia-Ohio) Quadrangle.

33. After peeling about an 18-inch high strip of bark from trees, Indians of the Ohio and Mississippi valleys utilized red ochre and charcoal to depict in picture writing the latest incidents of their daily lives, including war campaigns, hunting expeditions, religious thoughts, and even taunts aimed at their white enemies. McDermott, "Western Journals of Dr. George Hunter," 95; Paul A. W. Wallace, "Historic Indian Paths of Pennsylvania," *Pennsylvania Magazine of History and Biography* 76 (October 1952): 428-429; Sigfus Olafson, "The Painted Trees and the War Road, Paint Creek, Fayette County, W. Va.," *West Virginia Archeologist* 10 (September 1958): 3-6; James M. Adovasio, comp., *The Prehistory of the Paintsville Reservoir, Johnson and Morgan Counties, Kentucky*, Ethnology Monographs, no. 6 (Pittsburgh: Department of Anthropology, University of Pittsburgh, 1982), 50.

34. Rodney was mistaken as to the location, for Devil's Hole Creek is the modern-day Shade River in Meigs County, Ohio. The stream derived its earlier name from a rock shelter near its mouth called "The Devils Hole." John Melish, *Travels in the United States of America . . .*, 2 vols. Philadelphia: Printed for the Author, 1812), 2: 113; Dwight L. Smith and S. Winifred Smith, eds., "The Journey of a Pennsylvania Quaker to Pioneer Ohio," *Bulletin of the Cincinnati Historical Society* 26 (January 1968): 30; Zadok Cramer, *The Navigator; Containing Directions for Navigating the Monongahela, Allegheny, Ohio and Mississippi Rivers . . .*, 8th ed. (Pittsburgh: Cramer, Spear and Eichbaum, 1814), 96.

35. Later corrected to Ambersons by Rodney, Amberson's Island is today Buffington Island, situated opposite the mouth of West Virginia's Little Sandy Creek. Named for John Amberson (or Emerson) who attempted in 1785 to politically organize the Ohio Valley's squatter population, the island was purchased in 1797 by Joel Buffington—whom Rodney mistook for Amberson.

Buffington Island gained national notoriety in 1863 as the site of a Civil War battle, and for that reason remains today, after Blennerhassett, the Ohio's second most famous island. *Fifty Ohio Rarities: 1653-1802* (Ann Arbor, Mich.: Clements Library, 1953), 19, 21; U.S. Department of Navy, Office of the Chief of Naval Operations, Naval History Division, *Civil War Naval Chronology, 1861-1865,* 5 vols. (Washington: Government Printing Office, 1961-1965), 3: III-112, 118; Myron J. Smith, Jr., "Gunboats at Buffington: The U.S. Navy and Morgan's Raid, 1863," *West Virginia History* 44 (winter 1983): 97-110.

36. Presumably Joel Buffington.

37. Big Sandy Creek enters the Ohio River at Ravenswood, West Virginia. Ravenswood (West Virginia-Ohio) Quadrangle.

38. Rocky Island is Rodney's designation for a temporary low water situation. No island is indicated in Cramer. No island presently exists at the location. Cramer, *The Navigator,* 3d ed., 28; Ravenswood (West Virginia-Ohio) Quadrangle.

39. By his 8th edition, Cramer was calling Goose Island "George's or Goose Island." The island no longer exists. Cramer, *The Navigator,* 3d ed., 28; Cramer, *The Navigator,* 8th ed., 97; Ravenswood (West Virginia-Ohio) Quadrangle.

40. What Cramer first designates as Letart's Falls, he later more appropriately calls Letart's Rapids. The name "falls," as Rodney and other travelers indicated, was a misnomer as the spot exhibited nothing more than a strong current as easily detected as the boat channel. A 1795 traveler noted that the falls "took [its name] from a Frenchman, who was drown'd there many Years agoe." This was James Le Tort, an Indian trader present in the area before 1740. Cramer, *The Navigator,* 3d ed., 28; Cramer, *The Navigator,* 8th ed., 97-98; Thomas Chapman, "Journal of a Journey through the United States, 1795-6," *Historical Magazine and Notes and Queries, Concerning the Antiquities, History and Biography of America,* 2d series, vol. 5 (June 1869): 360; Victor Collot, *A Journey in North America . . . ,* 3 vols. (Paris: Arthur Bertrand, Bookseller, 1826; reprint ed., Firenze, Italy: O. Lange, 1924; reprint ed., New York: AMS Press, 1974), 1: 77-78; Hildreth, "History of a Voyage," 94; Charles A. Hanna, *The Wilderness Trail or the Ventures and Adventures of the Pennsylvania Traders on the Allegheny Path with Some New Annals of the Old West, and the Records of Some Strong Men and Some Bad Ones,* 2 vols. (New York: G. P. Putnam's Sons, 1911), 1: 166-168; Cuming, *Sketches of a Tour,* 120.

Letart Island is situated in the Ohio River between Letart Falls, Ohio, and Letart, West Virginia. New Haven (West Virginia-Ohio) Quadrangle.

41. West Creek joins the Ohio River on the West Virginia shore about a mile upstream from Racine, Ohio. New Haven (West Virginia-Ohio) Quadrangle.

42. While Sliding Hill does not appear on modern maps, Sliding Hill Creek enters the Ohio River on the West Virginia shore at Hartford City. Ibid.; Chester (Ohio-West Virginia) Quadrangle; Cramer, *The Navigator,* 3d ed., 29.

43. Eight Mile Island is situated in the Ohio River opposite Cheshire, Ohio. Cheshire (West Virginia-Ohio) Quadrangle.

44. Six Mile Island, having been joined by siltation to the West Virginia shore, does not appear on modern maps. Ibid., Addison (Ohio-West Virginia) Quadrangle; Cramer, *The Navigator,* 3d ed., 29.

45. Kyger Creek, variously spelled Tyger, Cyger, and Kayger, enters the Ohio River a mile above Addison, Ohio. Addison (Ohio-West Virginia) Quadrangle; Cramer, *The Navigator,* 3d ed., 29; Cramer, *The Navigator,* 8th ed., 100. Campaign Creek flows into the Ohio River at Addison, Ohio. Cramer, *The Navigator,* 3d ed., 29; Addison (Ohio-West Virginia) Quadrangle.

46. Kanawha River enters Ohio River at Point Pleasant, West Virginia. Gallipolis (Ohio-West Virginia) Quadrangle.

47. For a detailed account of George Washington's extensive western land claims, see Hugh G. Cleland, *George Washington in the Ohio Valley* (Pittsburgh: University of Pittsburgh Press, 1955), 233-330; Eugene E. Prussing, *The Estate of George Washington, Deceased* (Boston: Little, Brown, and Company, 1927), 301-348.

48. The October 10, 1774, Battle of Point Pleasant, the major engagement of Dunmore's War, pitted eleven hundred German and Scotch-Irish backwoods militia under Andrew Lewis against a thousand Indians led by Cornstalk. The former's victory helped to strengthen Virginia's charter claim to the land northwest of the Ohio River. Robert L. Kerby, "The Other War in 1774: Dunmore's War," *West Virginia History* 36 (October 1974): 8-12.

49. Elizabeth Hog (1769-1830), wife of Jesse Bennet (1769-1842), a prominent physician and militia officer of Mason County, (West) Virginia. Some medical authorities credit Dr. Bennet with performing the first Caesarean section in the United States, which he performed on his wife in 1794 in Rockingham County, Virginia. Aquilla L. Knight, "Life and Times of Jesse Bennet, M.D., 1769-1842," *Southern Historical Magazine* 2 (July 1892): 1-13; Dorothy Poling, "Jesse Bennet, Pioneer Physician and Surgeon," *West Virginia History* 12 (January 1951): 87-128; Joseph L. Miller, "Dr. Jessee [sic] Bennet, (1769-1842) Pioneer Surgeon. Dr. Aquilla Leighton Knight, (1823-

1897) Humanist, Old Virginia Doctors: 'Who Saw Life Steadily and Saw It Whole,'" *Virginia Medical Monthly, Official Organ of the Medical Society of Virginia* 55 (January 1929): 711-714.

50. Gallipolis Island, now much smaller in size, is situated adjacent to Gallipolis, Ohio. Gallipolis (Ohio-West Virginia) Quadrangle.

51. Gallipolis ("City of the Gauls") was founded in 1790 by a group of four hundred French fleeing the revolution which had engulfed their home-land the year before. Ill-fitted for wilderness living and attacked by sickness, the population dwindled rapidly until it numbered less than one hundred by the time of Rodney's visit. Lee Soltow and Margaret Soltow, "A Settle-ment That Failed: The French in Early Gallipolis, an Enlightening Letter, and an Explanation," *Ohio History* 94 (winter-spring 1985): 46-67.

5. Wood Nymphs and Other Adventures

1. Guyan Creek (Rodney's Little Quiendot, Cramer's Little Guyandot) enters the Ohio River on the West Virginia shore at the Mason County-Cabell County border. Cramer, *The Navigator,* 3d ed., 30; Glenwood (West Virginia-Ohio) Quadrangle.

2. Guyandotte River flows into Ohio River on the West Virginia shore at Huntington. Huntington (Ohio-West Virginia) Quadrangle.

3. Big Sandy River. Catlettsburg (Ohio-West Virginia-Kentucky) Quad-rangle.

4. The eastern spiny soft-shelled turtle *(Amyda ferox spinifera).* Archie F. Carr, *Handbook of Turtles: The Turtles of the United States, Canada, and Baja California* (Ithaca, N.Y.: Comstock Publishing Associates, 1952), 414, 426-431.

5. A few years later another traveler called it Hanging Rock. Cuming, *Sketches of a Tour,* 136.

6. Little Sandy River enters the Ohio River on the Kentucky shore at Greenup. Greenup (Kentucky-Ohio) Quadrangle.

7. Unable to save forts on the Hudson River, George Washington's small force was harried across New Jersey in November and December 1776. He was determined, if at all possible, to defend the Delaware River crossings and hence the American capital, Philadelphia. Rodney previously had re-corded how God's archangel had appeared in visions revealing that he, who commanded a small militia force at the time, would be instrumental in reversing Washington's misfortune. Which he was!

Pressure on Washington subsided, however, when, taking advantage of the British retirement into winter quarters, he launched a Christmas offensive across the Delaware River. He surprised and defeated British forces at Trenton and Princeton before encamping for the winter at Morristown.

Other accounts of Rodney's visions and performance in this campaign are found elsewhere in his papers. Hamilton, *Anglo-American Law*, 24-31.

8. Little Scioto River flows into the Ohio River on the Ohio shore at Sciotoville. New Boston (Ohio-Kentucky) Quadrangle.

9. Scioto River, which Rodney calls "Great Siota," falls into the Ohio River on the Ohio shore at Portsmouth. Friendship (Kentucky-Ohio) Quadrangle.

Subject to frequent flooding, Alexandria's location was not as secure as Rodney suggested. The settlement "gradually dwindled away" and by 1819 was described by a river traveler as "a small scabby and declining village. . . . composed of 3 houses. Those are going fast to decay—their roofs fractured and their window sashes filled with striped petticoats, old hats and pillows." Friendship (Kentucky-Ohio) Quadrangle; Nelson W. Evans, *A History of Scioto County, Ohio, together with a Pioneer Record of Southern Ohio* (Portsmouth, Oh.: Nelson W. Evans, 1903), 413, 472; Jonathan Devol, Journal of a Voyage on the Ohio River, entry for March 22, 1819, Jerry Barker Devol, Marietta, Ohio.

10. Turkey Creek enters the Ohio River on the Ohio shore near Friendship, Ohio. Friendship (Kentucky-Ohio) Quadrangle.

11. Kinniconick Creek comes into Ohio River at Garrison, Kentucky. Garrison (Kentucky-Ohio) Quadrangle.

12. Rodney's Vance Ville is the present-day Vanceburg, Kentucky. Salt Lick Creek flows into the Ohio River on the Kentucky shore at Vanceburg. Vanceburg (Kentucky-Ohio) Quadrangle.

13. Pond Run enters the Ohio River on the Kentucky shore opposite Rome (Stout Post Office), Ohio. Stout Run flows into the Ohio River near Rome, Ohio, and nearly opposite Pond Run. Concord (Ohio-Kentucky) Quadrangle.

Prestonville. According to Cramer, this is "Preston, or Graham's Station, in what is called Kennedy's bottom." There is no designation by any of these names on modern maps. If Rodney's distance calculation is correct, the location is beyond Taylor Chapel, Kentucky, and probably before Brush Creek Island. Cramer, *The Navigator*, 3d ed., 32; Concord (Ohio-Kentucky) Quadrangle.

14. Possibly a reference to Brush Creek Island, Manchester Island No. 1, and Manchester Island No. 2. Concord (Ohio-Kentucky) Quadrangle; Manchester Islands (Kentucky-Ohio) Quadrangle.

15. Sycamore Creek joins the Ohio River at Concord, Kentucky. Concord (Ohio-Kentucky) Quadrangle. Donaldson Creek falls into the Ohio River near Wrightsville, Ohio. Manchester Islands (Kentucky-Ohio) Quadrangle.

16. The two islands. Manchester Island No. 1 and Manchester Island No. 2; see note 14 above. The little village of Manchester is Manchester, Ohio. Manchester Islands (Kentucky-Ohio) Quadrangle.

17. Cabin Creek comes into Ohio River at Springdale, Kentucky. Orangeburg (Kentucky) Quadrangle. Crooked Creek enters the Ohio River at the Lewis County, Kentucky-Mason County boundary. Maysville East (Ohio-Kentucky) Quadrangle.

18. What "settlement" means here is uncertain. A few years later another traveler mentions "William Brookes's creek, below which is a floating mill, and Brookes's good house and fine farm." Cuming, *Sketches of a Tour*, 147.

19. Rodney later notes that the settlement was called Maysville as well as Limestone. Established in 1784, incorporated as a town and officially named "Maysville" three years later, Limestone's harbor, formed by a point of land which stretched into the river, was the finest on the Ohio. By the 1790s the settlement had become Kentucky's chief commercial port and main place of entry for emigration from the Ohio. Josiah Murdoch Espy, *Memorandums of a Tour Made by Josiah Espy in the States of Ohio and Kentucky and Indiana Territory in 1805* (Cincinnati: Robert Clarke & Co., 1870), 17; Edna M. Kenton, *Simon Kenton: His Life and Period, 1755-1836* (Garden City, N.Y.: Doubleday, Doran & Company, 1930), 60; G. Glenn Clift, *History of Maysville and Mason County* (Lexington, Ky.: Transylvania Printing Co., 1936), 46, 73.

20. Thomas Rodney to Caesar A. Rodney, October 3, 1803, in Gratz, "Thomas Rodney," 43.2 (1919): 127-129.

21. The town changed its name to Maysville in honor of John May, the principal local landowner. Federal Writers' Project, *Kentucky: A Guide to the Bluegrass State* (New York: Harcourt, Brace and Company, 1939), 363; Robert M. Rennick, *Kentucky Place Names* (Lexington: University Press of Kentucky, 1984), 193. Limestone Creek flows into the Ohio River on the Kentucky shore. Maysville West (Kentucky-Ohio) Quadrangle.

22. Charlestown, Kentucky—"Charleston" in 1800—was situated six miles downstream from Maysville at the mouth of Lawrence Creek. Rodney mistakenly identifies it as the seat of Mason County, which at the time was actually Washington. "Kentucky, Reduced from Elihu Barker's Large Map," in Carey, *Carey's General Atlas*, 40; Federal Writers' Project, *Kentucky*, 363; Clift, *History of Maysville and Mason County*, 72, 195-197; Lewis Collins,

Collins' Historical Sketches of Kentucky . . . , 2 vols. (Covington, Ky.: Collins & Co., 1874) 1: 21, 54, 56.

23. Eagle Creek flows into the Ohio River over a mile upstream from Ripley, Ohio. Maysville West (Kentucky-Ohio) Quadrangle.

24. Bracken Creek now falls into the Ohio River at Augusta, Kentucky. Augusta, Kentucky, also was known as Bracken Court House. Rennick, *Kentucky Place Names*, 10; Cramer, *The Navigator*, 3d ed., 34; Higginsport (Ohio-Kentucky) Quadrangle.

25. These sentences have been inserted here from their margin location in the manuscript.

26. Rodney's journal is interrupted here at the end of a manuscript page with a non-continuing page which is relocated to a more appropriate place in this day's entry. See note 27 below.

27. This paragraph has been relocated here from its original position in the manuscript. See note 26 above.

28. Indian Creek enters the Ohio River at Point Pleasant, Ohio. Laurel (Ohio-Kentucky) Quadrangle.

29. While Rodney's information is too nebulous to aid identification of this creek, the matter is further complicated by the fact that Little Indian Creek joins Ohio River at New Richmond, Ohio, some four miles downstream from Indian Creek. New Richmond (Ohio-Kentucky) Quadrangle; see also note 28 above.

30. Five Mile Creek falls into Ohio River on the Ohio shore opposite Silver Grove, Kentucky. Little Miami River enters Ohio River within the present limits of the city of Cincinnati and opposite Fort Thomas, Kentucky. Newport (Kentucky-Ohio) Quadrangle.

31. Columbia, Ohio, founded in 1788 by Benjamin Stites, was situated one-half mile below the mouth of the Little Miami. It is now a part of eastern Cincinnati. *History of Cincinnati and Hamilton County, Ohio.* . . . (Cincinnati: S. B. Nelson & Co., 1894), 33, 54-55; Beverley W. Bond, Jr., *The Foundations of Ohio* (Columbus: Ohio State Archaeological and Historical Society, 1941), 294-295.

32. Licking River flows into the Ohio River on the Kentucky shore. Covington (Kentucky-Ohio) Quadrangle.

6. Earthworks, Prehistoric Bones, and Two River Towns

1. Thomas Hill Williams "is a Meritorious young man out of business at present He has had a Classical Education and is a Correct Schollar and has read the Law He has wrote in Some of the Offices at Washington and

heretofore in Govr. Volunts [Blount's] office at Tennessee He is a Sober and Sedate young man and a man of Strong Talants—and understands Surveying &c." Thomas Rodney to Caesar A. Rodney, December 8-10, 1803, in Gratz, "Thomas Rodney," 43.3 (1919): 215.

Rodney's estimate was borne out, for Williams (1780-1840) had before him a brilliant career, serving as register of the land office for the Territory of Mississippi (1805); secretary of the territory, (1805-1806, 1807); acting governor (1806, 1809); collector of customs at New Orleans (1810); and U.S. senator from Mississippi (1817-1829). A native of North Carolina, Williams died a resident of Tennessee. Robert Williams to Thomas Jefferson, August 10, 1805, in Carter, *Territorial Papers, Territory of Mississippi*, 5: 417, et passim.; *Biographical Directory of the United States Congress, 1774-1989*, Bicentennial Edition, s.v. "Williams, Thomas Hill"; Richard Aubrey McLemore, *A History of Mississippi*, 2 vols. (Hattiesburg: University & College Press of Mississippi, 1973), 1: 250-253; Cecil L. Sumners, *The Governors of Mississippi* (Gretna, La.: Pelican Publishing Company, 1980), 38, 39.

2. Williams did not join the expedition until it reached Louisville. Thomas Rodney to Caesar A. Rodney, October 16, 1803, December 8-10, 1803, December 17, 1803, in Gratz, "Thomas Rodney," 43.2 (1919): 133; 43.3 (1919): 215, 216. See entries for October 8 and 15, 1803, below.

3. Born in Scotland in 1736 into a prosperous mercantile family, Arthur St. Clair attended the University of Edinburgh, entered the British army in 1757, and served in Canada during the French and Indian War. His 1760 marriage to Phoebe Bayard, a Boston heiress, gave him the means to purchase a 4,000 acre estate in western Pennsylvania's Ligonier Valley. Joining the American army at the outbreak of the Revolution, eventually he was made a major general. After the war he entered politics, was elected to the Continental Congress, becoming its president in 1787. The same year he was named governor of the Northwest Territory and served in that post until his rabid Federalist policies and opposition to Ohio statehood led to his dismissal by President Jefferson in 1802. St. Clair retired to his Ligonier Valley home where he died in poverty in 1818. *Dictionary of American Biography*, s.v. "St. Clair, Arthur," by Randolph C. Downes; William Henry Smith, ed., *The St. Clair Papers. The Life and Public Services of Arthur St. Clair . . .*, 2 vols. (Cincinnati: Robert Clarke & Co., 1882); Patrick J. Furlong, "St. Clair, Arthur," in *Dictionary of American Military Biography*, 3: 947-950.

4. Fort Washington, erected 1789-1790 as a protective stockade for the infant settlement, figured importantly in the 1790s Indian wars. As revealed by General Josiah Harmar, its source of building materials was unique:

"About 40 or 50 Kentucky Boats has begun, and will complete it [Fort Washington]—*Limestone* is the grand mart of Kentucky; whenever Boats arrive there, they are scarcely of any Value to the Owners—they are frequently set adrift in order to make room for . . . arrival of others—." The fort's roof and palisade were painted red as were a number of the town's houses—red paint was the cheapest and most available on the Ohio Valley frontier. Even before being abandoned by the United States Army in 1804, Fort Washington, as noted by Rodney, was falling into ruins. Only one blockhouse remained in 1810. Josiah Harmar to Henry Knox, January 14, 1790, Letter Book G, Josiah Harmar Papers, William L. Clements Library, Ann Arbor, Mich. See also Wiley Sword, *President Washington's Indian War: The Struggle for the Old Northwest, 1790-1795* (Norman: University of Oklahoma Press, 1985); Alexander Wilson to Alexander Lawson, April 4, 1810, in William Jardine, "Life of Alexander Wilson," in Alexander Wilson and Charles Lucian Bonaparte, *American Ornithology: or, The Natural History of the Birds of the United States*, 3 vols. (London: Chatto and Windus, 1876), 1: lxxv; Richard C. Knopf, Raymond S. Baby, and Dwight L. Smith, "The Re-Discovery of Fort Washington," *Bulletin of the Historical and Philosophical Society of Ohio* 11 (January 1953): 6; Wallace, *Thirty Thousand Miles*, 270.

5. Cincinnati was founded in 1788 opposite the mouth of the Licking River by Matthias Denman, a New Jersey land speculator. Initially called "Losantiville," its name was changed in 1790 by Arthur St. Clair to honor the American army's elite Society of the Cincinnati. Created the capital of the Northwest Territory in 1790, the settlement became an important military base the same year with the completion of Fort Washington. By 1800 its population had reached 750 and its future economic importance established as an export center for Ohio Valley farm produce. Incorporated as a town in 1802, it attained city status in 1819. Charles Cist, *Sketches and Statistics of Cincinnati in 1859* ([Cincinnati: Printed and Published for the Author,] 1859), 164; Lee Shepard, "When, and by Whom, Was Cincinnati Founded?" *Bulletin of the Historical and Philosophical Society of Ohio* 7 (January 1949): 28-34; Richard C. Wade, *The Urban Frontiers: The Rise of Western Cities, 1790-1830* (Cambridge: Harvard University Press, 1959), 26; John A. Jakle, *Images of the Ohio Valley: A Historical Geography of Travel, 1740 to 1860* (New York: Oxford University Press, 1977), 123.

6. James Findlay (1770-1835) and Jane Irwin Findlay had lived in Virginia and Kentucky before settling in Cincinnati. He had served in the legislative council of the Northwest Territory, and was now the receiver of public moneys in the recently established land office at Cincinnati. A lawyer by

profession, Findlay became prominent as a United States marshal, mayor of Cincinnati, a state militia and regular army general with service in defense against a potential Aaron Burr expedition and in the War of 1812, a member of Congress, and a Democratic candidate for state governor. War of 1812 Fort Findlay and the present-day city of Findlay, Ohio, were named in his honor. *Dictionary of American Biography,* s.v. "Findlay, James," by Reginald C. McGrane.

Doctor Sulman. John Sellman (1764-1827), a native of Annapolis, Maryland, was a surgeon's mate with Anthony Wayne's army when it came to Fort Washington in 1793. The next year he resigned to practice medicine in Cincinnati, where he remained for the rest of his life. Otto Juettner, *1785- 1909. Daniel Drake and His Followers: Historical and Biographical Sketches* (Cincinnati: Harvey Publishing Company, 1909), 29, 30, 32, 87.

7. For further details on the Cincinnati earthworks, see [S. Frederick] Starr, "Archaeology of Hamilton County, Ohio," *Journal of the Cincinnati Museum of Natural History* 23 (June 1960): 85-87, et passim; *History of Cincinnati and Hamilton County,* 26.

8. St. Clair "found a piece of Milled Coper Coin which he sent to Mr. Jefferson quite Legible which was found in the hill between the higher and lower part of the Town in Cutting a Street through it in doing which they Cut through an Indian Mound where several other Curiosities were found— a Pewter impression of the piece of Copper Coin was sent to one of the Eastern States and I think I remember to have seen a publication respecting it that it was a piece of German Coin." Thomas Rodney to Caesar A. Rodney, October 7, 1803, in Gratz, "Thomas Rodney," 43.2 (1919): 130.

9 See note 17 below.

10. Rodney had written a letter to his son from Cincinnati. Thomas Rodney to Caesar A. Rodney, October 7-8, 1803, in Gratz, "Thomas Rodney," 43.2 (1919): 129-131.

11. Mill Creek enters the Ohio River in Cincinnati. Covington (Kentucky-Ohio) Quadrangle.

12. Other than Rodney's mention of it here, identification of Bushes Ferry remains elusive. Rodney's reference to a French settlement is curious and probably mistaken. To date, there appears to be no documentary or archaeological evidence of French habitation on the site.

13. When Ohio became a state in 1803, the Ohio-Indiana Territory boundary was stipulated to start at the mouth of Great Miami River. Today, the Great Miami River enters the Ohio River a short distance upstream from the present-day border. John D. Barnhart and Dorothy L. Riker, *Indiana to*

1816: The Colonial Period (Indianapolis: Indiana Historical Bureau & Indiana Historical Society, 1971), 311-312; Lawrenceburg (Kentucky-Indiana-Ohio) Quadrangle.

14. The tamarind is the fruit of a tropical evergreen tree used in making candies, cakes, jellies, sauces, cooling drinks, and to concoct a mild laxative. It was imported in trading vessels from the West Indies. Thomas S. Elias, *The Complete Trees of North America: Field Guide and Natural History* (New York: Van Nostrand Reinhold Company, 1980), 650-651; *Academic American Encyclopedia*, 1993 ed., s.v. "tamarind."

15. Gunpowder Creek falls into the Ohio River on the Kentucky shore about two miles above Big Bone Creek. Rising Sun (Kentucky-Indiana) Quadrangle; see note 16 below.

16. Big Bone Creek enters the Ohio River at the Boone County, Kentucky-Gallatin County boundary. Patriot (Kentucky-Indiana) Quadrangle.

17. "Captn. Lewis had taken the Large Tusk lately found which is ten feet from the root to the point in a straight line and measured along the Centre of the Tooth or Tusk along the Curve is fifteen feet and weighs a hundred and eight pounds . . . I measured the face part of a head (the rest being gone) that was three feet a cross in the widest part—and I measured the Sockets of two Shoulder blades that were 9 Inches the widest way their form being oval." Thomas Rodney to Caesar A. Rodney, October 16, 1803, in Gratz, "Thomas Rodney," 43.2 (1919): 132-133.

Lying one and one-half miles east of the Ohio River, Big Bone Lick was an early attraction to white explorers and traders. Baron Charles De Longueuil was the first recorded visitor (1729). Christopher Gist, George Croghan, and Thomas Hutchins are among other famous names who stopped to view and take away bones of mammoths, mastodons, an American species of horse, bison, elk, ground sloths, and other prehistoric mammals which had died on the site.

The bulk of the remaining bones were removed by Dr. William Goforth (1766-1817) of Cincinnati in May 1803. He was swindled out of them by the notorious English traveler Thomas Ashe—also known as "the infamous Ashe"—"who sold them in Europe and embezzled the proceeds." On September 28, Meriwether Lewis arrived at the lick and secured for President Jefferson the greater part of what was left. These specimens later were lost in shipment. Ironically, it was Rodney who was to chronicle their disappearance. Big Bone Lick is today a Kentucky state park. Thomas D. Matijasic, "Big Bone Lick and the American Enlightenment," *Filson Club History Quarterly* 61 (October 1987): 466-477. See also Meriwether Lewis to Thomas

Jefferson, October 3, 1803, in Jackson, *Letters of the Lewis and Clark Expedition*, 126-132; Thomas Rodney to Caesar A. Rodney, October 16, 1803, in Gratz, "Thomas Rodney," 43.2 (1919): 132-133; Henry A. Ford and Kate B. Ford, comps., *History of Cincinnati, Ohio, with Illustrations and Biographical Sketches* (Cleveland, Oh.: L. A. Williams & Co., 1881), 295-296.

18. This sentence has been inserted here from its margin location in the manuscript.

19. For the coincidence of salt licks and animal bones in Kentucky, see R. S. Cotterill, *History of Pioneer Kentucky* (Cincinnati: Johnson & Hardin, 1917), 8-9.

20. Indian Creek joins the Ohio River a short distance downstream from Vevay, Indiana. Vevay South (Kentucky-Indiana) Quadrangle.

21. The Kentucky River flows into the Ohio River at Carrollton, Kentucky. Carrollton (Kentucky-Indiana) Quadrangle. The "pretty little town" was Port William, Kentucky, situated "on the bank of the Ohio on the uper side of Kty. River." Called Williamsport by Cramer, it was renamed Carrollton in 1838. Thomas Rodney to Caesar A. Rodney, October 16, 1803, in Gratz, "Thomas Rodney," 43.2 (1919): 132; see also Cramer, *The Navigator*, 3d ed., 35; Rennick, *Kentucky Place Names*, 51.

22. Today, the mouth of Little Kentucky River is somewhat less than a mile below the Kentucky River. Carrollton (Kentucky-Indiana) Quadrangle.

23. Daniel Boone and his family had moved to the Missouri River from Kentucky in 1799. John Mack Faragher, *Daniel Boone: The Life and Legend of an American Pioneer* (New York: Henry Holt and Company, 1992), 272, 277-278.

24. This is the only clue Rodney gives as to Buchanan's identity. Further information remains elusive. Rodney's reference to the clergyman "Pearson Landrum" is probably to Rev. Thomas Lendrum, who was "inducted" to Christ Church Parish in Queen Annes County, Maryland, May 26, 1773. The mother church was situated at Hibernia, within a mile of Centreville. As Lendrum was not its rector in 1773, he was probably assigned to one of its three progeny "chapels of ease," located within an eleven-mile radius of Centreville. Commission Book 82, Council of Maryland, *Maryland Historical Magazine* 27 (March 1932): 34; Arthur Pierce Middleton, *Tercentenary Essays Commemorating Anglican Maryland, 1692-1792* (Virginia Beach, Va.: Downing Company, 1992), 95-97.

25. The dateline is inserted here from its margin location in the manuscript and also from its additional location as a head note on the following manuscript page.

26. From Rodney's location description, this is probably Twelve Mile Island. Charlestown (Indiana-Kentucky) Quadrangle; Jeffersonville (Indiana-Kentucky) Quadrangle.

27. Cane is an exotic species of grass *(Arundinaria gigantea)* which grows from the Atlantic seaboard to Oklahoma and eastern Texas and north to the southern Ohio Valley. In Rodney's time, cane thrived in jungle-like profusion in the fertile Kentucky bottomlands bordering the Ohio. Also known as giant cane, southern cane, or canebrake bamboo, it reaches an average height of ten or twelve feet, occasionally reaching sixteen, its stems attaining a maximum two-inch diameter. Producing green leaves and stems year-round, cane was prized by Kentucky settlers as pasturage for their cattle and horses. Chester Raymond Young, ed., *Westward into Kentucky: The Narrative of Daniel Trabue* (Lexington: University Press of Kentucky, 1981), 166 n. 40; *The New Encyclopaedia Britannica,* 15th ed., s.v. "Arundinaria."

28. Six Mile Island is situated slightly upriver from Oak Park, Indiana. Jeffersonville (Indiana-Kentucky) Quadrangle.

29. Clarksville, Indiana, is situated between Jeffersonville and New Albany. Ibid.; New Albany (Indiana-Kentucky) Quadrangle.

30. Founded in 1778 by George Rogers Clark as a base of military operations against the British, the settlement's growth was assured in 1782 by the construction of Fort Nelson, by the geological blessing that it was elevated sufficiently to escape floods, and finally by its strategic economic location at the Falls of the Ohio: Louisville's being at "the foot of descending navigation" meant that "all the wealth of the western country must pass through her hands," i.e., cargoes had to be land-shipped around the falls when low water made them dangerous. In 1780 the settlement attained the status of a town, and by 1800 contained an estimated 350 to 800 inhabitants. The coming of the steamboat in the 1810s expanded the town's commercial base, to which industry, especially the distilling of liquor, soon was added, assuring it of its future role as one of the Ohio Valley's great cities and Cincinnati's perennial rival. *1778. History of the Ohio Falls Cities and Their Counties with Illustrations and Biographical Sketches,* 2 vols. (Cleveland, Oh.: L. A. Williams & Co., 1882), 1: 175-222; Hulbert, *The Ohio River,* 269-276; Wade, *The Urban Frontier,* 14-18, 64-65.

31. Thomas Rodney to Caesar A. Rodney, October 16, 1803, in Gratz, "Thomas Rodney," 43.2 (1919): 132-134.

32. Two years later Josiah Espy was to comment on the remarkable fossils preserved in this stretch of the falls: "The beach and whole bed of the river for two or three miles here is one continued body of limestone and

petrifactions. The infinite variety of the latter are equally elegant and astonishing. All kinds of roots, flowers, shells, bones, buffalo horns, buffalo dung, yellow-jacket's nests, etc. are promiscuously seen in every direction on the extensive beach at low water, in perfect form." *Memorandums of a Tour Made by Josiah Espy*, 13.

33. The mouth of Bear Grass Creek was the landing place for river craft to unload goods that required portage around the Falls and to obtain the services of a pilot to navigate the craft through the Falls. Cramer, *The Navigator*, 3d ed., 36; Jeffersonville (Indiana-Kentucky) Quadrangle.

34. See chapter 3, note 15 above.

35. The eagle was a United States ten-dollar gold piece first minted in 1795. R. S. Yeoman, *The Guide Book of United States Coins, 1990 . . .* , 43d rev. ed., Kenneth Bressett, ed. (Racine, Wis.: Western Publishing Company, 1989), 195.

36. For a contemporary description of the Falls (or Rapids) of the Ohio, see Cramer, *The Navigator*, 3d ed., 35-36; New Albany (Indiana-Kentucky) Quadrangle. For a 1778 sketch of the Falls of the Ohio which approximates the configuration that existed when Rodney saw them, see "A Plan of the Rapids, in the River Ohio," in Beverl[e]y W. Bond, Jr., ed., *The Courses of the Ohio River Taken by Lt. T. Hutchins, Anno 1766, and Two Accompanying Maps* (Cincinnati: Historical and Philosophical Society of Ohio, 1942), frontispiece.

This two-mile, twenty-five foot drop stretch of rapids—formed by an outcrop of limestone—presented the chief barrier to navigation on the Ohio during the late eighteenth and early nineteenth centuries. The various canal-building attempts—beginning in 1805—to circumvent the falls all failed until the Louisville and Portland Canal Company's canal was completed in 1830. R. Carlyle Buley, *The Old Northwest: Pioneer Period, 1815-1840*, 2 vols. (Indianapolis: Indiana Historical Society, 1950), 1: 435-436.

37. The configuration of the Falls of the Ohio and the island structure in the Ohio River has changed since Rodney's time. Goose Island eroded away in the 1937 flood. Cramer, *The Navigator*, 8th ed., 177-178; Jeffersonville (Indiana-Kentucky) Quadrangle; Samuel W. Thomas, *Views of Louisville Since 1766* (Louisville: Courier-Journal Lithographing Co., 1971), 54.

38. It was an age-old folk belief in Europe and America among those who looked to the sky for weather portents that "when a line joining the horns of the moon's crescent lies nearly perpendicular to the horizon, the moon cannot hold water, and is called a 'wet moon' and is a sign of wet weather; when it is almost horizontal, so that the crescent can gather and hold water,

it is called a 'dry moon' because, retaining the water above, fair weather blesses the earth." Gertrude Jobes and James Jobes, *Outer Space: Myths, Name Meanings, Calendars from the Emergence of History to the Present Day* (New York: Scarecrow Press, 1964), 28; see also Richard Inwards, ed., *Weather Lore: The Unique Bedside Book,* rev. ed. by E. L. Hawke (London: Rider and Company, 1950; reprint ed., London: S. R. Publishers, 1969), 91, 93, 96.

7. "Nothing but wilderness"

1. Salt River enters the Ohio River as the Hardin County, Kentucky-Jefferson County boundary. Kosmosdale (Indiana-Kentucky) Quadrangle.

2. Buck Creek falls into the Ohio River near Mauckport, Indiana. Mauckport (Indiana-Kentucky) Quadrangle.

3. Indian Creek joins the Ohio River about a mile downstream from New Amsterdam, Indiana. New Amsterdam (Kentucky-Indiana) Quadrangle.

4. Blue River enters the Ohio River as the Crawford County, Indiana-Harrison County boundary. Rodney's reference here is to Upper Blue River Island and Blue River Island. Cramer, *The Navigator,* 3d ed., 37; Leavenworth (Indiana-Kentucky) Quadrangle.

5. Hardins Creek is a branch of Sinking Creek which joins the Ohio River at Stephensport, Kentucky. Hardinsburg (Kentucky) Quadrangle; Rome (Indiana-Kentucky) Quadrangle.

6. Andersons River flows into the Ohio River as the Spencer County, Indiana-Perry County boundary. Tell City (Kentucky-Indiana) Quadrangle.

7. The difficult river passages which Rodney and a long line of eighteenth- and nineteenth-century travelers experienced found expression in John Randolph of Roanoke's classic remark that the Ohio was "frozen one half of the year, and dried up during the other." Randolph quoted in Ambler, *A History of Transportation,* 204–205; see also T. Addison Richards, *The Romance of American Landscape* (New York: Leavitt and Allen, 1854), 196.

8. Soon after Rodney's journey in 1803, here at the base of this huge bluff overlooking the river, the settlement of Hanging Rock was established. The two pillar-like appendages that tilted outward from the face of the cliff were called George Washington and Lady Washington. One fell in the earthquake of 1811 and the other was dynamited as a matter of safety. The settlement which came to be called Rockport was moved to its present location on the crest of the bluffs. Robert M. Taylor, Jr., Errol Wayne Stevens, Mary Ann Ponder, and Paul Brockman, *Indiana: A New Historical Guide* (Indianapolis: Indiana Historical Society, 1989), 219–220; Cramer, *The Navigator,* 8th ed., 127–129; John Woods, *Two Years' Residence in the Settlement on the English*

Prairie, in the Illinois Country, United States . . . (London: Longman, Hurst, Rees, Orme, and Brown, 1822), 124.

9. Five pages of notations of expenditures here are omitted. With this, Rodney had filled the book in which he was keeping his journal. The entry is continued in another book.

The continuation is prefaced: "On the Ohio at Great Rock on the N.W. shore in the next reach above the Yellow Banks, P.M., Munday, October the 24th 1803. The book which contains my journal from home to this place run out and not having another blank book have made this to persue my journal in from this remarkable rock and this time."

10. On November 22, 1497, Portuguese explorer Vasco da Gama (1469?-1524), searching for an all water route from Europe to India, rounded the Cape of Good Hope. While Rodney's precise reference is evasive, one source speculates he may have read the description in *The Lusiad,* the epic poem of Luis Vaz de Camoes, the central theme of which is da Gama's first voyage to India. William Julius Mickle, *The Lusiad; or, The Discovery of India. An Epic Poem. Translated from the Original Portuguese of Luis de Camoens* (Oxford: Jackson & Lister, 1778); Vincent Jones, *Sail the Indian Sea* (London: Gordon & Cremonesi Publishers, 1978), 50; Hamilton, *Anglo-American Law,* 64.

11. Yellow Banks, Kentucky—renamed Owensborough in 1816 and later Owensboro—was so called from the yellow appearance of its river bank. Rennick, *Kentucky Place Names,* 223.

12. Green River falls into the Ohio River on the Kentucky shore opposite Evansville, Indiana. Newburgh (Indiana-Kentucky) Quadrangle; Evansville South (Indiana-Kentucky) Quadrangle.

13. Pigeon Creek enters Ohio River on the Indiana shore at Evansville. Evansville South (Indiana-Kentucky) Quadrangle.

14. A quotation from Homer, *Odyssey,* book xviii, lines 229-232. See Maynard Mack, ed., *Alexander Pope, The Odyssey of Homer,* 2 vols. (London: Methuen & Co., 1967), 2: 178. Helpful in locating the simile: Harold Andrew Mason, *To Homer through Pope: An Introduction to Homer's Iliad and Pope's Translation* (London: Chatto & Windus, 1972), 82-85. The miscellany Rodney purchased before leaving Delaware included Alexander Pope's translation of Homer's epic poems. A convenient modern publication of Pope's Homer is Maynard Mack, ed., *Alexander Pope, The Iliad of Homer,* 2 vols. (London: Methuen & Co., 1967); Mack, *Alexander Pope, The Odyssey.*

15. Henderson or Hendersonville, also called "Red Banks," had become the seat of Henderson County, Kentucky, in 1798. It was named in honor

of Colonel Richard Henderson (1734-1785), one of Kentucky's most prominent pioneers, the founder of the Transylvania Land Company which, by
the 1795 "Treaty of Watoga," purchased from the Indians over half of what
became the state of Kentucky. This transaction later was canceled by the
state of Virginia, which compensated the Transylvania directors with a grant
of land twelve miles square on the Ohio below the mouth of the Green
River. Rennick, *Kentucky Place Names,* 137; Henderson (Kentucky-Indiana)
Quadrangle; Cramer, *The Navigator,* 8th ed., 130; *Appleton's Cyclopaedia of
American Biography,* s.v. "Henderson, Richard"; Cuming, *Sketches of a Tour,*
242. Henderson's grant is shown on a contemporary map, "Kentucky, Reduced from Elihu Barker's Large Map," in Carey, *Carey's General Atlas,* 40.

8. Treacherous Waters, Salt Works, and a Legendary Cave

1. Diamond Island, whose name is derived from its shape, was admired
in the nineteenth century for its natural beauty. Situated a mile downstream
from West Franklin, Indiana, it is the Ohio's second largest island. West
Franklin (Indiana-Kentucky) Quadrangle; Caborn (Indiana-Kentucky)
Quadrangle; Wilson (Kentucky-Indiana) Quadrangle; Smith Mills (Kentucky) Quadrangle; Cramer, *The Navigator,* 8th ed., 130, 132; Richards, *The
Romance of American Landscape,* 197-199; Gary L. Watson to Ray Swick, July
19, 1984.

2. Rodney's Six Mile Island may be Slim Island downriver about four
miles from Mount Vernon, Indiana. This surmise is fueled by Rodney's
location of the next island in the second paragraph below this one. Mount
Vernon (Indiana-Kentucky) Quadrangle; Uniontown (Kentucky-Indiana)
Quadrangle; Cramer, *The Navigator,* 8th ed., 132.

3. Highland Creek joins the Ohio River at Uniontown, Kentucky. Uniontown (Kentucky-Indiana) Quadrangle.

4. A few lines above, Rodney locates this settlement "near the mouth of
Highland Creek." A few lines below, he describes it as having "the best and
nicest harbor we have met with in the Ohio." Possibly, perhaps even probably,
this was Francisburg (or Francesburg), which merged with later established
Locust Port to become Uniontown. Rennick, *Kentucky Place Names,* 301.

5. Matthew Lyon (1750-1822) was born in Ireland and at the age of fifteen
emigrated to America, served two years in the American Revolution, and
then settled in Vermont where he became a successful businessman. He was
elected to the United States House of Representatives in 1797 as a Democratic-Republican. Moving to Kentucky in 1801, he represented that state in
Congress, 1803 to 1811. In 1820 he moved once more, relocating to Arkansas

where he was chosen a congressional territorial delegate, but died before he could take his seat. *Dictionary of American Biography*, s.v. "Lyon, Matthew," by William A. Robinson.

Samuel Hopkins (1753-1819) was born in Virginia and served in the American Revolution on the staff of General Washington and later as lieutenant colonel and colonel of the Tenth Virginia Regiment. Emigrating to Kentucky in 1796, he settled in Henderson County the following year, where he began a long and varied career. After studying law, Hopkins was admitted to the bar and presided as chief justice of the first court of criminal common law and chancery jurisdiction, 1799-1801; was a member of the Kentucky House of Representatives, 1800-1801 and 1803-1806; and of the state senate, 1809-1813. He served in the War of 1812 as Kentucky's commander in chief with rank of major general. (Rodney's informant's ranking of Hopkins as "general" doubtless refers to a militia title). After completing a term in Congress as a Democratic-Republican, 1813-1815, he retired to his plantation. *Biographical Directory of the United States Congress, 1774-1989*, Bicentennial Edition, s.v. "Hopkins, Samuel"; Edmund L. Starling, *History of Henderson County, Kentucky, Comprising History of County and City, Precincts, Education, Churches, Secret Societies, Leading Enterprises, Sketches and Recollections, and Biographies of the Living and Dead* (Henderson, Kentucky: n.p., 1887; facsimile reprint ed., Evansville, Indiana: Unigraphic, 1965), 796.

6. Wabash Island, named for its location at the mouth of Wabash River, is the Ohio's largest island. In 1803 the Ohio River contained 98 islands. Today it numbers 83, the missing ones having either eroded or been dredged away for sand and gravel. Uniontown (Kentucky-Indiana) Quadrangle; Wabash Island (Kentucky-Illinois-Indiana) Quadrangle; Gary L. Watson to Ray Swick, July 19, 1984. Wabash River falls into the Ohio River at the Indiana-Illinois boundary. Wabash Island (Kentucky-Illinois-Indiana) Quadrangle.

7. The Muskogee or Creek seem to have had towns principally all the way from Georgia's Atlantic Coast westward to central Alabama. John R. Swanton, *The Indian Tribes of North America*, Smithsonian Institution, Bureau of American Ethnology, Bulletin 145 (Washington: United States Government Printing Office, 1952), 160-168.

8. "What is Called the Shawnee Towns . . . instead of presenting anything like a Town or Houses is Nothing but a Ledge of Rocks forming a rising pavemnt from the water to the hill shore which makes it a fine Landing Place." Thomas Rodney to Caesar A. Rodney, November 3, 1803, in Gratz, "Thomas Rodney," 43.2 (1919): 135. Old Shawneetown (Shawneetown Sta-

tion), Illinois, is on the Ohio River, and Shawneetown (New Shawneetown Station) is situated over two miles from the river to the northwest. Shawneetown (Illinois-Kentucky) Quadrangle. Saline Creek enters Ohio River as the Gallatin County, Illinois-Hardin County boundary. Saline Mines (Illinois-Kentucky) Quadrangle.

9. The spring was "ten feet square." Thomas Rodney to Caesar A. Rodney, November 3, 1803, in Gratz, "Thomas Rodney," 43.2 (1919): 136.

10. "These things show that this Spring, has been the object of great attention perhaps thousands of years ago and by a People antecedent to the Present race of Indians—a Remnant of these People if report be true still remain on the banks of the *Misouri* a man at the Salt Works told me he had been 70 miles up that River as a Hunter, and heard a Mr. Evans, who had been up it 1800 say that he met with a nation of white People that Cultivated the Earth and were quite a Civilized People and very friendly and who spoke an unknown language different from that of all the Indians &c &c.—I said I had heard such story published of Mr. Boone he said he knew Boone & had been at his House on the Misouri but did not hear him mention it." Thomas Rodney to Caesar A. Rodney, November 3, 1803, in Gratz, "Thomas Rodney," 43.2 (1919): 137.

11. "The Eve" of the shed "is at least 8 ft high and the Sides all open." Ibid., 43: 135.

12. These sentences have been inserted here from their margin location on the manuscript's previous page.

13. This sentence has been inserted here from its margin location in the manuscript. Rodney wrote his son a few days later, "Hundreds of Parakeets are every day drinking this water. . . . they seem very fond of the Salt water." What the judge saw was the Carolina parakeet, the only one of five hundred species of parrots that is indigenous to the United States. It ranged from the Atlantic seaboard west to the Ohio and Mississippi and south to the Gulf of Mexico. On the frontier Ohio, the Carolina parakeet generally first was encountered by river travelers near the mouth of the Scioto although as late as 1810 it occasionally, though rarely, was seen as far north as Marietta. One foot in length, and arrayed in beautiful yellow, orange, and green plumage, the bird's fondness for farmers' seeds and orchards, its commercially valuable feathers, and its tendency to travel in flocks encouraged its slaughter in large numbers. It was driven into extinction by 1918, when the last known of the species died in the Cincinnati Zoo. Thomas Rodney to Caesar A. Rodney, November 3, 1803, in Gratz, "Thomas Rodney," 43.2 (1919): 136; Wilson and Bonaparte, *American Ornithology,* 1: 380;

Richard A. Bartlett, *The New Country: A Social History of the American Frontier, 1776-1890* (New York: Oxford University Press, 1974), 250; David Ehrlinger, *The Cincinnati Zoo and Botanical Garden from Past to Present* (Cincinnati: Cincinnati Zoo and Botanical Garden, 1993), 51.

14. Elsewhere, Rodney describes this in greater detail, as "a Crescent formed in a high Rocky Mountain with its open front to the River the wall of Rock around it perhaps 60 or 80 ft high and a Cavern under the bottom of the walls all round the Crescent nearly as deep under the wall as the length of the Cave & 10 or 15 ft. high in front in the bottom of the Crescent and perhaps Exactly midway a beautiful stream of pure water falls over the top of the wall at a part that appears a little lowered for that purpose here is formed a beautiful cascade or one of the finest shower baths that could be Contrived and here I injoyed it as such by leting it fall on my head—as the water falls it runs off in a stream under the front of the wall round the Crescent to the River behind this we walked under the wall perhaps 30 yds within the front which hung over us—In the Centre of this Crescent is a mound probably 60 ft. above the water of the River when full which gently declines all round the Crescent to the floor of the Caves at the front of the wall and from the front of the Crescent down to the river So that the whole together looks like a vast ampitheatre Presenting a dignity beyond the works of art. The wings on each side the front of this Crescent are Vast walls with perpendicular face 300, or 400 ft. above the water in the River This country abounds in Phenomona of this kind." Thomas Rodney to Caesar A. Rodney, November 4, 1803, in Gratz, "Thomas Rodney," 43.2 (1919): 139-140.

15. As may be discerned from Rodney's comments both in his journal and in a letter to his son—on November 4 he wrote of "the Cave in the Rock so much spoken of"—Cave in Rock was a noted Ohio River landmark by 1803. While its fame then doubtless derived from its uniqueness as a physical feature, nineteenth- and twentieth-century folklorists and writers of popular histories were to weave stories of its having served as the lair of river pirates. The only known contemporary mention of this role appears in the journal of Christian Schultz: "Formerly, perhaps it was inhabited by Indians; but since, with more probability, by a gang of bandits, headed by Mason and others, who a few years ago infested this part of the country, and committed a great number of robberies and murders."

Cave in Rock is located near Cave in Rock, Illinois. On a contemporary map it is designated simply as Great Cave. Cave in Rock (Kentucky-Illinois) Quadrangle; "Kentucky," in Carey, *Carey's General Atlas,* 40; Thomas Rodney to Caesar A. Rodney, November 4, 1803, in Gratz, "Thomas Rodney," 43.2

(1919): 138; Schultz, *Travels on an Inland Voyage,* 1: 201; Otto A. Rothert, *The Outlaws of Cave-in-Rock: Historical Accounts of the Famous Highwaymen and River Pirates Who Operated in Pioneer Days upon the Ohio and Mississippi Rivers and over the Old Natchez Trace* (Cleveland: Arthur H. Clark Company, 1924); Michael Allen, *Western Rivermen, 1763-1861: Ohio and Mississippi Boatmen and the Myth of the Alligator Horse* (Baton Rouge: Louisiana State University Press, 1990), 82-83.

16. Hurricane Island, the Ohio's third largest island, lies off the mouth of Hurricane Creek, which enters the Ohio River at Tolu, Kentucky. Cave in Rock (Kentucky-Illinois) Quadrangle; Rosiclare (Illinois-Kentucky) Quadrangle; Gary L. Watson to Ray Swick, July 19, 1984.

17. Tradewater River joins the Ohio River on the Kentucky shore as the Union County, Kentucky-Crittenden County boundary. Dekoven (Kentucky-Illinois) Quadrangle.

18. "Kentucky," in Carey, *Carey's General Atlas,* 40. Rodney mentions Carey's map a few times. As Mathew Carey published several atlases, it is not possible to determine precisely which one Rodney was using. For several published before 1803, any one of which he might have carried, see Philip Lee Phillips, *A List of Geographic Atlases in the Library of Congress,* 4 vols. (Washington: Government Printing Office, 1909-1920), numbers 683, 1172, 1213, 1362, 1364, 1365, 1367, 3565. The 1800 edition cited herein generally confirms Rodney's references.

9. The Last of the Ohio

1. Rodney's reference is to what Alexander Pope called "one of the noblest Simile's in all *Homer.*" It clearly inspired Rodney's descriptive passage of the tumbling rock. Mack, *Pope, The Iliad,* Book XIII, lines 187-200, and note for line 191.

2. The works of eighteenth-century Scottish poet James Macpherson are the sources of these names. The variant spelling occurring in editions of his work coupled with Rodney's creative spelling and difficult handwriting make for uncertainty in transcription. James Macpherson, *Fragments of Ancient Poetry, Collected in the Highlands of Scotland, and Translated from the Galic or Erse Language* (Edinburgh: G. Hamilton and J. Balfour, 1760), facsimile reprint, Augustan Reprint Society, *James Macpherson. Fragments of Ancient Poetry (1760)* (Los Angeles: William Andrews Clark Memorial Library, 1966), passim; Malcolm Laing, *The Poems of Ossian, &c. Containing the Poetical Works of James Macpherson, Esq. in Prose and Rhyme: With Notes and Illustrations,* 2 vols. (Edinburgh: Archibald Constable and Co.; London:

Longman, Hurst, Rees, and Orme, Cadell and Davies, and J. Mawman, 1805), facsimile reprint, *Poems of Ossian*, 2 vols. (Edinburgh: James Thin, Bookseller, 1971), passim; Trevor Royle, *Companion to Scottish Literature* (Detroit: Gale Research Company, 1983), 202-203, 233; Paul J. de Gategno, *James Macpherson* (Boston: Twayne Publishers, 1989), chapters 3 and 4.

Rodney sometimes tried his own hand at poetry. He titled one such effort "The Song of Mirno & his Children—from Ossian." Munroe, *Federalist Delaware,* 186.

3. Cumberland River falls into the Ohio River at Smithland, Kentucky. At the present time, Cumberland Island stretches over two miles downstream from the mouth of Cumberland River. Smithland (Kentucky-Illinois) Quadrangle; Little Cyprus (Kentucky-Illinois) Quadrangle.

4. Tennessee River enters the Ohio River at Paducah, Kentucky, as the Livingston County, Kentucky-McCracken County boundary. Paducah East (Kentucky-Illinois) Quadrangle.

5. Rodney wrote to his son from this location. Thomas Rodney to Caesar A. Rodney, November 3, 1803, in Gratz, "Thomas Rodney," 43.2 (1919): 134-137.

6. This sentence appears at the bottom of the manuscript page. Rodney designated it for insertion at this point in the entry.

7. Fort Massac was situated on the Indiana Territory shore at present-day Metropolis, Illinois. Built by the French in 1757, it was called Fort Ascension and then renamed in honor of the Marquis de Massiac, minister of marine. Abandoned the next year, the fort was soon destroyed by Indians. It was rebuilt in 1794 by the United States Army, which maintained it until after the War of 1812. Metropolis (Illinois-Kentucky) Quadrangle; André Michaux, "Journal of André Michaux, 1793-1796," in Reuben Gold Thwaites, ed., *Early Western Travels, 1748-1846: A Series of Annotated Reprints of Some of the Best and Rarest Contemporary Volumes of Travel . . . ,* 32 vols., (Cleveland, Oh.: Arthur H. Clark Company, 1904-1907), 3 (1904): 73 n. 139; Norman W. Caldwell, "Cantonment Wilkinsonville," *Mid-America* 31 (January 1949): 3-28; Francis Paul Prucha, *A Guide to the Military Posts of the United States, 1795-1895* (Madison: State Historical Society of Wisconsin, 1964), 91, and plate 15; Moulton, *Journals of the Lewis & Clark Expedition,* 2: 85 n. 2.

8. Daniel Bissell (d. 1833), commandant at Fort Massac, 1802-1808, was probably a native of Connecticut. He began his military service in 1791 and rose steadily in rank, obtaining that of brigadier general by the time of his death. Norman W. Caldwell, "Fort Massac: The American Frontier Post, 1778-1805," *Journal of the Illinois State Historical Society* 43 (winter 1950):

265-281; Francis B. Heitman, *Historical Register and Directory of the United States Army, From Its Organization September 29, 1789, to March 2, 1903*, 2 vols. (Washington: Government Printing Office, 1903), 1: 221; *Appleton's Cyclopaedia of American Biography*, s.v. "Bissel, Daniel."

9. Rodney wrote to his son from this location. Thomas Rodney to Caesar A. Rodney, November 4, 1803, in Gratz, "Thomas Rodney," 43.2 (1919): 137-140.

10. Little Chain of Rocks is mentioned by Cramer but is not designated on modern maps. Its approximate location was at Joppa, Illinois. Cramer, *The Navigator*, 3d ed., 40; Joppa (Illinois-Kentucky) Quadrangle.

11. Wilkinsonville, formerly known as Wilkinson's Landing or Cedar Bluffs, is now Metcalf's Landing, Illinois. Built as an outpost of the American Fort Massac, Cantonment Wilkinsonville having been abandoned—as Rodney mentions—as a military installation in 1802, was occupied by Indians. Caldwell, "Cantonment Wilkinsonville," 3-28; see note 7 above.

12. "Bradocks war." The French and Indian War (1754-1763), the final conflict of France and Great Britain for control of North America. Major General Edward Braddock (1695-1755) was commander-in-chief of the British Army in North America. He was mortally wounded in July 1755 in one of the war's early engagements—an attempt to capture the French Fort Duquesne on the present site of Pittsburgh. Lawrence Henry Gipson, *The British Empire before the American Revolution*, vol. 6: *The Great War for the Empire: The Years of Defeat, 1754-1757* (New York: Alfred A. Knopf, 1946), chapters 3, 4; Seymour I. Schwartz, *The French and Indian War, 1754-1763: The Imperial Struggle for North America* (New York: Simon & Schuster, 1994), 36, 44, 46, 47.

13. Elsewhere, Rodney described him as "my Interpreter . . . an Indian which they call a Spanish Indian . . . he told me his name was *Tom Brown* and that in fact he was only half Indian." Thomas Rodney to Caesar A. Rodney, November 16, 1803, in Gratz, "Thomas Rodney," 43.2 (1919): 141.

14. Elsewhere, Rodney described him as "a Negroman . . . Bella who talks very good American—he is of the Indian Color not black and was very Intelligent." Ibid.

15. Big Chain of Rocks is labeled Grand Chain on modern maps. A contemporary account describes the "'Grand Chain,' . . . [as] a large ledge of rocks which crossed the Ohio in a very oblique direction from the Kentucky to the Illinois shore." Cantonment Wilkinsonville was situated just above the head of Grand Chain of Rocks. The town of Grand Chain, Illinois, is located two miles from the river. Bandana (Kentucky-Illinois) Quadrangle; Cape

Girardeau (Missouri-Illinois-Kentucky) Quadrangle; Caldwell, "Cantonment Wilkinsonville," 3; Hildreth, "History of a Voyage," 105.

16. This paragraph, a separate page in Rodney's manuscript, was designated for insertion at this point in the entry.

10. Southward Bound on the "Prince of Rivers"

Although Louisiana Territory did not become the official designation until 1805, it is used herein to avoid confusion. Spain, which referred to it as a colony, transferred Louisiana to France, November 30, 1803, on the eve of Rodney's arrival in Natchez. France, which also referred to it as a colony, released its jurisdiction to United States, December 20, 1803.

1. The juncture of Ohio and Mississippi rivers is shown on Wyatt (Missouri-Illinois-Kentucky) Quadrangle; Wickliffe (Kentucky-Missouri) Quadrangle; U.S. Army Corps of Engineers, *Flood Control and Navigation Maps,* map 1.

2. Many of the Mississippi River islands of Rodney's time have since joined a shoreline, are now inland as the river has changed course, or have completely disappeared. Bragg, *Historic Names and Places,* 10-11.

3. Early travelers called the site of Columbus-Belmont Battlefield State Park (Columbus, Ky.) "Iron Banks" from the rich iron deposits its rust-colored bluff was believed to contain. After examining the location in 1721, however, Father Pierre de Charlevoix reported, "we found the coast extremely high, and the earth of a yellow colour, from whence some have imagined that there are mines of iron in this place." The name survives today as Iron Banks Light, a navigation light. "Kentucky," in Carey, *Carey's General Atlas,* 40; Arlington (Kentucky-Missouri) Quadrangle; Wickliffe SW (Missouri-Kentucky) Quadrangle; Federal Writers' Project, *Kentucky,* 325; Pierre de Charlevoix, *Journal of a Voyage to North America . . . ,* 2 vols. (London: R. and J. Dodsley, 1761; facsimile edition, Ann Arbor: University Microfilms, 1966), 2: 241; U.S. Army Corps of Engineers, *Flood Control and Navigation. Maps,* map 3; Bragg, *Historic Names and Places,* 13, 16-17.

4. Although the course of the river has since changed so that the island is now a part of the west bank, it is still designated Wolf Island. Wolf Island Bar, the "large sand bar," remains, however. U.S. Army Corps of Engineers, *Flood Control and Navigation Maps,* map 3.

5. Rodney is probably describing what is now known simply as Island No. 8. The present navigation channel is along the east side of the island, a consequence of modern floods. Ibid., map 4; Bragg, *Historic Names and Places,* 23-24.

6. New Madrid was founded in 1789 by the Indian agent and land speculator, George Morgan (1743-1810). The site of a French fur trading post, it initially was named "L'Anse a la graisse" ("Cove of grease," for its large number of bears and buffaloes). New Madrid became famous in American history as the epicenter of an 1811-1812 earthquake. So powerful it rang church bells in Boston, the New Madrid Earthquake was the most devastating ever recorded in the Mississippi Valley and eastern United States. In the early nineteenth century, New Madrid ranked, after Natchez, as the most important port between the mouth of the Ohio and New Orleans. The 1811 earthquake and floods have changed the town's location and the river's course since Rodney's time. Josiah Harmar to Henry Knox, Josiah Harmar Papers, May 8, 1789, Letter Book F; Max Savelle, *George Morgan: Colony Builder* (New York: Columbia University Press, 1932), 200-228; U.S. Department of Agriculture, *The New Madrid Earthquake*, by Myron L. Fuller, United States Geological Survey Bulletin 494 (Washington: Government Printing Office, 1912); New Madrid (Missouri-Kentucky) Quadrangle; Bragg, *Historic Names and Places*, 29-33; U.S. Army Corps of Engineers, *Flood Control and Navigation Maps*, map 5.

7. A contemporary map shows Obion River entering the Mississippi River in Tennessee at approximately 36°10' latitude. "A Map of the Tennessee State Formerly Part of North Carolina taken Chiefly from Surveys by Genl. D. Smith & Others," in Carey, *Carey's General Atlas*, 41.

Again, due to the considerable changes that have altered the course of the Mississippi River over the years, it is not precisely clear which stream Rodney mentions here. Obion *Creek* presently falls into the Mississippi River at Hickman, Kentucky, thirty-six miles upriver from New Madrid. Obion *River* presently enters the Mississippi River as the Dyer County, Tennessee-Lauderdale County boundary, 109 miles further downstream from Obion Creek. Hickman (Kentucky-Missouri-Tennessee) Quadrangle; New Madrid (Missouri-Kentucky) Quadrangle; Chic (Tennessee-Arkansas) Quadrangle; U.S. Army Corps of Engineers, *Flood Control and Navigation Maps*, maps 4, 9; Bragg, *Historic Names and Places*, 49-51.

8. This sentence has been inserted here from its margin location in the manuscript.

9. The general area of the former settlement, six miles upstream from Caruthersville, Missouri, is still called Little Prairie. Tennemo (Tennessee-Missouri) Quadrangle; Caruthersville SE (Tennessee-Missouri) Quadrangle; Caruthersville (Missouri-Tennessee) Quadrangle; U.S. Army Corps of Engineers, *Flood Control and Navigation Maps*, map 7; Bragg, *Historic Names and Places*, 42-43.

10. The pirogue was a dugout canoe often used on the Ohio and Mississippi rivers. "It was hollowed by fire or adz, usually from the sycamore, cypress, or cottonwood tree, and had one or both ends squared. Sometimes it was made from two logs, each formed to serve as a side. Its capacity could be increased by inserting planks between the two halves and spiking them in place, or by binding the planks with thongs and filling the interstices with clay or rosin. Another variation was a catamaran-like structure with a platform laid upon two pirogues, thus providing two covered cargo boxes in addition to the platform space. These dugouts were of all sizes. Some of the larger adaptations were fifty or more feet long and five feet in beam, and were able to hold thirty men and forty or fifty tons of freight. They were steered by a stern oar and propelled by poles, oars, or sails. Since portages were less frequent in the South than in the North, the weight of the pirogue was no great drawback so long as there was not a swift current to stem." Baldwin, *The Keelboat Age,* 41.

11. A term frequently used in the eighteenth and nineteenth centuries, especially by letter writers and diarists, to denote the present month; "ultimo" refers to the immediately previous month.

12. A contemporary map shows Forked Deer River flowing into the Mississippi River in Tennessee at approximately 35°50' latitude. "A Map of the Tennassee State," in Carey, *Carey's General Atlas,* 41. Currently, Forked Deer River converges with Obion River before the latter enters Mississippi River. See note 7 above. See also Blytheville (Arkansas-Tennessee-Missouri) 1:100 000 Quadrangle.

What Rodney calls Forked Deer River may have been what is now Middle Fork Forked Deer River which joins Mississippi River fourteen miles downstream from Obion River. Open Lake (Tennessee-Arkansas) Quadrangle. There is also currently a Lower Forked Deer River which flows into Mississippi River five miles further downstream. Open Lake (Tennessee-Arkansas) Quadrangle; Rosa (Arkansas-Tennessee) Quadrangle.

Identification of Catchey River remains elusive.

13. This is shown as the beginning of Chickasaw Bluffs on a contemporary map. "A Map of the Tennessee State," in Carey, *Carey's General Atlas,* 41. It is also referred to variously as Upper Chickasaw Bluff, Chickasaw Bluff No. 1, or First Chickasaw Bluff. This is one of four high bluffs along the Tennessee shore. Cramer, *The Navigator,* 8th ed., 182; Cuming, *Sketches of a Tour,* 262; U.S. Army Corps of Engineers, *Flood Control and Navigation Maps,* map 11; Bragg, *Historic Names and Places,* 58, 62.

14. A splinter group of Delaware Indians left Ohio in 1789 and with the

permission of the Spanish governor settled in present-day Cape Girardeau County in southeastern Missouri where they lived for several years. If these were indeed Delaware whom Rodney encountered, they may have been a hunting party from the Cape Girardeau settlement. C. A. Weslager, *The Delaware Indians: A History* (New Brunswick, N.J.: Rutgers University Press, 1972), 319, 353.

Elsewhere Rodney described them as "settled on the western Shore of the Misisipi about 20 miles above this Place," Chickasaw Bluffs, Fort Pickering. Thomas Rodney to Caesar A. Rodney, November 16, 1803, in Gratz, "Thomas Rodney," 43.2 (1919): 141.

15. In 1795, the Spanish established El Campo de Esperanza on the Arkansas shore of the river opposite Chickasaw Bluff No. 4. It served as a base for the Spanish river fleet while its commander negotiated with the Chicakasaw Indians and while Spanish workmen were constructing a fort on the bluff on the opposite shore. Abandoned by the Spanish, it became the village of Hopefield (a literal translation of the Spanish name). Bragg, *Historic Names and Places*, 75, 76; Gerald T. Hanson and Carl H. Monehon, *Historical Atlas of Arkansas* (Norman: University of Oklahoma Press, 1989), map 32, and narrative 32.

16. In 1739 the French built there a crude, short-lived fortification named Fort Assumption. In 1795 the Spanish occupied the mouth of Wolf River with Fort San Fernando de Barrancas for a little over two years. It was replaced by the American Fort Pike in 1797, but was soon abandoned in favor of another nearby location at the bluffs where Fort Adams was erected. Renamed Fort Pickering, it was finally abandoned in 1819. These were all situated within the area of present-day Memphis. Bragg, *Historic Names and Places*, 78-80; U.S. Army Corps of Engineers, *Flood Control and Navigation Maps*, map 14; Prucha, *Guide to the Military Posts*, 97, and plate 15.

17. Wolf River flows into the Mississippi River in northern Memphis, Tennessee. Memphis West (Tennessee-Arkansas) 1:100 000 Quadrangle.

18. Fort Pickering, see note 16 above. At that time the "Chickasaw Bluffs" were called the Fourth Chickasaw Bluff. Cramer, *The Navigator*, 8th ed., 187; Cuming, *Sketches of a Tour*, 267; Bragg, *Historic Names and Places*, 78-80; U.S. Army Corps of Engineers, *Flood Control and Navigation Maps*, map 14.

19. Possibly George Washington Carmichael. Heitman, *Historical Register*, 1: 283. First Lieutenant James B. Many, in Heitman, *Historical Register*, 1: 688. "Lt. Strong of Tenesse" is elsewhere referred to as Armstrong. Thomas Rodney to Caesar A. Rodney, November 16, 1803, in Gratz, "Thomas Rod-

ney," 43.2 (1919): 142. Lacking further clues, this may be Augustus Strong. Heitman, *Historical Register,* 1: 932.

20. This letter was written the day before. Thomas Rodney to Caesar A. Rodney, November 16, 1803, in Gratz, "Thomas Rodney," 43.2 (1919): 140-142.

21. Given Rodney's few clues here and what he wrote about the initial directions of his passage the next morning, it is probable that the night was spent somewhere along what are today called Council Chute, Council Bend, and Council Lake, at Commerce, Mississippi, vestiges of the former channel of the Mississippi River at this location. Bragg, *Historic Names and Places,* 87-89; U.S. Army Corps of Engineers, *Flood Control and Navigation Maps,* map 16.

22. This sentence has been inserted here from its margin location.

23. 33° latitude is the Louisiana-Arkansas boundary. Millikin (Louisiana-Mississippi) Quadrangle. Although this is clearly 33° latitude in the manuscript, Rodney is in error. He admitted difficulty in tracking progress in the lower Mississippi because of lack of a reliable guidebook and the sometimes confusing information he gathered from other travelers on the river. Even positioning him at 34° latitude seems to be too far; he was probably somewhere considerably above that as he would still have to reach the St. Francis River and Horseshoe Island before arriving at 34° latitude.

24. Rodney's identification of this as St. Francis River is disputed the next day by some upstream travelers. His sequence of encountering Horseshoe Island after passing the river's mouth, however, favors Rodney's identification. St. Francis River currently enters Mississippi River on the Arkansas shore considerably further upstream, a few miles upstream from Helena, Arkansas. Helena (Arkansas-Mississippi) Quadrangle; Stubbs Island (Mississippi-Arkansas) Quadrangle; Bragg, *Historic Names and Places,* 94; U.S. Army Corps of Engineers, *Flood Control and Navigation Maps,* map 18.

11. A Near Disaster and Journey's End

1. The ofttimes dramatic changes that have altered the course of the river over the years are well illustrated here. Rodney's Horseshoe Island is probably what is known on present-day navigation maps as Island No. 61. In 1848, when Horseshoe Bend was cut off by the river, the island was joined to the Arkansas shore. U.S. Army Corps of Engineers, *Flood Control and Navigation Maps,* map 20; Bragg, *Historic Names and Places,* 101-102.

2. Rodney was not alone in having difficulty with the word Ozark. Samuel Dorris Dickinson, "Colonial Arkansas Place Names," *Arkansas Historical Quarterly* 48 (summer 1989): 153. This is possibly Arkansas River which today

flows into the Mississippi River on the Arkansas shore six miles downstream from Rosedale, Mississippi. Dumas (Arkansas-Mississippi) 1:100 000 Quadrangle.

If this position is correct, Rodney was in error when he earlier located the Louisiana-Arkansas boundary. See chapter 10, note 24 above.

3. This, the only mention of Scott, probably refers to Joseph Scott, publisher of numerous geographical dictionaries, gazetteers, and maps. Rodney may have had a map from Scott's *An Atlas*. This work is noted in Phillips, *A List of Geographical Atlases,* as item 4521a.

4. Today commonly called "Spanish moss," "graybeard," or "long moss," this parasitic herb *(Tillandsia usneoides)* belongs to the pineapple family. Its grayish-green pendant stems and threadlike leaves grow to a length of 20 feet on trees from the American South to the Argentine deriving needed moisture and nutrients from air and rain. *The Marshall Cavendish Illustrated Encyclopedia of Plants and Earth Sciences,* 10 vols. (New York: Marshall Cavendish, 1988), 5: 644-646; *Academic American Encyclopedia,* 1993 ed., s.v. "Spanish moss."

5. A ring-shaped piece of iron, flat on one side and convex on the other and eight to nine inches in diameter, used in a game by the same name. Popular in eighteenth and nineteenth-century America, quoits was similar to the modern game of horseshoes. Players, standing on a designated line, endeavored to toss the quoit around a one-inch high peg or metal rod stuck in the ground, or to come as close to it as possible. Quoits has nearly died out except for a version played by children using rings of rope or rubber. Darwin A. Hindman, *Complete Book of Games and Stunts* (New York: Bonanza Books, 1956), Book II, p. 206; *Webster's Sports Dictionary* (Springfield, Mass.: G. & C. Merriam Company, 1976), 339.

6. Rodney describes *Leptochloa dubia,* commonly known as green sprangletop. Thriving in warm, moist, or marshy sites, it is regarded as good forage grass. Frank W. Gould and Robert B. Shaw, *Grass Systematics,* 2d ed. (College Station: Texas A&M University Press, 1983), 154, 287-288; J. McNeill, "Diplachne and Leptochloa (Poaceae) in North America," *Brittonia* 31 (July-September 1979): 399-404.

7. Rodney's losses included "my Mamoths tooth and all my Fosil Curiosities." Thomas Rodney to Caesar A. Rodney, December 5, 1803, in Gratz, "Thomas Rodney," 43.3 (1919): 209.

8. To be cooled sufficiently for drinking, tea and coffee, at this time and well into the twentieth century, often were poured into, and sipped from, a deep-rimmed saucer. The custom perhaps was encouraged by the fact that

until the mid-eighteenth century—and as late as 1830—cups for coffee and tea lacked handles, making them uncomfortable to hold when those liquids were hot. Such "dish" drinking gave rise to the popular expression, "I'm saucered and blown," meaning ready to begin drinking. Michael Smith, *The Afternoon Tea Book* (New York: Atheneum, 1986), 69.

9. Except that it happened somewhere beyond Horseshoe Island, of conjectural identification itself, pinpointing the location of Rodney's mishap is impossible. Rodney was uncertain himself. There were scarcely any place names in this wilderness, and other river travelers were unreliable sources of information.

Aggravated by natural disaster and altered by human rechanneling and dredging, the meandering course of today's Mississippi is significantly different in form and distance from when Rodney sailed down it in 1803. Sketches in Bragg, *Historic Names and Places,* passim; and U.S. Army Corps of Engineers, *Flood Control and Navigation Maps,* passim, offer many illustrations of the changes that have occurred in the river between Rodney's journey and today.

10. Rodney reported the accident after he reached Natchez: "Our Boat run on a Secret Snag which instantly Rushed through her bottom and made a hole 6 inches Square or more when we were 150 miles from any Inhabitants—we lost many things by not being able with our Skiff to get them out before our Boat Sunk but saved our most material things by Great Dexterity & Exertion—We Seemed however to be in a distress Situation with out any resource but in ourselves—Presently after we Left the boat the Current over set her and Tore her off the Snag which occasioned her ankor to fall out and that held her from being Carried away by the Torrent of the Misisipi we then towed her to the shore and had to Encamp on a mud bank all night—and next day we Turned her bottom upward mended the break ourselves and then Righted her again and Bailed her and Slept in her again the next night and the next morning proceeded on again and Met with no further Mischief—and tho we were all in the water and wet during this business none of us Caut Cold or were unwell—." Thomas Rodney to Caesar A. Rodney, December 2, 1803, in Gratz, "Thomas Rodney," 43.3 (1919): 208-209.

11. "Little Lonely Isle." Whether Rodney is describing the island or indicating its name is not possible to determine. Whether either or both, its survival to the present is at best conjectural.

12. Rodney is correct in his earlier mention that the mouth of Yazoo River lay upstream from Walnut Hills. Later rechanneled, it today enters the

Mississippi River at Vicksburg, Mississippi. Federal Writers' Project, *Mississippi: A Guide to the Magnolia State* (New York: Viking Press, 1938), 275; Jackson (Mississippi-Louisiana) 1:100 000 Quadrangle; U.S. Army Corps of Engineers, *Flood Control and Navigation Maps*, maps 32 and 33. See also note 14 below.

13. This sentence is inserted here from its margin location in the manuscript.

14. Walnut Hills, situated on a high bank on the Mississippi's east side, was given its name by the English who controlled the region as part of West Florida, 1763 to 1781. The Spanish built Fort Nogales on the site in 1791, and were succeeded in 1798 by the United States which renamed the locale Walnut Hills and the military post Fort Henry. Newitt Vick, a Methodist minister from Virginia, began the first civilian settlement in 1819 although the town was not called Vicksburg until 1825. It had become a significant river port by the time of the Civil War during which it endured a bitterly contested siege that made it nationally famous. Federal Writers' Project, *Mississippi*, 269; McLemore, *A History of Mississippi*, 1: 162, 192; Thomas Ashe, *Travels in America, Performed in 1806, For the Purpose of Exploring the Rivers Allegheny, Monongahela, Ohio, and Mississippi, and Ascertaining the Produce and Condition of Their Banks and Vicinity*, 3 vols. (London: Richard Phillips, 1808), 3: 186-187; Bragg, *Historic Names and Places*, 159-163. See also note 12 above.

15. Rodney is confused in the hours recorded in this paragraph.

16. This sentence has been inserted here from its margin location.

17. The harbor town of Grand Gulf, Mississippi, established here in 1828, initially flourished and then fell into decline. As with many locations on the Mississippi, the river's channel has changed and Grand Gulf is no longer on the river. The many changes that have occurred in the course of the river between the time of Rodney's journey and the present which make it very difficult to plot his progress on today's map are well illustrated here in the vicinity of Grand Gulf. Harris Gaylord Warren, "Population Elements of Claiborne County, 1820-1860," *Journal of Mississippi History* 9 (April 1947): 83-84; Bragg, *Historic Names and Places*, sketches, p. 173; U.S. Army Corps of Engineers, *Flood Control and Navigation Maps*, map 35.

18. Irish born Peter Bryan Bruin (c.1754-1827), who became a merchant in colonial Virginia, served as an officer in the Revolutionary War, and was for several months a prisoner of war, in 1788 settled with his family on a Spanish land grant in the Natchez district. When the area was organized as the American Mississippi Territory, Bruin was appointed as one of its three

territorial judges. Timothy Pickering to Andrew Ellicott, May 11, 1798, in Carter, *Territorial Papers, Territory of Mississippi*, 5: 34; Rowland, *Courts, Judges, and Lawyers*, 12-13.

Thomas Ashe, who stopped in 1806 to make a courtesy call, described Bruin's residence as "hospitable and comfortable." It was situated at "Bayeau Pierre," eleven miles downstream from the "Grand Gulph." Ashe further stated that "There is no settlement so extensive as the Colonel's above him on the river. He keeps one hundred negroes, and makes by their labor, ten thousand dollars a year. He principally cultivates cotton. The wheat, corn, &c. which he raises are only for his domestic use." Ashe, *Travels in America*, 3: 189-190. See also William S. Coker, "Peter Bryan Bruin of Bath: Soldier, Judge and Frontiersman," *West Virginia History* 30 (July 1969): 579-585.

19. Irish-born and educated David Ker (d. 1805) migrated with his family to colonial North Carolina where he was variously a minister, a merchant, an academy teacher, a university professor and administrator, and a founder of the University of North Carolina. Moving to Natchez, he founded a school for girls and served as a sheriff and clerk of court before receiving appointment as a territorial judge. David Ker to Thomas Jefferson, October 3, 1801, in Carter, *Territorial Papers, Territory of Mississippi*, 5: 84; Rowland, *Courts, Judges, and Lawyers*, 18-19.

20. Edward Turner (1778-1860) of Kentucky was register of the land office at Natchez. Despite Bruin's estimate of his capabilities, Turner's legal practice and career moved him steadily upwards, culminating as attorney general in Mississippi. Thomas Jefferson to Albert Gallatin, March 20, 1803, in Carter, *Territorial Papers, Territory of Mississippi*, 5: 206; Rowland, *Courts, Judges, and Lawyers*, 77, 79, 248, 256; *Appleton's Cyclopaedia of American Biography*, s.v. "Turner, Edward."

Cato West. John Steele, Petition to Congress, October 5, 1803, in Carter, *Territorial Papers, Territory of Mississippi*, 5: 243.

William C. C. Claiborne (1775-1817) served as governor of Mississippi Territory from 1801 to 1804. *Dictionary of American Biography*, s.v. "Claiborne, William Charles Coles," by Isaac Joslin Cox.

21. Robert Williams of North Carolina was the other land commissioner. Thomas Rodney to Robert Williams, August 7, 1803, Historical Society of Delaware. See note 23 below.

22. Coles Creek today enters the Mississippi River from Mississippi at approximately the northern tip of Adams County, Mississippi, and opposite the Tensas Parish, Louisiana-Concordia Parish boundary. Natchez (Missis-

sippi-Louisiana) 1:100 000 Quadrangle; Bragg, *Historic Names and Places*, 182; U.S. Army Corps of Engineers, *Flood Control and Navigation Maps*, map 37.

During this day's river passage, Rodney had sailed past the future site of a settlement that would bear his name. See Introduction, note 7 above.

23. Robert Williams (1773-1836) served as the third governor of Mississippi Territory, 1805-1809. He was a member of the U.S. House of Representatives from North Carolina from 1797 to 1803. Carter, *Territorial Papers, Territory of Mississippi*, 5: 238 n. 27; *Biographical Directory of the United States Congress, 1774-1989*, Bicentennial Edition, s.v. "Williams, Robert." See also note 21 above.

24. Ferdinand Leigh Claiborne, a brother to William C. C. Claiborne, was a merchant in Natchez. Rowland, *Encyclopedia of Mississippi History*, 1: 423-424. Garrett, Wood & Co. was a Natchez mercantile house. Merchants of Natchez to Congress, Petition, January 22, 1802, in Carter, *Territorial Papers, Territory of Mississippi*, 5: 138-139.

25. The territorial capital had been moved by action of the legislature from Natchez to Washington, which became the first state capital in 1817. McLemore, *History of Mississippi*, 1: 197; Federal Writers' Project, *Mississippi*, 333.

26. Edward Turner. See note 20 above.

27. Thomas Rodney to Thomas Jefferson, December 2, 1803, in Carter, *Territorial Papers, Territory of Mississippi*, 5: 295-296.

28. Under dateline Natchez, December 5, 1803: "The Commissioners who were appointed by the President for hearing and determining all disputed claims to lands in the Mississippi Territory, have arrived in this city." Wilmington, Delaware, *Mirror of the Times, & General Advertiser*, December 31, 1803.

29. The final three pages of the manuscript, here omitted, contain a table of distances on the Mississippi River from the mouth of the Ohio River to the mouth of the Mississippi that Rodney copied from "The Misisipi Pilot." He commented, as he had already noted in the journal, that distances would vary considerably depending on the seasonal differences of the depth of the water in the river. The distances "were increased one third in our voiage by the rivers being low, in roundg all the great sand bars which spred out from every point where the river turned."

BIBLIOGRAPHY

Manuscripts

Backus-Woodbridge. Papers. Ohio Historical Society. Columbus, Ohio.

Claiborne, Richard. Genealogical Notes and Manuscripts. Lolita H. Bissell. Nashville, Tennessee.

Claiborne, Richard, John Hopkins, and George Pickett. Indenture, July 5, 1798. Deed Book I, 453-458. Monongalia County Courthouse. Morgantown, West Virginia.

Devol, Jonathan. Journal of a Voyage on the Ohio River. Jerry Barker Devol. Marietta, Ohio.

Drowne, Solomon. Journal. Brown University. Providence, Rhode Island.

Harmar, Josiah. Papers. William L. Clements Library. Ann Arbor, Michigan.

Haward, Peter. Journal. Hunterdon County Historical Society. Flemington, New Jersey.

Hildreth, Samuel P. Papers. Marietta College Library, Marietta, Ohio.

Lawton, James. Memoirs. Ruth Lawton Lee (Mrs. Robert E. Lee). Belpre, Ohio.

Little, Nathaniel W. Journal. William L. Clements Library. Ann Arbor, Michigan.

Rodney, Thomas. Letters. Historical Society of Delaware. Wilmington, Delaware.

Sargent, Winthrop. Journal. Massachusetts Historical Society. Boston, Massachusetts.

Maps

United States, Department of Defense. Army Map Service. Gettysburg.
1:50 000

United States. Department of the Interior. Geological Survey. Topographic Maps. 1:24 000 scale unless otherwise noted. The appropriate quadrangles are cited in the documentation to indicate the present-day location of Rodney's progress westward.

Books and Articles

Academic American Encyclopedia. 1993 ed. S.v. "Spanish moss," "tamarind."

Adovasio, James M., comp. *The Prehistory of the Paintsville Reservoir, Johnson and Morgan Counties, Kentucky.* Ethnology Monographs, no. 6. Pittsburgh: Department of Anthropology, University of Pittsburgh, 1982.

Albert, George Dallas. *History of the County of Westmoreland, Pennsylvania, with Biographical Sketches of Many of Its Pioneers and Prominent Men.* Philadelphia: L. H. Everts & Co., 1882.

Allen, Michael. "Beyond the 'Endless Mountains': The View from the Ohio River." *Queen City Heritage* 53 (fall 1995): 33-39.

———. *Western Rivermen, 1763-1861: Ohio and Mississippi River Boatmen and the Myth of the Alligator Horse.* Baton Rouge: Louisiana State University Press, 1990.

Ambler, Charles Henry. *A History of Transportation in the Ohio Valley with Special Reference to Its Waterways, Trade, and Commerce from the Earliest Period to the Present Time.* Glendale, Cal.: Arthur H. Clark Company, 1932.

Angle, Paul M., ed. *Illinois: Guide & Gazetteer.* Chicago: Rand McNally & Company, 1969.

Appleton's Cyclopaedia of American Biography. S.v. "Bissell, Daniel," "Henderson, Richard," "Turner, Edward."

Ashe, Thomas. *Travels in America, Performed in 1806, For the Purpose of Exploring the Rivers Alleghany, Monongahela, Ohio, and Mississippi, and Ascertaining the Produce and Condition of Their Banks and Vicinity.* 3 vols. London: Richard Phillips, 1808.

Backus, Reno W., comp. *The Backus Families of Early New England.* Duluth, Minn.: Service Printers, 1966.

Baldwin, Leland D. *The Keelboat Age on Western Waters.* Pittsburgh: University of Pittsburgh Press, 1941.

Barnhart, John D. *Henry Hamilton and George Rogers Clark in the American Revolution with the Unpublished Journal of Lieut. Gov. Henry Hamilton.* Crawfordsville, Ind.: R. E. Banta, 1951.

Barnhart, John D., and Dorothy L. Riker. *Indiana to 1816: The Colonial Period.* Indianapolis: Indiana Historical Bureau & Indiana Historical Society, 1971.

Bartlett, Richard A. *The New Country: A Social History of the American Frontier, 1776-1890.* New York: Oxford University Press, 1974.

Beers, D. G. *Atlas of Franklin County, Pennsylvania, from Actual Surveys under the Direction of D. G. Beers.* Philadelphia: Pomeroy & Beers, 1868.

Beers, S. N., and D. G. Beers. *Atlas of Westmoreland County, Pennsylvania, From Actual Surveys.* Philadelphia: A. Pomeroy, 1867.

Bevan, Wilson Lloyd, and E. Melvin Williams, eds. *History of Delaware Past and Present.* 4 vols. New York: Lewis Historical Publishing Company, 1929.

Biographical Directory of the United States Congress, 1774-1989: The Continental Congress, September 5, 1774, to October 21, 1788, and the Congress of the United States, from the First through the One Hundredth Congresses, March 4, 1789, to January 3, 1989, Inclusive. Bicentennial Edition. S.v. "Hopkins, Samuel," "Rodney, Thomas," "Williams, Robert," "Williams, Thomas Hill."

Bissell, Lolita H. *Cliborn-Claiborne Records.* Nashville, Tenn.: Williams Printing Company, 1986.

Bond, Beverley W., Jr. *The Foundations of Ohio.* Columbus: Ohio State Archaeological and Historical Society, 1941.

————, ed. *The Courses of the Ohio River, Taken by Lt. T. Hutchins, Anno 1766, and Two Accompanying Maps.* Cincinnati: Historical and Philosophical Society of Ohio, 1942.

Bragg, Marion. *Historic Names and Places on the Lower Mississippi River.* Vicksburg: Mississippi River Commission, 1977.

Brigham, Clarence S. *History and Bibliography of American Newspapers, 1690-1820.* 2 vols. Worcester, Mass.: American Antiquarian Society, 1947.

Buley, R. Carlyle. *The Old Northwest: Pioneer Period, 1815-1840.* 2 vols. Indianapolis: Indiana Historical Society, 1950.

Caldwell, Norman W. "Cantonment Wilkinsonville." *Mid-America* 31 (January 1949): 3-28.

————. "Fort Massac: The American Frontier Post, 1778-1805." *Journal of the Illinois State Historical Society* 43 (winter 1950): 265-281.

Carey, Mathew. *Carey's General Atlas.* Philadelphia: Mathew Carey, [1810].

Carr, Archie F. *Handbook of Turtles: The Turtles of the United States, Canada, and Baja California.* Ithaca, N.Y.: Comstock Publishing Associates, 1952.

Carter, Clarence Edwin, comp. and ed. *The Territorial Papers of the United States.* Vol. 5. *The Territory of Mississippi, 1798-1817 [sic].* Washington: Government Printing Office, 1937.

————. *The Territorial Papers of the United States.* Vol. 6. *The Territory of Mississippi, 1809-1817.* Washington: Government Printing Office, 1938.

————. "The Transit of Law to the Frontier: A Review Article." *Journal of Mississippi History* 16 (July 1954): 183-192.

Carter, W. C., and A. J. Glossbrenner. *History of York County from Its Erection to the Present Time; (1729-1834).* New ed. Edited by A. Monroe Aurand, Jr. Harrisburg: Aurand Press, 1930.

Cayton, Andrew R. L. *The Frontier Republic: Ideology and Politics in the Ohio Country, 1780-1825.* Kent, Oh.: Kent State University Press, 1986.

Cayton, Andrew R. L., and Paula R. Riggs. *City into Town: The City of Marietta, Ohio, 1788-1988.* Marietta, Oh.: Dawes Memorial Library, Marietta College, 1991.

Chapman, Thomas. "Journal of a Journey through the United States, 1795-6." *Historical Magazine and Notes and Queries, Concerning the Antiquities, History and Biography of America.* 2d series, vol. 5 (June 1869): 357-368.

Cist, Charles. *Sketches and Statistics of Cincinnati in 1859.* [Cincinnati: Printed and Published for the Author,] 1859.

Cleland, Hugh G. *George Washington in the Ohio Valley.* Pittsburgh: University of Pittsburgh Press, 1955.

Clift, G. Glenn. *History of Maysville and Mason County.* Lexington, Ky.: Transylvania Printing Co., 1936.

Coker, William S. "Peter Bryan Bruin of Bath: Soldier, Judge and Frontiersman." *West Virginia History* 30 (July 1969): 579-585.

Collins, Lewis. *Collins' Historical Sketches of Kentucky. History of Kentucky: by the Late Lewis Collins, Judge of the Mason County Court. Revised, Enlarged Four-Fold, and Brought Down to the Year 1874, by His Son, Richard H. Collins. . . .* 2 vols. Covington, Ky.: Collins & Co., 1874.

Collot, Victor. *A Journey in North America, Containing a Survey of the Countries Watered by the Mississipi [sic], Ohio, Missouri, and Other Affluing Rivers. . . .* 3 vols. Paris: Arthur Bertrand, Bookseller, 1826; reprint ed., Firenze, Italy: O. Lange, 1924; reprint ed., New York: AMS Press, 1974.

Commission Book 82. *Maryland Historical Magazine* 26 (June 1931): 138-158; 26 (September 1931): 244-263; 26 (December 1931): 342-361; 27 (March 1932): 29-36.

Cook, Roy Bird. "Fort Belleville, A Forgotten Frontier Post." *West Virginia History* 9 (October 1947): 57-69.

Cotterill, R. S. *History of Pioneer Kentucky.* Cincinnati: Johnson & Hardin, 1917.

County Atlas of Bedford, Pennsylvania; from Recent and Actual Surveys and Records under the Superintendence of F. W. Beers. New York: F. W. Beers & Co., 1877.

Cramer, Zadok. *The Ohio and Mississippi Navigator Comprising an Ample Account of Those Beautiful Rivers, from the Head of the Former, to the Mouth of the Latter.* . . . 3d ed. Pittsburgh: Zadok Cramer, 1802. Reprinted with 4th ed. in *The Ohio and Mississippi Navigator of Zadok Cramer.* Morrison, Ill.: Karl Yost, 1987.

———. *The Navigator; Containing Directions for Navigating the Monongahela, Allegheny, Ohio and Mississippi Rivers; with an Ample Account of These Much Admired Waters, from the Head of the Former to the Mouth of the Latter.* . . . 8th ed. Pittsburgh: Cramer, Spear and Eichbaum, 1814. Facsimile reprint as Zadok Cramer, *The Navigator,* 8th ed. (Ann Arbor, Mich.: University Microfilms, 1966).

Creigh, Alfred. *History of Washington County from Its First Settlement to the Present Time, First under Virginia as Yohogania, Ohio, or Augusta County until 1781, and Subsequently under Pennsylvania.* . . . 2d ed. Harrisburg, Pa.: B. Singerly, 1871.

Crumrine, Boyd, ed. *History of Washington County, Pennsylvania, with Biographical Sketches of Many of Its Pioneers and Prominent Men.* Philadelphia: L. H. Everts & Co., 1882.

Cuming, Fortescue. *Sketches of a Tour to the Western Country, through the States of Ohio and Kentucky; A Voyage down the Ohio and Mississippi Rivers, and a Trip through the Mississippi Territory, and Part of West Florida, Commenced at Philadelphia in the Winter of 1807, and Concluded in 1809.* . . . Pittsburgh: Cramer, Spear & Eichbaum, Franklin Head Bookstore, 1810.

Cunnington, Phillis, and Catherine Lucas. *Costume for Births, Marriages & Deaths.* New York: Barnes & Noble Books, 1972.

Day, Sherman. *Historical Collections of the State of Pennsylvania; Containing a Copious Selection of the Most Interesting Facts, Traditions, Biographical Sketches, Anecdotes, Etc.* . . . Philadelphia: George W. Gorton, 1843.

de Charlevoix, Pierre. *Journal of a Voyage to North America.* . . . *Containing the Geographical Description and Natural History of That Country, Particularly Canada.* . . . *In a Series of Letters to the Duchess of Lesdiguieres.* 2 vols. London: R. and J. Dodsley, 1761; facsimile ed., Ann Arbor: University Microfilms, 1966.

de Gategno, Paul J. *James Macpherson.* Boston: Twayne Publishers, 1989.

Denon, Vivant. *Travels in Upper and Lower Egypt, During the Campaigns of General Bonaparte. Translated from the French. To Which Is Prefixed, An Historical Account of the Invasion of Egypt by the French. By E. A. Kendal.* 2 vols. London: F. Cundee, 1802.

Dickinson, Samuel Dorris. "Colonial Arkansas Place Names." *Arkansas Historical Quarterly* 48 (summer 1989): 137-168.

Dictionary of American Biography. S.v. "Claiborne, William Charles Coles," by Isaac Joslin Cox; "Clark, William," by Louise Phelps Kellogg; "Findlay, James," by Reginald C. McGrane; "Greene, Nathanael," by Randolph G. Adams; "Lewis, Meriwether," by Louise Phelps Kellogg; "Lyon, Matthew," by William A. Robinson; "Putnam, Rufus," by Beverley W. Bond, Jr.; "Rodney, Caesar," by George H. Ryden; "Rodney, Thomas," by George H. Ryden; "St. Clair, Arthur," by Randolph C. Downes.

Dillon, Richard H. *Meriwether Lewis: A Biography.* New York: Coward-McCann, 1965.

Dohan, Mary Helen. *Our Own Words.* New York: Alfred A. Knopf, 1974.

Dorman, John Frederick, comp., in collaboration with Claiborne T. Smith, Jr. *Claiborne of Virginia: Descendants of Colonel William Claiborne: The First Eight Generations.* Baltimore, Md.: Gateway Press, 1995.

Eckman, Jeannette. *Delaware: A Guide to the First State.* 2d ed. New York: Hastings House, 1955.

Egle, William Henry. "The Federal Constitution of 1787: Sketches of the Members of the Pennsylvania Convention." *Pennsylvania Magazine of History and Biography* 10 (1886): 446-460; 11 (1887): 69-79, 213-222, 249-275, 499-500.

————. *History of the Commonwealth of Pennsylvania, Civil, Political, and Military, from Its Earliest Settlement to the Present Time, Including Historical Descriptions of Each County in the State, Their Towns, and Industrial Resources.* 3d ed. Philadelphia: E. M. Gardner, 1883.

Ehrlinger, David. *The Cincinnati Zoo and Botanical Garden from Past to Present.* Cincinnati: Cincinnati Zoo and Botanical Garden, 1993.

Elias, Thomas S. *The Complete Trees of North America: Field Guide and Natural History.* New York: Van Nostrand Reinhold Company, 1980.

Espy, Josiah Murdoch, *Memorandums of a Tour Made by Josiah Espy in the States of Ohio and Kentucky and Indiana Territory in 1805.* Cincinnati, Oh.: Robert Clarke & Co., 1870.

Eudy, John Carroll. "The Political Intrigues of Thomas Rodney: Territorial Politics, 1807-1809." *Journal of Mississippi History* 40 (November 1978): 329-339.

————. "Thomas Rodney, 1744-1811: Patriot in the Mississippi Territory." In Dean Faulkner Wells and Hunter Cole, eds., *Mississippi Heroes,* pp. 2-26. Jackson: University Press of Mississippi, 1980.

Evans, Nelson W. *A History of Scioto County, Ohio, together with A Pioneer Record of Southern Ohio.* Portsmouth, Oh.: Nelson W. Evans, 1903.

Faragher, John Mack. *Daniel Boone: The Life and Legend of an American Pioneer.* New York: Henry Holt and Company, 1992.

Farrand, Max, ed. *A Journey to Ohio in 1810, as Recorded in the Journal of Margaret Van Horn Dwight.* New Haven: Yale University Press, 1913.

Federal Writers' Project. *Kentucky: A Guide to the Bluegrass State.* New York: Harcourt, Brace and Company, 1939.

———. *Mississippi: A Guide to the Magnolia State.* New York: Viking Press, 1938.

———. *Tennessee: A Guide to the State.* New York: Viking Press, 1939.

———. *The WPA Guide to Illinois: The Federal Writers' Project Guide to 1930s Illinois.* Rev. ed. New York: Pantheon Books, 1983.

Fifty Ohio Rarities: 1653-1802. Ann Arbor, Mich.: Clements Library, 1953.

Ford, Henry A., and Kate B. Ford, comps. *History of Cincinnati, Ohio, with Illustrations and Biographical Sketches.* Cleveland, Oh.: L. A. Williams & Co., 1881.

Forsyth, Gideon C. "Geological, Topographical and Medical Information Concerning the Eastern Part of the State of Ohio." *The Medical Repository, Comprehending Original Essays and Intelligence Relative to Medicine, Chemistry, Natural History, Agriculture, Geography, and the Arts. . . .* 2d hexade, 6 (February, March, April 1809): 350-358.

Frank, William P., and Harold B. Hancock. "Caesar Rodney's Two Hundred and Fiftieth Anniversary: An Evaluation." *Delaware History* 18 (fall-winter 1978): 63-74.

Freidel, Frank, ed. *Harvard Guide to American History.* 2 vols. Cambridge, Mass.: Belknap Press of Harvard University Press, 1974.

Fuller, Myron L. *See* U.S. Department of the Interior.

Furlong, Patrick J. "St. Clair, Arthur." In Roger J. Spiller, ed., *Dictionary of American Military Biography,* 3: 947-950. 3 vols. Westport, Conn.: Greenwood Press, 1984.

Gibbens, Alvaro F. *Wood County Formation: A Century of Progress: History of Divisions, Courts, Buildings, Past and Present, and Engravings of the Same.* Morgantown, W.Va.: Acme Press, 1899.

Gibson, George H., ed. "William P. Brobson Diary, 1825-1828." *Delaware History* 15 (April 1972): 55-84; 15 (October 1972): 124-155; 15 (April 1973): 195-217; 15 (October 1973): 295-311.

Gipson, Lawrence Henry. *The British Empire before the American Revolution.*

Vol. 6: *The Great War for the Empire: The Years of Defeat, 1754-1757.* New York: Alfred A. Knopf, 1946.

Gould, Frank W., and Robert B. Shaw. *Grass Systematics.* College Station, Tex.: Texas A&M University Press, 1983.

Gratz, Simon. "Thomas Rodney." *Pennsylvania Magazine of History and Biography* 43.1 (1919): 1-23; 43.2 (1919): 117-142; 43.3 (1919): 208-227; 43.4 (1919): 332-367; 44.1 (1920): 47-72; 44.2 (1920): 170-189; 44.3 (1920): 270-284; 44.4 (1920): 289-308; 45.1 (1921): 34-65; 45.2 (1921): 180-203.

Hamilton, William Baskerville. *Anglo-American Law on the Frontier: Thomas Rodney & His Territorial Cases.* Durham, N.C.: Duke University Press, 1953.

———. *Thomas Rodney, Revolutionary & Builder of the West.* Durham, N.C.: Duke University Press, 1953.

Hanna, Charles A. *The Wilderness Trail or the Ventures and Adventures of the Pennsylvania Traders on the Allegheny Path with Some New Annals of the Old West, and the Records of Some Strong Men and Some Bad Ones.* 2 vols. New York: G. P. Putnam's Sons, 1911.

Hanson, Gerald T., and Carl H. Monehon. *Historical Atlas of Arkansas.* Norman: University of Oklahoma Press, 1989.

Harris, Thaddeus Mason. *The Journal of a Tour into the Territory Northwest of the Alleghany Mountains.* . . . Boston: Manning & Loring, 1805.

Heitman, Francis B. *Historical Register and Dictionary of the United States Army, From Its Organization September 29, 1789, to March 2, 1903.* 2 vols. Washington: Government Printing Office, 1903.

Hildreth, Samuel Prescott. "A Brief History of the Settlement at Belville, in Western Virginia: With an Account of Events There, and Along the Borders of the Ohio River in That Region of Country, from the Year 1785 to 1795: Including Biographical Sketches of Some of the Western Pioneers." *The Hesperian; A Monthly Miscellany of General Literature, Original and Select* 3 (June 1839): 25-34; 3 (July 1839): 109-115; 3 (August 1839): 194-199; 3 (September 1839): 269-277; 3 (October 1839): 352-354; 3 (November 1839): 431-435.

———. "History of a Voyage from Marietta to New Orleans in 1805." *American Pioneer* 1 (March 1842): 89-105; 1 (April 1842): 128-145.

———. "Early Emigration, Or, The Journal of Some Emigrant Families 'across the Mountains,' from New England to Muskingum, in 1788." *American Pioneer* 2 (March 1843): 112-134.

———. *Memoirs of the Early Pioneer Settlers of Ohio, with Narratives of Inci-*

dents and Occurrences in 1775. Cincinnati, Oh.: H. W. Derby, 1854; reprint ed., Baltimore, Md.: Clearfield Company, 1995.

———. *Pioneer History: Being an Account of the First Examinations of the Ohio Valley, and the Early Settlement of the Northwest Territory. Chiefly from Original Manuscripts. . . .* Cincinnati, Oh.: H. W. Derby & Co., 1848.

Hindman, Darwin A. *Complete Book of Games and Stunts.* New York: Bonanza Books, 1956.

History of Cincinnati and Hamilton County, Ohio: Their Past and Present, Including Early Settlement and Development. . . . Cincinnati, Oh.: S. B. Nelson & Co., 1894.

History of Cumberland and Adams Counties, Pennsylvania. Containing History of the Counties, Their Townships, Towns, Villages, Schools, Churches, Industries, Etc. . . . Chicago: Warner, Beers & Co., 1886.

Howe, Henry. *Historical Collections of Virginia; Containing A Collection of the Most Interesting Facts, Traditions, Biographical Sketches, Anecdotes, &c. Relating to Its History and Antiquities, Together with Geographical and Statistical Descriptions. To Which Is Appended an Historical and Descriptive Sketch of the District of Columbia.* Charleston, S.C.: Babcock & Co., 1845.

Hulbert, Archer Butler. *The Ohio River: A Course of Empire.* New York: G. P. Putnam's Sons, 1906.

———. "Western Ship-Building." *American Historical Review* 21 (July 1916): 720-733.

Hutchins, Thomas. *A Topographical Description of Virginia, Pennsylvania, Maryland, and North Carolina.* London: Thomas Hutchins, 1778; reprint ed., edited by Frederick Charles Hicks, Cleveland: Arthur H. Clark Company, 1904.

Inwards, Richard, comp. *Weather Lore: The Unique Bedside Book.* Rev. ed. by E. L. Hawke. London: Rider and Company, 1950; reprint ed., London: S. R. Publishers, 1969.

Jackson, Donald, ed. *Letters of the Lewis and Clark Expedition with Related Documents, 1783-1854.* Urbana: University of Illinois Press, 1962.

Jakle, John A. *Images of the Ohio Valley: A Historical Geography of Travel, 1740 to 1860.* New York: Oxford University Press, 1977.

Jardine, William. "Life of Alexander Wilson." In Alexander Wilson and Charles Lucian Bonaparte, *American Ornithology; or, The Natural History of the Birds of the United States.* 3 vols. London: Chatto and Windus, 1876, 1: ix-cv.

Juettner, Otto. *1785-1909. Daniel Drake and His Followers: Historical and Biographical Sketches.* Cincinnati: Harvey Publishing Company, 1909.

Jobes, Gertrude, and James Jobes. *Outer Space: Myths, Name Meanings, Calendars, from the Emergence of History to the Present Day.* New York: Scarecrow Press, 1964.

Jones, Vincent. *Sail the Indian Sea.* London: Gordon & Cremonesi Publishers, 1978.

Kenton, Edna M. *Simon Kenton: His Life and Period, 1755-1836.* Garden City, N.Y.: Doubleday, Doran & Company, 1930.

Kerby, Robert L. "The Other War in 1774: Dunmore's War." *West Virginia History* 36 (October 1974): 1-16.

Knight, Aquilla L. "Life and Times of Jesse Bennet, M.D., 1769-1842." *Southern Historical Magazine* 2 (July 1892): 1-13.

Knopf, Richard C., Raymond S. Baby, and Dwight L. Smith. "The Re-Discovery of Fort Washington." *Bulletin of the Historical and Philosophical Society of Ohio* 11 (January 1953): 2-12.

Laing, Malcolm. *The Poems of Ossian, &c. Containing the Poetical Works of James Macpherson, Esq. in Prose and Rhyme: With Notes and Illustrations.* 2 vols. Edinburgh: Archibald Constable and Co.; London: Longman, Hurst, Rees, and Orme, Cadell and Davies, and J. Mawman, 1805. Facsimile reprint as *Poems of Ossian.* 2 vols. Edinburgh: James Thin, Bookseller, 1971.

Landis, Charles I. "History of the Philadelphia and Lancaster Turnpike. The First Long Turnpike in the United States." *Pennsylvania Magazine of History and Biography* 42 (1918): 1-28, 127-140, 235-258, 358-360; 43 (1919): 84-90, 182-190.

Lomask, Milton. *Aaron Burr.* Vol. 2: *The Conspiracy and Years of Exile, 1805-1836.* New York: Farrar, Straus, Giroux, 1982.

Loos, John L. "Clark, William." In Roger J. Spiller, ed., *Dictionary of American Military Biography,* 1: 182-185. 3 vols. Westport, Conn.: Greenwood Press, 1984.

———. "Lewis, Meriwether." In Roger J. Spiller, ed., *Dictionary of American Military Biography,* 2: 635-638. 3 vols. Westport, Conn.: Greenwood Press, 1984.

McDermott, John Francis, ed. "The Western Journals of Dr. George Hunter, 1796-1805." *Transactions of the American Philosophical Society* n.s. 53 (July 1963): 1-133.

Mack, Maynard, ed. *Alexander Pope, The Iliad of Homer.* 2 vols. London: Methuen & Co., 1967.

———, ed. *Alexander Pope, The Odyssey of Homer.* 2 vols. London: Methuen & Co., 1967.

McLemore, Richard Aubrey, ed. *A History of Mississippi*. 2 vols. Hattiesburg: University & College Press of Mississippi, 1973.

McNeill, J. "Diplachne and Leptochloa (Poaceae) in North America." *Brittonia* 31 (July-September 1979): 399-404.

Macpherson, James. *Fragments of Ancient Poetry, Collected in the Highlands of Scotland, and Translated from the Galic or Erse Language*. Edinburgh: G. Hamilton and J. Balfour, 1760; facsimile reprint ed., Augustan Reprint Society, *James Macpherson. Fragments of Ancient Poetry (1760)*, Los Angeles: William Andrews Clark Memorial Library, 1966.

The Marshall Cavendish Illustrated Encyclopedia of Plants and Earth Sciences. 10 vols. New York: Marshall Cavendish, 1988.

Mason, Harold Andrew. *To Homer through Pope: An Introduction to Homer's Iliad and Pope's Translation*. London: Chatto & Windus, 1972.

Massey, George Valentine, II. "Priscilla Kitchen, Quakeress, of Salem, Mass., and Kent County, Del., and Her Family." *New England Historical and Genealogical Register* 106 (January 1952): 38-50.

Matheny, H. E. *Wood County, West Virginia, in Civil War Times with an Account of the Guerrilla Warfare in the Little Kanawha Valley*. Parkersburg, W.Va.: Trans-Allegheny Books, 1987.

Matijasic, Thomas D. "Big Bone Lick and the American Enlightenment." *Filson Club History Quarterly* 61 (October 1987): 466-477.

Melish, John. *Travels in the United States of America, in the Years 1806 & 1807, and 1809, 1810, & 1811; Including an Account of Passages betwixt America and Britain, and Travels through Various Parts of Great Britain, Ireland, and Upper Canada.* . . . 2 vols. Philadelphia: Printed for the Author, 1812.

Michaux, André. "Journal of André Michaux, 1793-1796." In *Early Western Travels, 1748-1846: A Series of Annotated Reprints of Some of the Best and Rarest Contemporary Volumes of Travel*. . . , vol. 3 (1904): 25-104. Reuben Gold Thwaites, ed. 32 vols. Cleveland, Oh.: Arthur H. Clark Company, 1904-1907.

Michaux, François André. *Travels to the Westward of the Allegany Mountains, in the States of the Ohio, Kentucky, and Tennessee, in the Year 1802.* . . . London: Richard Phillips, 1805.

Mickle, William Julius. *The Lusiad; or, The Discovery of India. An Epic Poem. Translated from the Original Portuguese of Luis de Camoens*. Oxford: Jackson & Lister, 1778.

Middleton, Arthur Pierce. *Tercentenary Essays Commemorating Anglican Maryland, 1692-1792*. Virginia Beach, Va.: Downing Company, 1992.

Miller, Joseph L. "Dr. Jesse [*sic*] Bennet, (1769-1842) Pioneer Surgeon,

Dr. Aquilla Leighton Knight, (1823-1897) Humanist, Old Virginia Doctors: 'Who Saw Life Steadily and Saw It Whole.'" *Virginia Medical Monthly, Official Organ of the Medical Society of Virginia* 55 (January 1929): 711-714.

Missouri Writers' Project. *Missouri: A Guide to the "Show Me" State.* New York: Duell, Sloan and Pearce, 1941.

Mitcham, Howard. "Old Rodney: A Mississippi Ghost Town." *Journal of Mississippi History* 15 (October 1953): 242-251.

Mombert, J. I. *An Authentic History of Lancaster County in the State of Pennsylvania.* Lancaster, Pa.: J. E. Barr & Co., 1869.

Moulton, Gary E., ed. *The Journals of the Lewis & Clark Expedition.* Lincoln: University of Nebraska Press, 1983—.

Munroe, John A. *Federalist Delaware, 1775-1815.* New Brunswick, N.J.: Rutgers University Press, 1954.

The New Encyclopaedia Britannica. 15th ed. S.v. "Arundinaria."

Newton, J. H., G. G. Nichols, and A. G. Sprankle. *History of the Pan-Handle: Being Historical Collections of the Counties of Ohio, Brooke, Marshall and Hancock, West Virginia.* Wheeling, W.Va.: J. A. Caldwell, 1879.

Norona, Delf. *Wheeling: A West Virginia Place-Name of Indian Origin.* Moundsville, W.Va.: West Virginia Archeological Society, 1958.

Nourse, James. "Journey to Kentucky in 1775, Diary of James Nourse, Describing His Trip from Virginia to Kentucky One Hundred and Fifty Years Ago." *Journal of American History* 19 (April-May-June 1925):121-138; 19 (July-August-September 1925):251-260; 19 (October-November-December 1925):351-364.

Ohio River Navigation Charts: Foster, Ky., to New Martinsville, W. Va. Huntington, W.Va.: U.S. Army Engineer District, 1970.

Olafson, Sigfus. "The Painted Trees and the War Road, Paint Creek, Fayette County, W. Va." *West Virginia Archeologist* 10 (September 1958): 3-6.

Patterson, John Gerald. "Ebenezer Zane, Frontiersman." *West Virginia History* 12 (October 1950): 5-45.

Peattie, Donald Culrose. *A Natural History of Trees of Eastern and Central North America.* Boston: Houghton Mifflin Company, 1950.

Pemberton, Robert L. *A History of Pleasants County, West Virginia.* St. Marys, W.Va.: Oracle Press, 1929.

Pennsylvania Writers' Project. *Pennsylvania: A Guide to the Keystone State.* New York: Oxford University Press, 1940.

Phillips, Philip Lee. *A List of Geographical Atlases in the Library of Congress.* 4 vols. Washington: Government Printing Office, 1909-1920.

Poling, Dorothy. "Jesse Bennet, Pioneer Physician and Surgeon." *West Virginia History* 12 (January 1951): 87-128.

Preston, Laura Curtis. *History and Some Anecdotes of the Settlement of Newbury, Washington County, Ohio.* Marietta, Oh.: Marietta Journal Print, 1909.

Prucha, Francis Paul. *A Guide to the Military Posts of the United States, 1795-1895.* Madison: State Historical Society of Wisconsin, 1964.

Prussing, Eugene E. *The Estate of George Washington, Deceased.* Boston: Little, Brown, and Company, 1927.

Putnam, Eben, comp. *A History of the Putnam Family in England and America: Recording the Ancestry and Descendants of John Putnam of Danvers, Mass., Jan Poutman of Albany, N.Y., Thomas Putnam of Hartford, Conn.* Salem, Mass.: Salem Press Publishing and Printing Co., 1891.

Ravenhold, Reimert Thorolf. "Triumph Then Despair: The Tragic Death of Meriwether Lewis." *Epidemiology* 5 (May 1994): 366-379.

Rennick, Robert M. *Kentucky Place Names.* Lexington, Ky.: University Press of Kentucky, 1984.

Richards, T. Addison. *The Romance of American Landscape.* New York: Leavitt and Allen, 1854.

Rothert, Otto A. *The Outlaws of Cave-in-Rock: Historical Accounts of the Famous Highwaymen and River Pirates Who Operated in Pioneer Days upon the Ohio and Mississippi Rivers and over the Old Natchez Trace.* Cleveland: Arthur H. Clark Company, 1924.

Rowland, Dunbar, ed. *Courts, Judges, and Lawyers of Mississippi, 1798-1935.* Jackson, Miss.: Press of Hederman Bros., 1935.

———. *Encyclopedia of Mississippi History: Comprising Sketches of Counties, Towns, Events, Institutions and Persons.* 2 vols. Madison, Wis.: Selwyn A. Brant, 1907.

Royle, Trevor. *Companion to Scottish Literature.* Detroit: Gale Research Company, 1983.

Rupp, I. Daniel. *The History and Topography of Dauphin, Cumberland, Franklin, Bedford, Adams, and Perry Counties. . . .* Lancaster City, Pa.: Gilbert Hills, 1846.

Safford, William H. *The Blennerhassett Papers, Embodying the Private Journal of Harman Blennerhassett, and the Hitherto Unpublished Correspondence of Burr, Alston, Comfort Tyler, Devereaux, Dayton, Adair, Miro, Emmett, Theodosia Burr Alston, Mrs. Blennerhassett, and Others. . . .* Cincinnati, Oh.: Moore, Wilstach, Keys & Co., 1861.

Savelle, Max. *George Morgan: Colony Builder.* New York: Columbia University Press, 1932.

Schultz, Christian, Jr. *Travels on an Inland Voyage through the States of New-York, Pennsylvania, Virginia, Ohio, Kentucky and Tennessee . . . With Maps and Plates.* 2 vols. in 1. New York: Isaac Riley, 1810.

————. *Travels on an Inland Voyage through the States of New-York, Pennsylvania, Virginia, Ohio, Kentucky and Tennessee. . . .* 2 vols. New York: Isaac Riley, 1810; reprint ed., 2 vols. in 1, Ridgewood, N.J.: Gregg Press, 1968.

Schwartz, Seymour I. *The French and Indian War, 1754-1763: The Imperial Struggle for North America.* New York: Simon & Schuster, 1994.

Scott, Joseph. *An Atlas of the United States.* Philadelphia: F. & R. Bailey, B. Davis, & H. & P. Rice, 1796.

Seelye, John. *Beautiful Machine: Rivers and the Republican Plan, 1755-1825.* New York: Oxford University Press, 1991.

1778. History of the Ohio Falls Cities and Their Counties, with Illustrations and Biographical Sketches. 2 vols. Cleveland, Oh. L. A. Williams & Co., 1882.

Shepard, Lee. "When, and by Whom, Was Cincinnati Founded?" *Bulletin of the Historical and Philosophical Society of Ohio* 7 (January 1949): 28-34.

Showman, Richard K., ed. *The Papers of General Nathanael Greene.* Chapel Hill: University of North Carolina Press, 1976—.

Smith, Dwight L., ed. "The Ohio River in 1801: Letters of Jonathan Williams, Junior." *Filson Club History Quarterly* 27 (July 1953): 199-222.

Smith, Dwight L., and S. Winifred Smith, eds. "The Journey of a Pennsylvania Quaker to Pioneer Ohio." *Bulletin of the Cincinnati Historical Society* 26 (January 1968): 2-40; 26 (April 1968): 174-210.

Smith, Michael. *The Afternoon Tea Book.* New York: Atheneum, 1986.

Smith, Myron J., Jr. "Gunboats at Buffington: The U.S. Navy and Morgan's Raid, 1863." *West Virginia History* 44 (winter 1983): 97-110.

Smith, William Henry, ed. *The St. Clair Papers. The Life and Public Services of Arthur St. Clair: Soldier of the Revolutionary War; President of the Continental Congress; and Governor of the North-Western Territory, with His Correspondence and Other Papers.* 2 vols. Cincinnati, Oh.: Robert Clarke & Co., 1882.

Soltow, Lee, and Margaret Soltow. "A Settlement That Failed: The French in Early Gallipolis, an Enlightening Letter, and an Explanation." *Ohio History* 94 (winter-spring 1985): 46-67.

Starling, Edmund L. *History of Henderson County, Kentucky, Comprising History of County and City, Precincts, Education, Churches, Secret Societies, Leading Enterprises, Sketches and Recollections, and Biographies of the Living and Dead.* Henderson, Kentucky: n.p., 1887; facsimile reprint ed., Evansville, Ind.: Unigraphic, 1965.

Starr, [S. Frederick]. "Archaeology of Hamilton County, Ohio." *Journal of the Cincinnati Museum of Natural History* 23 (June 1960): 1-130.

Stein, Christin L. *Monument Place: A Palace for Lydia, June 29-October 11, 1992.* Oglebay Institute Exhibit Catalogue. Wheeling, W.Va.: n.p., 1992.

Sumners, Cecil L. *The Governors of Mississippi.* Gretna, La.: Pelican Publishing Company, 1980.

Swanton, John R. *The Indian Tribes of North America.* Smithsonian Institution, Bureau of American Ethnology, Bulletin 145. Washington: United States Government Printing Office, 1952.

Sweeney, John A. H., ed. "The Norris-Fisher Correspondence: A Circle of Friends, 1779-82." *Delaware History* 6 (March 1955): 187-232.

Swick, Ray. "Aaron Burr's Visit to Blennerhassett Island." *West Virginia History* 35 (April 1974): 205-219.

————. "'The Smoky Time': Ohio Frontier Valley." *History Today* 27 (April 1977): 234-239.

Sword, Wiley. *President Washington's Indian War: The Struggle for the Old Northwest, 1790-1795.* Norman: University of Oklahoma Press, 1985.

Taylor, Robert M., Jr., Errol Wayne Stevens, Mary Ann Ponder, and Paul Brockman. *Indiana: A New Historical Guide.* Indianapolis: Indiana Historical Society, 1989.

Thomas, Samuel W. *Views of Louisville Since 1766.* Louisville: Courier-Journal Lithographing Co., 1971.

Thomson, W. W., ed. *Chester County and Its People.* Chicago: Union History Company, 1898.

Thwaites, Reuben Gold. *See* Michaux, André.

U.S. Army Corps of Engineers, Mississippi River Commission. *Flood Control and Navigation Maps of the Mississippi River, Cairo, Illinois, to the Gulf of Mexico, Including Navigation Charts [of the] Middle Mississippi River below Hannibal, Missouri.* 29th ed. Vicksburg, Miss.: U.S. Army Corps of Engineers, 1961.

U.S. Department of Navy, Office of the Chief of Naval Operations, Naval History Division. *Civil War Naval Chronology, 1861-1865.* 5 vols. Washington: Government Printing Office, 1961-1965.

U.S. Department of the Interior. *The New Madrid Earthquake,* by Myron L. Fuller. United States Geological Survey, Bulletin 494. Washington: Government Printing Office, 1912.

Wade, Richard C. *The Urban Frontier: The Rise of Western Cities, 1790-1830.* Cambridge: Harvard University Press, 1959.

Wallace, Paul A. W. "Historic Indian Paths of Pennsylvania." *Pennsylvania Magazine of History and Biography* 76 (October 1952): 411-439.

——, ed. *Thirty Thousand Miles with John Heckewelder.* Pittsburgh: University of Pittsburgh Press, 1958.

Warren, Harris Gaylord. "Population Elements of Claiborne County, 1820-1860." *Journal of Mississippi History* 9 (April 1947): 75-87.

Webster's Sports Dictionary. Springfield, Mass.: G. & C. Merriam Company, 1976.

Wells, Dean Faulkner, and Hunter Cole. *See* Eudy, John Carroll.

Weslager, C. A. *The Delaware Indians: A History.* New Brunswick, N.J.: Rutgers University Press, 1972.

White, Helen M. "Seven Islands Dot Pleasants County's River Frontage." *Parkersburg (W.Va.) News,* November 22, 1962.

Wilmington (Del.) Mirror of the Times, & General Advertiser. December 31, 1803.

Wilson, Alexander, and Charles Lucian Bonaparte. *See* Jardine, William.

Windell, Marie, ed. "James Van Dyke Moore's Trip to the West, 1826-1828." *Delaware History* 4 (September 1950): 68-104.

Woods, John. *Two Years' Residence in the Settlement on the English Prairie, in the Illinois Country, United States. . . .* London: Longman, Hurst, Rees, Orme, and Brown, 1822.

Woofter, Albert J., [and Ray Swick]. "All Ohio's Islands Have Special Place in History." *Parkersburg (W.Va.) News.* June 14, 1987.

Writers' Program. *Arkansas: A Guide to the State.* New York: Hastings House, 1941.

——. *Indiana: A Guide to the Hoosier State.* New York: Oxford University Press, 1941.

Yeoman, R. S. *A Guide Book of United States Coins, 1990: Fully Illustrated Catalog and Valuation List—1616 to Date. . . .* 43d ed. Kenneth Bressett, ed. Racine, Wis.: Western Publishing Company, 1989.

Young, Chester Raymond, ed. *Westward into Kentucky: The Narrative of Daniel Trabue.* Lexington: University Press of Kentucky, 1981.

INDEX

Thomas Rodney's variable spellings of place names and names of persons are enclosed in parentheses following the proper spellings. His phonetic spellings, when they are difficult to understand, are also listed with cross references to the correct spellings.

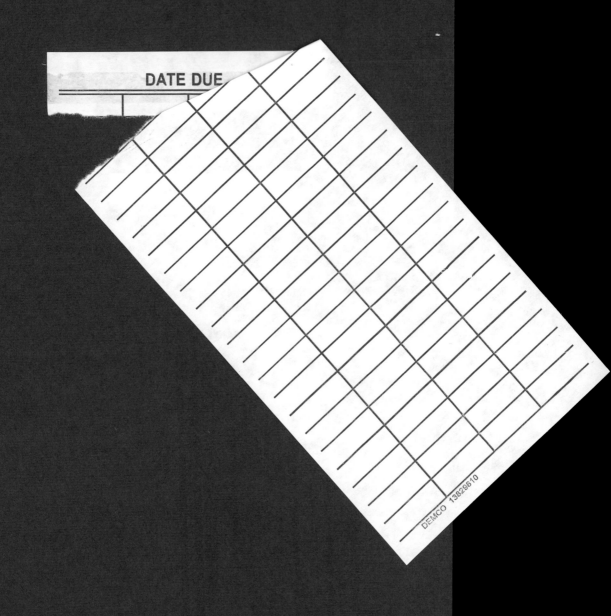

DATE DUE

DEMCO 13829610